educate
your brain

Use mind-body balance
to learn faster, work smarter
and move more easily
through life

KATHY BROWN

Educate Your Brain:
Use mind-body balance to learn faster, work smarter,
and move more easily through life

Copyright © 2012 by Kathy Brown

Book and cover design by Norma Strange and Lisa Hewitt
Movement and Author Photographs: Laird Brown

Published by Balance Point Publishing LLC
Phoenix, Arizona
www.balancepointpublishing.com

Brain Gym® is a registered trademark of
Brain Gym® International/Educational Kinesiology Foundation
(800) 356-2109 from the United States and Canada
(805) 658-7942 from all other countries
info@braingym.org
www.braingym.org

The term Brain Gym®, whether used by itself or as a modifying phrase, describes a specific set of movements, processes, programs, materials, and educational philosophy, the rights to which are held by the Educational Kinesiology Foundation (Brain Gym® International) of Ventura, California.

ISBN-13: 978-1-938550-00-3
Library of Congress Control Number: 2012941479

This book is intended for informational and educational purposes only and should not be construed as a health guide or a manual for self-treatment. Before beginning any exercise program, it is always advisable to check with your physician or other professional health-care practitioner.

Publisher's Cataloging-in-Publication

    Brown, Kathy
        Educate your brain : use mind-body balance to learn
    faster, work smarter, and move more easily through life
    / Kathy Brown ; foreword by Paul E. Dennison.
        p. cm.
    Includes bibliographical references and index.
    LCCN 2012941479
    ISBN 978-1-938550-00-3

      1. Learning--Physiological aspects. 2. Mind and
    body. 3. Movement education. 4. Learning, Psychology
    of.   I. Title.

QP408.B76 2012   612.8'2

QBI12-200013

Acknowledgments

It has been a privilege to be a student of Brain Gym® and its parent discipline, Educational Kinesiology (Edu-K). These programs have taught me so much about myself and have given me a means of supporting others in making personal change at a level I never thought possible. Many people have contributed to the body of knowledge that is Brain Gym/Edu-K and, therefore, to my ability to share the information contained in this book, and I would like to offer my heartfelt gratitude to them all.

First and foremost, I want to thank Paul E. Dennison, Ph.D., whose gifts, challenges, wisdom, and focused intention over so many years gave birth to the concept of Brain Gym and its powerful practices, as well as the entire discipline of Educational Kinesiology, and his wife, Gail E. Dennison, who embodies the vision, language, and artistry of these programs, infusing them with her own gentle spirit. I especially appreciate the personal guidance Paul has offered, supporting me as I refined my knowledge of some of his key concepts.

Great thanks must go next to the talented and inspiring Brain Gym/Edu-K teachers I've had over the years, too many to mention them all, who consistently model acceptance of and respect for the learner and teach with such dedication. In particular, I am grateful to Carla Hannaford, Ph.D., whose many courses and books have provided much of the factual information and understanding that ends up being shared in the workshops I teach and, therefore, this book.

Special thanks go to my good friends Colleen Carroll Gardner, Brain Gym mentor, guide, and angel, whose strong vision of this book helped birth it into print; Dianne Williams, who supported me in the initial creative visioning of its content and direction; and Cristina Whitehawk, my first Brain Gym instructor and now dear colleague, who pointed me toward my future and continues to inspire me along the way.

I am also grateful to the many Brain Gym consultants who have shared their experiences about Brain Gym through books, articles, talks, and conference presentations, and those I've learned with as we trained together in this amazing process. Thanks also go to my many students and clients who have allowed me to bring their stories to life in this book.

Tremendous appreciation and love go to my dear friend, colleague, and editing partner, Deborah Scott Studebaker, whose perceptive co-visioning and brilliant language skills unfailingly brought out the best in the text as we journeyed together, reconsidering and revising every page, and to Laird Brown Photography for the many images illustrating this text.

Thanks also go to Cindy Goldade (and before her, Judy Grant), chair of the Edu-K Product Review Team, and the many team members who spent countless hours reviewing and commenting on the text, through each revision.

My greatest gratitude goes to my husband, Laird, who is my most dedicated supporter and cheerleader. Through all aspects of my decision to change careers, my training in Brain Gym, the growth of my business as a Licensed Brain Gym® Instructor/Consultant, and the writing of this book, he has been only positive and encouraging, celebrating every success I've achieved.

I must conclude with my gratitude to you, the reader. Thank you for your interest in Brain Gym. May you use a bit of Brain Gym to transform your own corner of the world.

Table of Contents

~ Continued on next page

Table of Contents

~ Continued from previous page

Foreword

It was in the late 1990s—the "decade of the brain"—that I first began hearing about Kathy Brown, an enthusiastic Brain Gym® instructor in Arizona who was bringing "learning through movement" to life through school workshops and classroom visits. Once I got to know Kathy personally, I found her to be an accomplished teacher and an exceptional advocate for learners. Watching her present key Brain Gym concepts in our advanced-level courses, I was impressed with her creativity and her gift for conveying the simplified essence of each topic she covered.

When I heard that she was writing a book about her experiences with the Brain Gym program, I knew immediately that this would be a work written by a caring educator who would answer the questions commonly asked by those who wonder how such simple physical activities can benefit learners. Knowing Kathy's commitment, I was certain she would seek those answers from a wide variety of sources. I am delighted to report that this well-referenced book is all that it promised to be.

Educate Your Brain offers an important look at how movement shapes the brain. This book is for all parents, teachers, life-students, sports enthusiasts, and business professionals who believe that each of us can access the opportunity to learn, grow, and be all that we can be. The inspiring case studies, many of them the kind of small miracles that represent true learning, document the happy experiences of students and clients of all ages as they rediscover the relationship between their physical structure and function. This marvelous book will have a positive impact on all who explore the many innovative concepts it includes.

As an author of books and course manuals about the Brain Gym work, I know how challenging it can be to create vivid images that convey the subtleties of Brain Gym theory and practice. I found it a joy to read this book, and I warmly acknowledge Kathy Brown, who held her vision for it through the many years it took to write. I know that Kathy's readers will be equally captivated by her story and all that she passionately shares in the telling of it.

~Paul E. Dennison

Origins
of the Brain Gym Program

Brain Gym® and its parent discipline Educational Kinesiology (Edu-K) developed out of more than seventeen years of research by Paul E. Dennison, originally a public school teacher and reading specialist, beginning in 1969 when he was director of the Valley Remedial Group Learning Centers in California. His primary clients were adults and children who had significant academic challenges: many were identified as dyslexic.

Paul Dennison's own history as a "challenged learner" gave him an acute awareness of the emotional and psychological impact of learning difficulties, as well as a great respect for the inner workings of the learning process. With his doctorate in the relationship between thinking skills and beginning reading ability, and his ongoing exploration of learning theory and left-right brain function, he began collaborating with experts in visual and motor development, searching for keys that would allow each client to succeed and grow.

> Paul Dennison beautifully describes his personal story in his book *Brain Gym® and Me—Reclaiming the Pleasure of Learning*.

At every turn, these collaborations reinforced the importance of physical movement to learning: Paul Dennison observed how a baby's first reflexive and developmental movements take her through the stages of patterning necessary for physical coordination and fine-motor control. Specific activities from developmental vision training encouraged eye-hand coordination, eye-teaming, and visual focus. Muscle-lengthening techniques from dance and physical therapy released muscle tension and restored the body to its natural alignment. And activities from

> Any movement-based program that works with "the brain" is actually addressing the entirety of the mind-body system. You'll learn more about this dynamic relationship as you explore the concepts presented throughout this book.

the Touch for Health program developed by the late John Thie, D.C., enhanced the equilibrium of the mind-body system.

To further support the learning process, Paul Dennison and his wife and partner Gail E. Dennison, a writer, artist, and movement educator, adapted activities from some of these disciplines and created other activities based on their understanding of the needs of the learner. Their clients of all ages not only overcame many physical coordination issues but simultaneously improved in reading, writing, math, listening, focus, and a host of other academic and social skills.

It became clear to the Dennisons that these activities were strengthening the foundational skills (e.g., smooth eye tracking and focus, postural control, left-right coordination, spatial orientation, auditory processing) that are required for success in academics and more.

> *Five Steps to Easy Learning* is a process unique to Edu-K that anchors new learning to movement experiences. Please see Chapter 12, "Make Lasting Change with Edu-K Balancing" for further information on this balance process.

Eventually, the Dennisons developed a very specific activity sequence that was even more effective than using the individual movements alone. It became known as Edu-K's *Five Steps to Easy Learning*, which is also called the "balance" process since it does just that: it brings both mental ability and physical coordination back into balance, creating a state of equilibrium.

Out of these discoveries, the Dennisons arrived at a profound awareness: learning readiness can be cultivated through physical movement by "bringing together the thinking intelligence and the coordination of the body."[1]

> Brain Gym® is the entry-level course of Educational Kinesiology. However, the terms *Brain Gym*® and *Edu-K* are often used interchangeably.

Over time, the Dennisons' collaboration and exploration grew into an entire discipline known as Educational Kinesiology (Edu-K): the study of movement in relation to achievement. Out of this rich system, they created the core Brain Gym® program to teach the basics of Edu-K in a way that is clear, effective, and easy to learn.

Brain Gym and Edu-K

At the foundation of the Edu-K system are twenty-six simple, enjoyable Brain Gym movements. People of all ages use these activities throughout the day to relieve stress, or as a quick mind-body warm-up before studying, writing, or sports—whatever the activity may be—bringing them back to feeling comfortable and productive.

The Edu-K five-step balance process takes the Brain Gym movements to a new level and supports deep and rapid change. An Edu-K balance can be done to overcome an obstacle you're experiencing: a skill you can't quite accomplish, a self-defeating habit you wish to eliminate, or a potential within yourself you'd like to develop. In Edu-K, this is called "balancing for" a specific goal, and the process is simply called "a balance."

Edu-K balances are experienced with a trained facilitator, either one-on-one or in groups. Children often choose to balance for coordination in skills such as kicking the ball in soccer, or academic skills such as reading easily or quickly recalling math facts. Adults often choose to address confidence in public speaking, or easily dealing with a certain person or situation. Groups (office staffs, project committees, athletic teams) may balance for easy communication or finding simple resolutions as challenges arise. Edu-K balancing typically results in immediate, sometimes dramatic, change.

Introduction
Moving Into Potential

Do we ever glimpse what our potential really is? Can we envision what it would possibly feel like to operate more comfortably and effectively, even in circumstances that currently feel challenging? Can we see this same ability not only in ourselves, but in our friends, family, and colleagues, and the children, students, or clients with whom we work?

This book is dedicated to the premise that making dynamic change in how we learn, process, and move through life can be simpler than we might ever have thought. The mind-body system has innate intelligence that is ready and waiting to be tapped; by following its lead, we can resolve even longstanding blocks to learning and achievement.

We are constantly educating our brain. Every time we repeat an action or thought, we spontaneously forge and reinforce pathways linking neurons in our mind-body system, creating networks that encourage those very behaviors to become automatic.

This can be for good or ill. We can memorize math facts or poetry, or become adept at soccer, piano, or managing paperwork, thus constantly reinforcing our sense of self as skilled and competent. We can also learn to feel overwhelmed by these same tasks, repeatedly seeing ourselves as incapable, hopeless, or unworthy. In addition, we may unknowingly wait a lifetime for "missing" neural lessons, intended to be experienced during infancy and childhood, which prepare us for efficient, joyful learning and participation in our world.

All of this education—or lack thereof—happens without our direct intention, casting its impression on our mind-body system and affecting how we move forward in life.

But what if we could *consciously* educate our brain? What if we could engage in a process that supports us in developing our innate abilities, overcoming stuck, counterproductive behaviors, and aligning with how we truly want to be?

This is my experience of the Brain Gym® program, and the subject of this book.

This unique system has the capacity to *draw out* from within us our own ability to move with ease through new learning; to develop integrated patterns of thought and action where once there was hesitation and confusion; to reveal the confidence and self-esteem that come with ability, productivity, and fulfillment of our potential to grow and learn.

Modern science tells us that *where our attention is focused* is the key to determining how our experience will affect our brain.[1] The Dennisons' philosophy is truly my experience as well: movement done with *focused intention for specific change* is the key to taking on new patterns of thought and behavior that bring us to comfort, competence, and joy.

Imagine the possibilities:

- Twenty-five wiggling, distracted third graders do four Brain Gym activities and immediately become calm, focused, and ready to learn.

- A college student must pass a crucial test she has already failed once. After a Brain Gym session, the material makes sense to her; she studies easily, and passes the exam.

- A child who struggles when reading aloud does the Brain Gym warm-up; he then reads fluently, and with expression.

- A woman's fear of driving has kept her limited to her own immediate neighborhood; following a Brain Gym session, she confidently drives home on the freeway.

- A fourth-grader diagnosed with fetal alcohol syndrome has never put spaces between the words he writes; after just a few Brain Gym movements, he writes with perfect spacing.

- Battling co-workers begin a planning meeting with a group Brain Gym session and then come up with creative, cooperative solutions that meet everyone's needs.

These are all shifts I experienced in my work with learners young and old. Initially, changes like these were astounding to me; I would never have imagined I'd see similar outcomes again and again.

Having had to work hard to achieve academically myself, and then teaching school for twenty-three years, I believed that overcoming learning obstacles was inevitably a struggle, and that change was always slow and incremental. I know now that I was wrong.

Who is this book for?

This book is for everyone: workers, parents, educators, students, athletes—anyone who wants to be more comfortable, capable, and effective at what he or she does, or who wants to support others (clients, students, children, friends) in learning or moving more easily.

Many people think of the Brain Gym program first in regard to children, and it is indeed very effective at helping children develop all kinds of academic, coordination, and interpersonal skills.

But the secret is out, and now adults are now using Brain Gym movements and processes in an ever-expanding number of ways. Brain Gym helps workers stay more focused and productive on the job. Athletes use it to stay more physically coordinated and mentally ready to perform at their peak. It helps people in all walks of life bring new energy and creative management skills to their day's events.

What's ahead

In this book you'll find simple tools to begin a practice of Brain Gym movements for yourself, or with your family, friends, or students. Together we'll cover:

- the four-step warm-up called PACE

- a sampling of other Brain Gym movements, and information on why each one may have such a beneficial effect

- the source of many learning, attitude, and performance challenges, why we are impelled to behave the way we do under stress, and what we can do about it

- simple processes that you can use immediately, and information to help you understand your experience

- ideas for applying the Brain Gym system in the areas of business, education, personal growth, home life, physical movement, and recovery from stress, distress, and trauma

- how and where to learn more

This Introduction offers just a quick glimpse of the Brain Gym program. Each of the topics mentioned here will be addressed in full within the pages to come. So I invite you to turn the page and join me for "A Brain Gym Beginning."

After reading this book you may find you'd like to know even more about
the Brain Gym®/Edu-K program.
Visit www.braingym.org to explore the possibilities!

PACE

Positive • Active • Clear • Energetic

A three-minute warm-up
for whole-brain living and learning

Chapter 1
A Brain Gym Beginning

I sat down to begin writing this book and a most surprising thing happened: I found myself absolutely stuck. I knew exactly what I wanted to say. I knew the basic structure I wanted the book to have. I had been making notes for months and refining the content through frequent talks and presentations. I had tremendous enthusiasm for actually beginning. And yet there I sat, staring at a blank computer screen, with a completely blank mind.

So I got up and did four simple movements, taking about three minutes in all. At the end of that time, I sat back down at my desk feeling refreshed. Ideas flowed effortlessly through my fingertips to the keyboard and onto the computer monitor—and became these very words.

What had I done? A simple Brain Gym® warm-up that allowed me to shift from stuck to energetic, and ready to begin.

How can movement bring about a change like this?

It's easy to recognize that our human body is designed to benefit from movement (exercise builds muscle tissue), but the concept that movement also benefits the many functions of the brain is only now beginning to be widely appreciated. John J. Ratey, M.D., author of *A User's Guide to the Brain*, says: "Mounting evidence shows that movement is crucial to. . . brain function, including memory, emotion, language, and learning. . . [O]ur 'higher' brain functions have evolved from movement and still depend on it."[1]

I experience this concept at work every time I do Brain Gym. I find that certain movements have a consistent, beneficial effect on my ability to perceive, evaluate, focus, respond, and function in my world.

Okay—what movements did you do?

I did a quick, four-step Brain Gym warm-up called "PACE" that prepares us for learning and achievement. I sipped some water, gave a quick massage to the points just below each collarbone, stood and slowly raised one knee at a time while touching it with the opposite elbow, and then sat for perhaps a minute with ankles crossed and arms criss-crossed in front of my chest.

"PACE" is an acronym that stands for *Positive, Active, Clear,* and *Energetic*. Each word describes the purpose of one of these four initial Brain Gym activities.

The PACE warm-up may sound quite simple—in fact, it's elegantly simple—yet the changes we may experience from it are sometimes profound. See what you experience as we explore a few Brain Gym movements together.

▶ First: Scan your body.

This will give you a "before" picture: how you feel right now. Allow your awareness to move slowly from head to foot and notice whatever presents itself. Just close your eyes or look gently into the distance as you scan your body.

What do you notice?

• How is your breathing: deep? shallow?

• Are there any aches, pains, or tight muscles making themselves known?

• Do you feel evenly balanced as you sit or stand? Are you comfortable?

• Is your mind agitated, foggy, or somewhere in between?

• What emotions are present?

• Anything else?

Get a clear picture of this "before" state and set it aside for now.

Sipping Water

Second: Experience the PACE activities.

1. Have a sip of water—or several sips. Take your time and allow yourself to really satisfy your thirst.

2. Rub your Brain Buttons. Just underneath your collarbones and on either side of the sternum (breastbone) are two spots that may be a bit softer than the surrounding area. Make a large "U" with the thumb and fingers of one hand and massage these two points simultaneously, while you rest your other hand over your navel. As you rub these spots you can move your eyes slowly, side to side. Do this for perhaps twenty to thirty seconds, switching hands halfway through.

Brain Buttons

3. Do the Cross Crawl. Standing, slowly raise one knee at a time and bring the opposite elbow or hand over to touch it: right elbow to left knee, left elbow to right knee. Alternate side to side in this way, for about a minute. (This can also be done sitting or lying down.)

4. Stand or sit in Hook-ups. Begin by crossing your ankles. Hold your arms out in front of you, thumbs downward. Cross your wrists and bring the palms of your hands together (you could "pat hands" in this position) and loosely interlace your fingers. Slightly bend your elbows and rotate your clasped hands down, in toward your body, then up, and allow them to rest against your chest. Relax your shoulders, loosening your clasped hands if necessary. Breathe easily, bringing your tongue to the roof of your mouth when you inhale, relaxing it when you exhale.

After resting in Hook-ups Part I for a minute or two (or as long as you like), uncross your hands and feet and bring the fingertips of both hands together. Remain this way for another 30 seconds or so, continuing this same breathing technique.

The Cross Crawl

Third: Scan your body again.

What do you notice now about:

- your breathing
- those aches, pains, or tight muscles
- your balance and level of comfort as you sit or stand
- the pace at which your mind is working
- emotions that are present
- anything else?

Compare this with the "before" picture you set aside a few moments ago. What changes do you notice?

Hook-ups,
Part I and II

As in any new practice you explore, please be sure to do the activities described in this book in a way that is comfortable for you and is in line with any recommendations your doctor may have. It is possible to modify any of the movements for easier participation. Consider using less pressure, doing the activity sitting or lying down, or to a lesser degree, to meet your particular needs. If you are not able to do these movements on your own due to any limiting factor, it's fine for someone else to assist you. You will want to maintain clear communication with your "helper" to be sure that he or she is facilitating in a way that is in line with your comfort level and doctors' recommendations, as above.

People who do these four Brain Gym movements often feel a shift in at least one area: their breathing becomes fuller and deeper, physical tension diminishes or even vanishes, posture becomes more balanced and comfortable, racing thoughts slow down or troubling thoughts fade, and stress leaves as a sense of well-being emerges. People tend to feel more calm, focused, and at ease. They often find that their eyes move more comfortably as they read and that what they're reading makes more sense. Then they have this question: *Why did I feel a change?* Simple: You allowed your body to move.

Okay, it's not quite that simple! It was the integrating nature of the movements you were doing. This easy, enjoyable Brain Gym warm-up can have a profound effect on how we function and how we feel, preparing us to move at our best pace and rhythm.

While we talk about *PACE* as an acronym for

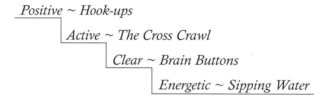

Positive ~ Hook-ups

Active ~ The Cross Crawl

Clear ~ Brain Buttons

Energetic ~ Sipping Water

...what we really do is "ECAP": we climb the stairs starting at the bottom—essentially "stepping up into PACE."

In the next four chapters, you can explore each element of this warm-up in greater depth and learn why these movements may have so many positive effects. Or, you may choose to skip to Chapter 6, "How Simple It Is," for more information on how these four movements combine to be such a power-packed routine.

Chapter 2

Water: Charge Up Your Body's Battery

~ PACE: Positive, Active, Clear, **Energetic**

How does it feel to have an *Energetic* day? You know the kind I mean: where you easily accomplish your tasks with a sense of productivity and a positive attitude. One important part of the answer may be *consuming enough water*. When I feel lethargic or low in energy, I perk up considerably—sometimes even dramatically—once I've had sufficient water. Then, whatever I'm doing seems to become easier; I feel refreshed, alert, motivated, and more comfortable overall. What is water's role in this energetic equation?

Our nervous system, in charge of sending important messages throughout the body, relies on electrical impulses to do a large part of its work. Jim Robbins, author of *A Symphony in the Brain*, describes each neuron (nerve cell) as a "microscopic battery" whose membrane "builds up a charge electrochemically and then releases it, over and over again."[1] In order for this electrical messaging system to operate, we must be sufficiently hydrated.

Sipping Water

An energetic beginning

I love that the PACE warm-up begins with Sipping Water. This simple action refreshes our neural system, through which we bring in sensorimotor feedback and issue commands for skilled action. I believe this enhances the ability to monitor our own inner state—and make appropriate adjustments—as we go through a Brain Gym® session, or through our busy day.

> ▶ I invite you to pause for a sip of water, even if you don't feel thirsty. Hold the water in your mouth for a moment before swallowing. If you're inspired to, take another sip—or two or three. What do you notice?

Over the years, I've developed a habit of drinking water throughout the day, and this has brought me to a whole new appreciation of the benefits of this simple act. Now I have a heightened awareness of when my "water meter" feels low. When I find myself feeling cranky or losing productivity, I quite often look back and realize it's been an hour or more since I consumed any water. Then, just a few sips help me return to a state of clarity and effectiveness.

I consistently get similar feedback from clients and students. And I've received many email messages from amazed teachers who report that, when their students sip water throughout the day, it greatly improves their ability to focus, learn, and behave appropriately. They say it's as if they're teaching a "whole new class."

How could this be? Science tells us that, without enough water in our system, neural messages don't get through as quickly or easily (see below). How effective can we be in this state? Is it possible that when we're not adequately hydrated, we have less access to our innate skills and sensory signals? If so, would this change how we respond to the world around us and affect how ready we are to learn?

A bit of background

Water is vital for appropriate electrical activity within our body. Every living cell needs to have positively charged ions outside it and negatively charged ions inside it. This difference maintains the cell's *polarity*, also called *membrane potential*. Neurons are specialized cells that carry electrical messages throughout our body, and they need to have "good membrane potential" in order to do this job well.

> Electrical impulses generated by living tissue, especially nerve cells, are sometimes described as *bioelectrical*.

The ions necessary for membrane potential (sodium, potassium, and chloride) come from the salts in our diet. Some come from regular table salt (sodium chloride) and others occur naturally in fruits, vegetables, and animal products. When salts we have consumed come in contact with water, they separate into their component ions, or electrolytes. In this way, the ions are made available to our body, maintaining the membrane potential of our cells, so our neural system is able to conduct the electrical messages that help our body to function.

> The term *electrolytes* may be familiar to you as a component of popular sports beverages, which replace the salts eliminated through sweat during exercise.

The need for water

When clients come to my office for a Brain Gym balance session, the first thing we do is sip some water—the first step of the PACE warm-up. Sometimes a client's reaction is, "Oh, I never get thirsty." The truth is, if we go long enough without water, we can lose our thirst trigger.[2] Once a "never-thirsty" person starts drinking water, she often can't believe how much of it her body wants. I've seen people surprise themselves by reaching again and again for their water glass during their session.

While members of the medical community may not agree on exactly how much water a person needs, I frequently find recommendations for consuming eight to ten glasses per day. Clearly, we need to replace what we release through respiration, elimination, and perspiration. We do get water from foods and other liquids in a healthy diet; however, in my experience, there's nothing that quite takes the place of a drink of pure water.

> "Lower membrane potential, while making us more alert to smaller stimuli, disables our capacity to selectively focus and control our sensory input. At such times, learning is very difficult." [3]
> ~ Carla Hannaford
> *Smart Moves*

A bit about liquids

Some people discount what they hear about their body's need for water. They may think it's not very interesting as a beverage. And many of us have been conditioned to think that if it's not flavored, carbonated, or caffeinated, it's not much fun.

Adults often ask, "But coffee has water in it. Doesn't that count?" Well, yes and no. Coffee, non-herbal teas, and most soft drinks generally contain caffeine. Caffeine acts as a diuretic, so it encourages your body to release fluids. That means if you drink a cup of coffee or a glass of iced tea, you might not gain the full benefits of the equivalent amount of water. I love a good cup of coffee, and I often enjoy iced tea when I go out for lunch, but I'm always thirsty afterward! If you're like me, you may find that you do just fine drinking caffeinated beverages as long as you balance them with actual water. The key is to truly notice how you feel and how well you operate with varying levels of hydration; then you can develop a routine for consuming water that really works for you.

Water as an issue in schools

As someone who taught elementary school for many years, I'm very familiar with the challenge of *when* to consume beverages. I remember feeling all but captive in my classroom once the school day began, since I could not leave my students unsupervised to go to the restroom. (Keep in mind that in those days I was a devoted tea and cola drinker, which my body experiences as diuretic.) The bottom line was that I hardly drank any liquids at all during the school day. This is not optimal for a teacher's health.

Of course, the other challenge in schools concerns children's needs for water. Besides the fact that they're starting to turn up their noses at "city water," it's hard for children to get the amount they really need from a drinking fountain. (Have you ever been able to really quench your thirst at a fountain?) For students, there's the added pressure of trying to grab a drink with ten others in line behind them, telling them to hurry up because the bell is about to ring!

> Water quality varies widely by region and city. It's important to know your locale and act accordingly. In my opinion, though, drinking readily available water is often better than drinking no water.

A growing number of teachers ask students to bring water bottles from home, or provide them in the classroom, and encourage students to sip water throughout the day. This is excellent, especially in light of what we're learning about the positive effects of water on our capacity to focus and learn.

About the benefits of water

Scientists are only beginning to study the effects of water on cognitive ability; however, one excellent paper was recently published. In a peer-reviewed article for the highly regarded journal *Appetite*, authors David Benton and Naomi Burgess (Department of Psychology, University of Wales) describe their research on water consumption and children's cognitive processing. Both immediate memory and delayed memory showed a statistically significant improvement after a drink of water.[4]

Electro-encephalograph (EEG) machines measure electrical impulse levels in the brain, which register as alpha, beta, theta, or delta waves, denoting different levels of consciousness found in humans.

A study by Sue Maes Thyret, a Brain Gym consultant in Ontario, Canada, illustrates the benefit of drinking water. She attached her electroencephalograph (EEG) machine to volunteers in order to measure the effects on the brain of various Brain Gym movements. In a presentation at one of the international Brain Gym conferences, she showed images of two EEG readings from the same person, taken about fifteen seconds apart. The first image showed high alpha and theta brain waves that indicate inwardly focused, relaxed, passive attention. The second showed mid-range beta waves that indicate alert outer focus, attention, and memory retention. What had this person done to make such a shift in fifteen seconds? *He'd taken a sip of water.*

A closing thought on water

I received this email from an occupational therapist who had just completed a Brain Gym® 101 course:

> I work regularly with Lara, a girl with developmental delay who has been in therapy since she was born, so that would be eleven years. Her mother is very much the doubting-Thomas type, especially with regard to trying new ways to help. After working with Lara today, I was chatting with the mother for about a half an hour, during which time Lara became unfocused and dazed without something to engage her mind and body. I remembered what you'd said about water and focus, so I suggested to the mother that water might help right now, and explained why. As usual, she immediately dismissed the idea as having no credence. By now, Lara was slouching heavily against her, staring into space, and wasn't able to answer any of our questions. The mother finally relented and gave Lara some water—and all of a sudden there was this energetic child again! She stood up straight,

focused easily on her mother, and started trying to engage her mother in conversation. It was truly powerful to watch—and for this mother to see—the changes in her daughter after just having a sip of water!

So many benefits come from something so simple—drinking water. Now that our body is more energized, let's move on to clearer thinking with the Brain Buttons.

Chapter 3
Brain Buttons: Clear Out the Cobwebs

~ PACE: Positive, Active, **Clear**, Energetic

Imagine having one simple Brain Gym® movement that you could do almost anytime to bring more clarity to your vision and the feeling of energy and coordination to your whole body. You do—and it's right at your fingertips! So take a moment to experience the Brain Buttons once again, the movement that represents *Clear* in the PACE warm-up:

Brain Buttons

▶ At the top of your ribcage are your collarbones. Find these horizontal bones and then let your fingers slip downward about an inch or so, until they're resting over your uppermost ribs, just on either side of your sternum, or breastbone. These spots may feel like slight indentations, or softer than the surrounding area.

Make a large "U" with your hand and place the thumb on one of the spots, and the fingertips on the other. Massage these points gently but firmly as you rest your other hand over your navel, and allow your eyes to track gently side to side. Do this for perhaps twenty to thirty seconds. (If you experience tenderness, rub gently until it is released or reduced.) Then switch hands for another twenty to thirty seconds. What do you notice?

When I rub my Brain Buttons on a stressful day, I often find myself exhaling deeply as I feel my body relax. I may notice my shoulders dropping and my posture straightening. Sometimes I feel a release of tension at the back of my neck. Then even my eyes relax, and it's easier to scan lines of print, or more fully see the world around me. Typically, I feel more awake and focused.

A bit of background

There are many perspectives from which to appreciate this simple Brain Buttons activity. Paul and Gail Dennison focus their exploration on how it supports our posture and spatial orientation. They say this movement provides "a stable physical reference for moving the eyes left and right," and helps to "establish the midfield. . . as the central area of reference for horizontal movement toward and away from the midline."[1]

Other people may explain the benefits of this movement by referring to concepts from the world of applied kinesiology, developed in the 1960s by the esteemed chiropractor George Goodheart, D.C. This discipline refers to the concept of *switching*, or *neurological disorganization*, in which we may experience confusion between such things as left and right. In his text on applied kinesiology, David S. Walther describes how various aspects of neurological disorganization are associated with learning challenges, such as the tendency to reverse letters like "d" and "b," and difficulty reading left-to-right.[2]

Applied kinesiology describes how the state of left/right switching may also lead to "ocular lock." When our brain is not able to synchronize the movements of our eyes, looking in a specific direction (different in each person or case) may result in eyestrain, dizziness, and even extreme drowsiness. Common activities producing ocular lock are reading and driving, both of which require shifting the eyes from side to side. The effort required to focus while in this state can result in excessive muscle tension in the back of the neck.[3]

> More information on the K-27s and the "meridian system" of the body can be found in the Addendum.

In applied kinesiology, the "correction" for both these conditions is to rub the "K-27" points of acupuncture—just under the collarbones, near the sternum—while covering or massaging the navel area. Sound familiar?

Two key benefits of Brain Buttons

One of the frequent outcomes of the Brain Buttons movement, as mentioned above, is release of *ocular lock*, which can prevent us from using both eyes comfortably and fully.

I taught the Brain Buttons movement to a roomful of workshop participants and asked them to share what they noticed. One woman commented, "I had no idea that I was holding so much stress, but when I started rubbing my Brain Buttons, I felt a major release of tension in the back of my neck! My upper body posture sort of moved into alignment, and then everything in the room around me shifted from fuzzy to clear. It was like I'd just cleaned my glasses!"

The Dennisons sometimes describe the Brain Buttons movement as a "mini balance for crossing the midline." This was vividly demonstrated as I worked one day with a young client.

Jacob, age 7, arrived for his session with his mother, who had learned about the Cross Crawl movement and had been doing it at home with him. As soon as he set foot in my office, he wanted to show me what he could do, but it was clearly a struggle. Getting his arm to the opposite knee took a surprising amount of planning and effort, and he almost fell down in the process. So I asked, "Jacob, would you like to try a little something that might make the Cross Crawl easier?" and he readily agreed. I showed him where his Brain Buttons were, and he took some time rubbing them. When he was finished, he Cross Crawled again—this time with much improved coordination and balance. He was delighted!

Ongoing opportunity for noticing

People have various responses to rubbing their Brain Buttons, and they're sometimes quite subtle. I always remind workshop participants to give themselves time to experience the difference this movement can make. Your ability to notice these changes will deepen with practice. Prepare to be surprised!

One day, I gave three consecutive workshops for a local corporation, focusing on the PACE process as a means of managing stress. All three sessions were coordinated by the same person, a very tightly-wound human resources director. During the first two workshops, he smiled and nodded politely as he did the Brain Gym movements along with the group but didn't say anything in particular. During the third workshop, however, his face absolutely lit up when he rubbed his Brain Buttons. He said, "Wow! I didn't feel anything doing this the other times, but now my brain feels warm! And I feel so awake and full of energy! What's going on?" My guess: This was the third time he'd rubbed his Brain Buttons that day, and his body had finally relaxed to the point where he could experience its benefits.

While rubbing your Brain Buttons is an important part of the four-step PACE process, as with any Brain Gym movement, it's fine to do it on its own.

One evening, after a very demanding day, I was sitting in a theater with my husband, listening to a classical chorale performance. It was wonderful—and long. And the room was dark. Before long, my head was nodding and I was struggling to keep my eyes open. Then I thought about Brain Buttons. I quietly brought my hand up and gave those spots a bit of a rub and instantly found myself wide awake! I could not believe how alert I had become. I was reminded of turning on my computer in the morning—I hear the familiar "hmmm!" and the monitor lights up—and that's exactly how my brain felt. I felt completely alert and refreshed throughout the rest of the evening.

While a truly remarkable occurrence like this may not happen every day, I continue to experience smaller, helpful shifts all the time. I often use this movement (sometimes nonchalantly) during long meetings, and in a wide variety of similar situations, to maintain a clear focus and remain at my best. It's even been described to me as a "lifesaver" when driving:

Arlene was fairly new to Brain Gym, and she'd been telling her husband about the benefits of some of the Brain Gym movements. He consistently made light of her "new thing." Late one night, he arrived home after a long drive back from a meeting. He looked at her, glanced away, and sheepishly muttered, "Okay, it works." Arlene really wasn't sure what he'd said and asked him to repeat it. This time he grinned and said, "It works. It works. I was really drowsy at the wheel and thought I'd give that rubbing thing a try. It really woke me up. What other Brain Gym tricks have you got?"

Now that rubbing our Brain Buttons has readied us to think more clearly and feel more alert, let's move on to the Cross Crawl.

Chapter 4

The Cross Crawl:
Power Up Your Hemispheres

~ PACE: Positive, **Active**, Clear, Energetic

Before I became a student of the Brain Gym® program, I never gave the hemispheres of my brain a second thought beyond knowing that some people, like me, were "right brained" and others were "left brained." Then I learned how important it is that both hemispheres work together, that this capacity must actually be developed (through early movement experiences like infant crawling)—and that when this connection is lacking or insufficient, all kinds of cognitive and coordination problems can arise. The best thing I learned, however, is that people of any age can nurture this *Active* right-left communication through simple cross-lateral movement.

The Cross Crawl

▶ Here's an opportunity to experience the Cross Crawl once again, while you're learning more about it. Stand (or sit or lie down) and slowly raise one knee at a time as you bring the opposite elbow or hand over to it. Alternate back and forth, elbow to the opposite knee.

What do you notice? Was the Cross Crawl easy for you to do, or did it require a bit of thought or planning in order to bring your hand to the opposite knee?

I've learned that the Cross Crawl can be challenging for people under stress, for those whose daily activities call primarily on one side of the brain (most often the detail-oriented left hemisphere), or for those whose infancy and childhood didn't include the kinds of movement that are necessary for whole-brain development.

Doing the Cross Crawl in any position is good; doing it while standing, and especially slowly (s-l-o-w-l-y), is most beneficial because it calls on more of your body-balance mechanism (the vestibular system), improving physical balance and coordination. Some children will only be able to do the Cross Crawl quickly. You'll want to help them slow down over time, so they're moving consciously, rather than reflexively. They'll enjoy playful Cross Crawling, switching back and forth between fast and slow. In her book *Move into Life*, movement expert Anat Baniel describes the benefit of *slow* movement: "Slow gets the brain's attention and gives it time to distinguish and perceive small changes and form new connections. Fast, you can only do what you already know. To be aware and to create new patterns, you need to *feel*, and that requires slowing down." [1]

Coordination and communication

Does the Cross Crawl develop our hemispheres' ability to communicate and share information? I believe it does, based on what I see in my clients and students. Even if their Cross Crawl at first feels awkward, as they continue on, it typically becomes quite smooth and fluid; at the same time, they report feeling more coordinated, more skilled at eye-teaming, and more able to learn and think.

To understand all the benefits of the Cross Crawl, it's important to back up a bit and describe the process we go through to develop fluid communication between the two sides of our brain.

A bit of background

The outermost structure of the human brain, or *cerebrum*, is divided into two matching halves, or hemispheres. Each hemisphere is further divided into four *lobes* with regions devoted to movement, visual processing, auditory processing, and planning and conceptualizing. Special nerve fibers connect these various brain areas so they can coordinate their efforts.

This myelination occurs not just in the corpus callosum, but throughout the rest of the brain and body, wherever axons spread to deliver neural messages.

In order for us to function optimally, many of these fibers need to connect regions in both hemispheres, so they can act in concert (i.e., both eyes working together). However, these lateral connecting fibers must pass through a small, compressed structure called the *corpus callosum*. Imagine the residents of two huge cities traveling back and forth across a single bridge!

"In highly myelinated neurons, impulses travel at 100 meters per second. Therefore, the more practice, the more myelin, and the faster the processing—until it becomes easy and familiar, like driving fast on a superhighway." [2]
~ Carla Hannaford
Smart Moves

Fortunately, our body has an ingenious method of speeding up this neural commute: It lays down myelin, an insulating substance, on frequently used neural pathways, allowing messages to zip along them quickly and efficiently, improving the two hemispheres' ability to share and coordinate information.

The two sides of our brain must *learn* to work together—and this active connection is developed *through physical movement*.

Why do we need the cooperation of both hemispheres?

We do most of our work and play in the space directly in front of us, where our two visual fields overlap. Here we use both eyes for reading and bringing in other information about our world; our two hands coordinate for catching a ball; our writing hand tracks through this space to put words on paper. Paul Dennison calls this area *the midfield*. Key opportunities for learning and communication occur here in the midfield, all of which require readiness and integration to make the most of them.

> Paul Dennison fully describes the midfield on page 93 of his book *Brain Gym® and Me: Reclaiming the Pleasure of Learning.*

However, if both sides of our brain aren't sharing information easily, we may lack coordination in using both hands (or both feet or both eyes) as we work and play. For example, a young child in this state may have challenges in catching a ball; his eyes must cooperate to converge on the ball as it comes toward him and guide closure of his hands—right on his midline. And tying shoes can also be problematic, as it can take considerable time for him to learn how to hold a loop with one hand and wrap it with the lace held in the other.

As the child grows older, the acts of reading and writing require that both eyes (and the hand holding the pencil) start at the left side of the page and travel fluidly across to the right side. If his eyes don't team and track well, they may have only one preferred zone for functioning—so he may position his writing paper or book to the extreme right or left. Or he may actually move the book back and forth in front of him, or move his whole head instead of just his eyes. And one of the most common midline issues I've found is the tendency of some children to reverse letters, such as "d" and "b."

> A further exploration of reading challenges can be found in Chapter 11, "Ready for Reading."

Building a midline bridge

Effortlessly crossing your elbow over to the opposite knee, as we do in the Cross Crawl, requires the simultaneous use of both sides of the brain. Children (or adults) who have not developed sufficient cross-lateral patterning may find that coordinating the movement of both sides of the body is stressful for them: it's much easier to use only one side of their body at a time. Someone in this state may find himself expending extra effort to coordinate the movement of opposite limbs, or simply end up bringing his elbow to his same-side knee. This is called a *homolateral*, or one-sided, state.

Many times, I've had to gently and repeatedly guide a person's arm over to her opposite knee. Some people actually need to be "motored" through the Cross Crawl by having someone physically lift and connect first their right knee and left hand, and then left knee and right hand, as they sit in a chair or lie on the floor. I sometimes see this in people who've suffered a stroke, as well as others who may not have developed enough neural patterning between their brain hemispheres.

Warren, age eight, had significant school issues. He had great difficulty in reading and was physically very awkward—always tripping over some object in front of him, or even his own feet. When I asked him to Cross Crawl, he dutifully raised his left knee and moved his right elbow toward it. It was as if there was a transparent wall between his right and left sides. His elbow stopped moving across his body, right at the midline. With the downward motion he'd already begun with his elbow, he almost fell. Warren was not "just misbehaving." He really wanted to Cross Crawl and was doing his best; he simply could not cross the midline.

No wonder Warren was having such a hard time in school. To read a line of print, both of his eyes had to cooperate and flow across the page. To write a sentence, his hand and eyes had to work together in the midfield as he wrote. Clearly, even attempting these activities was very tiring for him.

Over the next few weeks, as Warren did the Cross Crawl daily in his classroom and at home, his coordination improved significantly. Before long, he was spontaneously reaching for the opposite knee. And, simultaneously, his reading and writing improved!

So—we've developed an effective "brain bridge" through a childhood filled with integrating, cross-lateral movement, and we're ready to roll through a lifetime of activities. Or are we? We are—unless we're under chronic stress or consistently involved in activities that call on mainly one hemisphere of our brain.

Whole-brain challenges under stress

The effect that stress has on the body is fairly widely known, but the effect it has on the brain, and therefore on our ability to think and act effectively, is only beginning to be appreciated. To understand how and why, let's explore a bit about our survival response.

When we experience stress, our brain stem (survival center) shows increased blood flow and electrical activity, while that of the frontal lobes is considerably diminished.[3] This not only limits our cognitive functioning, but it may affect the *kinds* of tasks we find challenging on a difficult day.

Please see Chapter 9, "Theory in Action," for more on the concepts of "switching off" and hemisphere dominance.

Many people typically favor the processing style of one hemisphere over the other, resulting in labels such as "right-brain dominant" or "left-brain dominant." However, when the entire area of the frontal lobes is less active, this difference in processing style may be noticed even more dramatically, giving rise to the feeling that our non-dominant hemisphere has "switched off" under stress.

This is why people often find themselves feeling less capable when they're under stress: They're no longer in a whole-brain operating state, so they're "trying" to function without all their natural capacities available.

I was actually relieved when I learned this, because it explained so much about the challenges I experienced as a student. Under stress, my ability to focus (a function of the frontal lobes) was limited. As a very right-brained learner, when I was under stress, the capacities of my left hemisphere seemed to vanish, leaving me with very little access to the part of my brain which functions most naturally with details. This made schoolwork even more difficult for me.

> My husband is the opposite: a very left-brained learner, he loses the "big picture" capacities of his right hemisphere when under stress, but maintains his ability to function beautifully with details.

Learning this information about the brain gave me a way to understand that it wasn't that I simply didn't care enough or try hard enough in my studies: if I was under stress, my brain was bound to behave in this way. I wish I had known then that simple cross-lateral movement could bring my two hemispheres into more balanced participation. Even now, when I need to attend to details, such as elements of accounting or data entry in my computer, I always do some Cross Crawl first, so I can approach my task in a whole-brain state.

And, as much Brain Gym as I've done since those days, I still can find myself operating in a stressed, homolateral way. At the end of a long, demanding day, or in challenging circumstances, I may start to Cross Crawl and find myself bringing my elbow down to my same-side knee instead! Then I'm really happy to have such an effective tool at the ready: I can do some Cross Crawl and end up mentally refreshed and ready to go.

The issue of "priming" just one hemisphere

We may also find ourselves operating in a one-sided way because major elements of our career, favored pastimes, or other frequent tasks primarily call on one hemisphere. Math, for example, is a very left-hemisphere-intense activity. I facilitated a workshop for an association of certified public accountants, using the principles of the PACE warm-up to address stress management issues. When we got to the Cross Crawl, many of the people in the room initially brought their arm to their same-side knee. Eventually everyone got the pattern, but for some it took more than a minute or two, and for a few, considerable coaching! One accountant I know practices piano daily and takes art lessons, specifically to keep more balance between her hemispheres—and in her life.

Pressed by a variety of budgetary and academic proficiency issues, many schools have squeezed out the whole-brain activities of art, music, physical education, and even recess. This results in increased amounts of time spent sitting, sitting, sitting, working with details. It's no surprise that so many children are at a loss when asked to practice creative writing and critical thinking skills! These activities require use of the whole brain.

One of the most intensely left-brain activities young children experience is phonics. I have worked with students who are simply incapable of *reading* after doing phonics practice. However, if they do some Cross Crawl or other Brain Gym® Midline Movements after phonics or, better still, do these movements as part of their phonics lesson, they flow much more easily into reading. Perhaps this is because they are storing and using their phonics skills in a more whole-brain way.

The Cross Crawl in daily life

Life is full of occasions when we want to be at our best. From business meetings or creative endeavors to sports, reading, and writing—any time we're experiencing stress or simply want to enjoy our activities more fully—having "both brains" available will give us an advantage. I invite you to add a bit of Cross Crawl to your life and see for yourself what a difference it makes.

And now, let's finish our exploration of the PACE warm-up with the next Brain Gym movement, Hook-ups.

Chapter 5

Hook-ups: Move Out of Your Brain Stem and into the Flow

~ PACE: **Positive**, Active, Clear, Energetic

How often do you find yourself more or less in a state of stress, or even overwhelm? If you're like me, even with the best of intentions to stay even and calm, life's events can tend to mount up; only later do I realize how tense I've become. Shifting into "survival mode" can limit our ability to focus, comprehend, and make rational choices. Not the best scenario for ease and productivity!

To shift out of survival and back to a *Positive* state, we can use a movement called Hook-ups. This is the single Brain Gym® activity, shared by a friend so long ago, that made an immediate difference in my stress level, and left me wanting to know more about what the entire Brain Gym program had to offer.

> ▶ **Hook-ups Part I:**
>
> Sit comfortably (or stand or lie down) and cross your ankles. Hold your hands out in front of you, rotated so that your thumbs are down. Now cross your wrists so the palms of your hands could pat each other. Loosely interlace your fingers; then bend your elbows and bring your clasped hands down and toward you, allowing them to come to rest against your chest. (If this arm position is challenging for any reason, simply cross your wrists over your chest.) If you like, you can lightly touch your tongue to the roof of your mouth just behind your teeth when you inhale, and let it relax as you exhale.

Hook-ups Part I

Cook's Hook-ups
A variation for Part I

In my experience, many people find that there is no one "right" way for them to do Hook-ups. Some people cross their wrists and ankles in the same direction (both right over left, or both left over right), and some seem to get the most out of crossing wrists and ankles in opposite directions (ankles left over right, wrists right over left). Some prefer to cross in one direction for a bit and then release and cross differently. Anyone's preferences in this may change from day to day or hour to hour; it's fun to notice differences and consistencies in how we spontaneously choose to cross.

Some people prefer this variation for Part I, called Cook's Hook-ups: Sitting comfortably, cross your right ankle over your left knee. Grasp your right ankle with the left hand and cross your right hand over to wrap your fingers around the ball of the right foot. (This may be done in the opposite way, reversing left and right for these directions.)

▶ Hook-ups Part II:

Whether you prefer Hook-ups Part I or the Cook's Hook-ups variation, after a minute or so (or as long as you like), conclude with Part II. Uncross your ankles and wrists and bring the fingertips of both hands together. Continue to touch your tongue to the roof of your mouth (relaxing it on the exhalation) as you breathe deeply for another minute or so. Sit this way for several moments, until you feel "settled."

What do you notice?

Hook-ups Part II

"Cook's Hook-ups" got its name from Wayne Cook, a pioneering researcher of bioenergetic force fields, who theorized that this body position helped to counterbalance the negative effects of electromagnetic fields.[1]

After using Hook-ups, most people feel markedly calmer, less overwhelmed. Their shoulders relax as tense muscles release, and they breathe more deeply. Their racing thoughts slow down; they feel more present and focused.

The more stressed you are when you begin this activity, the more obvious a change you will likely notice. To explore why the Hook-ups movement may leave us in such a positive state, let's begin by looking at our survival system.

Our body's survival wiring

Throughout our lives, we experience stressful situations: exams, arguments, deadlines, embarrassment, heavy traffic, etc. The challenge is that no matter what kind of stress we may be facing, our body readies itself to handle a *physical threat* and prepares to defend itself at all costs. Two main survival impulses are to attack or run away (fight or flight). In either case, our body adds a big boost of adrenaline so we can attack with force, or run away fast. Sometimes our clever body chooses "freeze," where we stop in our tracks as if to fade into the background like a scared fawn. We may be frozen, but that same boost of adrenaline still surges through our system.

A bit of background

At the base of our brain is the brain stem, which is often called the "survival center." It's hard-wired at birth for automatic reactions that increase our chances of physical survival.

When we perceive a threat (whether real or imagined) the body starts directing blood flow toward the brain stem—and away from the frontal lobes, or forebrain, where we perform higher-order thinking skills. (If your house were on fire, you probably wouldn't need your knowledge of calculus, for example.) This state of stress actually can be measured. It registers on an electroencephalograph machine (EEG) as "high beta" brain waves, associated with narrow focus, anxiety, physical tension, and readiness for quick physical movement. All of this leaves us primed for reaction unencumbered by conscious thought.[3]

> "Whenever a brain region is activated, its blood vessels dilate and in one to five seconds the area in question receives a fresh influx of oxygenated blood." [2]
> ~ Stanislaus Dehaene
> *Reading in the Brain*

Returning to a positive state

How do we prepare to deal appropriately with a psychological or emotional challenge in life when our brain is primed to deal with a physical emergency? How do we release the feeling of "overwhelm" and return to a calm, positive state? We can use Hook-ups.

Why do so many people experience this as helpful? First, we can consider the physiological element. When we're under stress, our energy reserves go to the brain stem, leaving the cortex less active. Because our hands are so sensitive and articulate, large portions of our brain's sensory and motor cortex are devoted to them (far out of proportion to their size relative to the rest of the body). When we interlace our fingers, we activate that entire territory—in both hemispheres simultaneously. Essentially, this brings energy out of our brain stem and into our thinking brain.

Secondly, some who are familiar with Chinese medicine explain Hook-ups in terms of the *meridian system*. This ancient discipline identifies fourteen main meridians, or subtle energy flows, in the body. Two of these are on the body's central midline, front and back; the other twelve run either up or down along specific routes between our torso and fingertips or toes, in matched sets on either side of the body. Some believe that connecting our hands and feet in this particular Hook-ups pattern encourages the subtle energy to flow through areas formerly blocked by tension, and that touching the fingertips together in Hook-ups Part II helps balance activity between the two sides of the brain and the rest of the body.

> You'll find more on the meridian system, a key element in the practice of acupuncture, in Appendix D.

A third explanation simply focuses on *where we place our focus*. We spend so much time paying attention to external elements of our lives: *that* job, *that* task, *that* person, *that* responsibility, *that* deadline. When we live our lives like this, we forget to pay attention to ourselves, and we start overriding the authentic thoughts or feelings that might get in the way of accomplishing all this "important stuff." When we sit in Hook-ups, we cross our ankles and intertwine our arms, right over our own midline. We bring all that outward focus right back inside, to the present moment, and we can begin to more deeply notice our own thoughts and feelings again.

Regardless of the model we employ to explain its benefits, people most often find sitting in Hook-ups to be very soothing. In fact, this is clearly demonstrated on an EEG machine. Subjects in Hook-ups have been shown to move quickly into the alpha or theta states of deep relaxation.[5]

As we relax, the brain stem's fear-based grip on our awareness begins to release and we have more access to the forebrain (and reason) again. Once we are no longer in the midst of a fear reaction, we can see the situation from a safer, more balanced perspective, and the feeling of overwhelm simply falls away.

Two days after I was introduced to Hook-ups, a friend called me on the phone, sounding extremely upset. She was in tears as she told me that the company she worked for was downsizing and she was sure she'd be let go. She'd just bought a new home and was worried she'd have to sell it, and on top of all that, she and her longtime boyfriend had just broken up. I asked if she'd like to try something that might help, and a small, teary "Okay. . . " came back over the phone. I described how to move into the Hook-ups posture, and waited. After perhaps fifteen seconds, a completely different voice—a grounded, deeper, confident voice—came over the line, saying, "What *IS* this?" I knew what had happened, but I chose just to ask, "Why?" She replied, "Well, nothing in my life has changed in the last few seconds, but it's just not overwhelming now. I can handle it." And she did.

Yes, my friend's life still had ups and downs as she dealt with all these matters, but she now had a tool that could help her stay on a more even keel with calm, reasoned responses instead of hasty, emotional reactions. Sitting in Hook-ups had allowed her to return to a more comfortable, functional state where it was easier to hold her life's events in perspective and deal with them proactively. Hook-ups also works wonders in the classroom:

A friend of mine teaches orchestra at two elementary schools and one high school. Her strings program was so popular that one year she found herself with a class of thirty-three enthusiastic third-grade violin students. *Thirty-three*—all in one room with violins that needed tuning, not to mention just being active third-graders! As you can imagine, she was rapidly going crazy with all these youngsters wanting individual attention. I said, "Teach them Hook-ups. Call it 'pretzel sitting.' They'll think it's fun." So she did. "It's amazing," she told me later. "The children calm down and become almost. . . serene! Then they listen so well and class goes smoothly. When I'm working with one section, I have the others 'pretzel sitting.'" My friend also taught "pretzel sitting" to her high-school orchestra students that day. The next day, she could hardly hold class because they all wanted to tell her how they'd used Hook-ups to their advantage in the previous twenty-three hours.

I love teaching Brain Gym movements, especially Hook-ups, to children because of the many profound ways that stress affects them, too. Using Hook-ups is a positive way for a child to manage his own thoughts and behaviors. As one boy said to me, "I never knew I could do something about being angry besides hit. Now I can use Hook-ups." What power this gives to children—to us all—to be able to *choose* to be calm and focused—and to know how to get there.

Regarding attitudes, behavior, and learning

Hook-ups is a powerful tool for learning. It's very difficult to learn under stress, because in this state, we have so little access to the territory where higher order thinking skills occur. Rather than a helpful flow of information through the higher structures of the brain (from visual input to processing, memory, analysis, and finally to expression through writing or speech), we're limited to functioning through lower structures, especially the brain stem.

Bruce D. Perry, M.D., a child psychiatrist specializing in trauma recovery, describes it this way:

> When we are calm it is easy to live in our cortex, using the highest capacities of our brains to contemplate abstractions, make plans, dream of the future, read. But if something attracts our attention and intrudes on our thoughts, we become more vigilant and concrete, shifting the balance of our brain activity to subcortical areas to heighten our senses in order to detect threats. As we move up the arousal continuum toward fear, then, we necessarily rely on lower and faster brain regions. In complete panic, for example, our responses are reflexive and under virtually no conscious control. Fear quite literally makes us dumber, a property that allows faster reactions in short periods of time and helps immediate survival.[7]

Anyone who is constantly under stress (overwhelmed with difficult financial situations; dealing with divorce, illness, or death in the family; living in a violent neighborhood) is most likely operating in survival mode, stuck in the brain stem. Students operating in survival mode may find it all but impossible to pay attention in class, since their unconscious hyper-vigilance has them on high alert for every sound and movement around them. Muscles on the outsides of the eyes may tug hard so they are ready to spot danger on the periphery; bringing the eyes back to center (to read or write) may be uncomfortable and challenging to sustain. Focus and listening may require much more effort, and since there's limited access to logic, the ability to deal with the material at hand will be limited. Over time, this can lead to poor school skills, low achievement, frustration, and acting out, not to mention increased sensitivity to direction—or correction—from a teacher, since the student is primed to perceive a threat in any movement or sound. These behaviors match many of those listed as "observable traits" of Attention Deficit Hyperactive Disorder, or ADHD.[8]

Children under stress who don't act out may disengage—and not act at all. The fear reactions of the mind-body system—and resulting poor achievement and low self-image—may be incredibly overwhelming. With the constant flood of adrenaline and other accompanying hormones, our body tires of hyper-vigilance and simply gives in to the hopeless feeling that nothing can be done about the situation—so why try? This may be labeled as Attention Deficit Disorder, or ADD (essentially ADHD without the hyperactive component). My personal belief is that this is the source of much of the depression that young children are experiencing in our complex, demanding society.

> It's common to talk about the mind or the body separately; however, when we focus on how united they really are, we speak of the *mind-body system.*

The gift of releasing a learned stress response

Typically, people are very understanding when someone has a fear of snakes, small spaces, or heights. But what about reactions that manifest to a similar degree, perhaps to math, English grammar, or school in general? These kinds of aversions may be a learned response to stress, yet parents and teachers often consider them "unreasonable."

Even for an overall good student, a stressful learning moment can create a lasting learning block. Think back to a subject you avoid, or something that was difficult for you to learn. I must have had a challenging time with one particular math fact, because when I have to remember seven times six, I actually feel my stomach sink while I retrieve the answer. I have no active memory of trauma surrounding it—like being badly embarrassed for not knowing this one fact—but some part of me certainly remembers the stress of it.

> I could use Brain Gym® balancing to quickly resolve this small learning block, but I keep it around as a bit of a curiosity. It's not really in the way, and it's useful to me as a reminder of the results of learning under stress.

Through incidents like this, stress and trauma may "teach" children that they're uncoordinated, lacking in intelligence, or have little of value to offer. In this way, they end up with involuntary reaction patterns that follow them into adulthood, "saving" them long after the scenarios of their lives have changed.

However, it's possible to release these learned patterns. The Brain Gym movements and processes are very helpful in bringing the mind-body system back into a state of integration—a bit at a time. And as we release stress again and again through such movements as Hook-ups, we're gently educating our mind-body system about the mode in which we want it to work: fully integrated, coordinated, ready to learn and achieve.

Chapter 6
PACE: Bringing It All Together

So you've now learned the PACE warm-up: Sipping Water, Brain Buttons, the Cross Crawl, and Hook-ups. I hope you've allowed yourself to fully experience each movement and notice the changes it can bring.

The simplicity of PACE can be a bit deceptive. PACE, like all of Brain Gym,® is not costly, time-consuming, or elaborate; it is easy to learn and requires no special equipment. In just a few moments, the basics can be implemented right where you work, study, or play every day. For these very reasons, some people say it looks too simple to be doing anything. "Elegantly simple" is the phrase that Carla Hannaford, neurobiologist and author of *Smart Moves*, uses to characterize it.

Doing the four movements of PACE helps us find our own unique timing and flow—described by the Dennisons as "the relaxed, unstressed, self-initiated pace that allows for optimal learning."[1] As we settle in to our own best pace for living, we give ourselves permission to slow down and become present. Then we can give our best to whatever we do.

When we make PACE a daily practice, we remind ourselves again and again about how to be in our best rhythm for learning and moving. People who use PACE regularly will tell you how well it works, no matter their age or ability level. Here's the story of an impressive shift experienced by a group of children with learning challenges:

I was invited to do some demonstration work in the special-education classroom of an elementary school. The teacher, Mrs. Cole, had heard about Brain Gym and was interested to see it in action.

When I arrived, she was engaged with a group of third- and fourth-grade students who had a variety of learning challenges. Their labels included such things as low IQ, severely learning disabled, minimally mentally retarded, and fetal alcohol syndrome. As much as this teacher cared, and as hard as she worked to draw out their best, these children learned very slowly. Two boys in particular, Brandon and Cody, found certain aspects of learning very challenging. Brandon, diagnosed with fetal alcohol syndrome, had never left spaces between the words he wrote in a sentence without direct coaching. And Cody, who was labeled minimally mentally retarded, had struggled with letter size and formation for years. These boys had improved only moderately in academics over the two years they'd spent getting special help from this very skilled and caring teacher.

I introduced the PACE process to the group and, with the fun and giggles that truly engage young children, had them do all the steps with me. The children were very cooperative and enthusiastic—and very awkward in their movements. Many had significant difficulty in accomplishing the Cross Crawl, as is often the case with learning-challenged children. The entire process of explaining, demonstrating, and doing the movements took about twenty minutes.

Mrs. Cole handed out paper so each child could write me a thank-you note, which became that day's writing lesson. The room became pin-drop quiet as twelve heads bent over desktops and much writing appeared on paper, with remarkably good spelling and few requests for help. Mrs. Cole surveyed the students' work with an amazed look on her face. She sat next to Cody and asked him, "Do you notice anything different about your writing?" Astonished, he looked up and said, "Yes— it's good! The letters are all the right size!"

Let's all

Drink some water

Rub our Brain Buttons

Do the Cross Crawl

Sit or stand in Hook-ups

And see how we think and learn!

Then looking at Brandon's paper, Mrs. Cole was stunned to see that, *for the first time ever,* all of his letters were actually written on the line, and he had put spaces between his words. Not only that, but he was writing and writing, sentence after coherent sentence—this, from a boy who'd never written more than a line or two without help.

Almost every child's sentence content, handwriting, and spelling had improved after "just" PACE. By the time I left, Mrs. Cole had copied my PACE instructions off the board, made a simple poster chart of them, and hung it on the wall. She said, "We're doing this every day from now on!"

She was as good as her word. The next day, she had water bottles for all her students and led them in PACE. Before long, the children began automatically getting drinks of water when they arrived and working out a system so everyone could have his or her turn leading the group in the movements. Major changes began appearing in the achievement of almost every child in the group. This teacher was amazed to see how much difference just a little integrating movement had made for each of these very special learners.

And PACE is just as effective with adults. I use it all the time, and so do thousands of people around the world—at home, at work, and at school. I love showing adults how just a little bit of PACE works wonders.

I sometimes give stress-management workshops to adults in business or school settings. I explain what happens to the brain under stress, introduce the basics of Brain Gym, and then lead the participants through the PACE process.

At a recent presentation, before I led everyone in the PACE movements, I had them pick up an article I'd distributed and read a few paragraphs to themselves. I asked them to notice what their reading was like. People made comments including:

"I have no idea what I just read."

"I had to read one sentence three times."

"My eyes were jumping all over the page."

"My head hurts, and so do my eyes."

After they did the PACE movements, I had them read again, from a different point in the article. Almost everyone noticed a significant change, saying things like:

"I only had to read it once this time."

"The first time I was only reading words. This time it made sense!"

"The words look sharper on the page, and they're easier to read."

"Did you just turn up the lights in here?"

Imagine how easily your workday would progress if you really understood what you read the first time. And just think about how many children are dealing with reading issues in school. What would happen if, every day, students got into their best learning rhythm before beginning their schoolwork, and refreshed their PACE throughout the day?

Numbers, please?

A growing collection of studies attests to the effectiveness of Brain Gym movements and processes, especially now that they're being used by more and more educators. Brain Gym publications regularly offer information on current research, and more is being done all the time.

The Lazy 8s movement is a lateral 8, which may be drawn on a surface with a pencil, pen, or marker (excellent preparation for writing), or in the air, in front of the face (sometimes preferred before reading). In either case, the hand is followed by the eyes. You can learn more about the Lazy 8s movement in Appendix E.

Young learners

Here's one of my favorite studies on the outcome of using PACE with young children. Teacher consultant Debra Honegger compared two groups of first-grade students in Novi, Michigan, to see what the effects of using Brain Gym would be. The first group did the PACE warm-up at least three times a week, had water bottles on their desks at all times, did the Lazy 8s movement before writing, and used other Brain Gym movements as desired.

At three points during the year, their writing ability was evaluated. The children were assigned a topic, then given one minute to prepare and three minutes to write. The results were assessed using four different measures: number of letters written, words written, correct word sequences, and words correctly spelled. Here are the outcomes, comparing the Brain Gym and non-Brain Gym groups.[2]

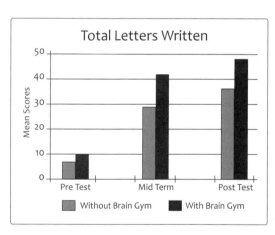

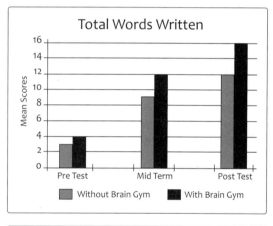

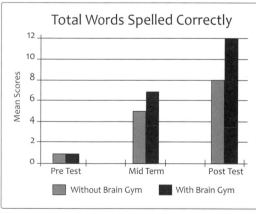

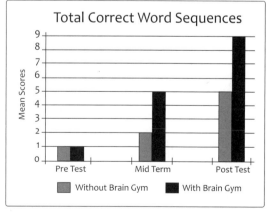

Special-ed students

In another study, Carla Hannaford assessed the progress of fifth-grade special-education students, using the Brigance Inventory of Basic Skills. Tests were administered at the beginning and end of the school year. These students used Brain Gym activities throughout the day for a few minutes each time, and some received individual balance sessions. Here are their results for both reading and math.[3] In my experience, it's rare to see such significant progress with special-ed students.

Brigance Inventory

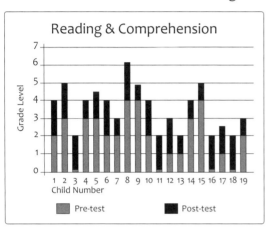

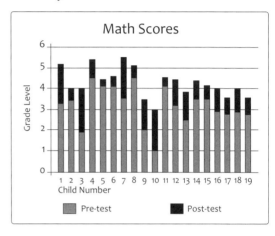

Motor skills

This study organized by an occupational therapist in New South Wales, Australia, shows the outcome of Brain Gym use with children who have significant motor issues. They were assessed using the TOMI (Test of Motor Impairment), which measures levels of manual dexterity and ball skills, as well as static and dynamic balance—all of which are markers for developmental delay and learning challenges. (Keep in mind that, with motor impairment, a reduction in value shows improvement: the level of impairment is going down.)[4]

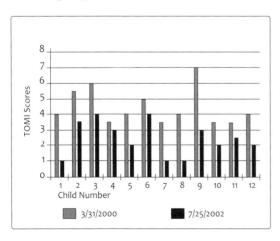

Adult learners

And here's a study of the effects of PACE when used by adults:

PACE has been shown to lower anxiety and raise skill test scores. A multiple-baseline study was done by Jan Irving, Ph.D., for her doctoral thesis, in which three randomly divided groups of first-year nursing students were introduced to the PACE process at different points in the semester. The students were taking the same course content and the same skill assessments.

As these charts show, prior to learning the PACE process, each group reported high anxiety before skill performance tests, and some group members actually failed these assessments. At the point at which the students of each group began using the PACE movements in class, reports of high anxiety in that group went down 69.5% and scores on skill assessments rose 18.7%.[5]

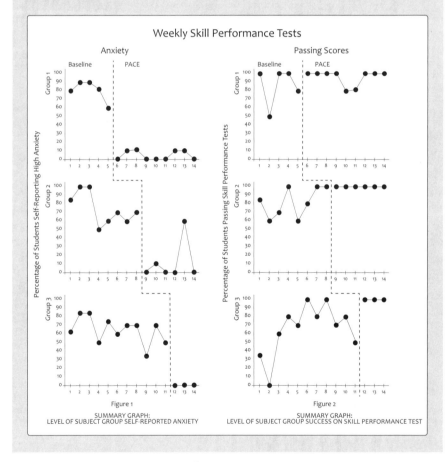

Figure 1
SUMMARY GRAPH:
LEVEL OF SUBJECT GROUP SELF-REPORTED ANXIETY

Figure 2
SUMMARY GRAPH:
LEVEL OF SUBJECT GROUP SUCCESS ON SKILL PERFORMANCE TEST

Please see www.braingym.org for more information on research studies.

Experience trumps skepticism

I love sharing the PACE process with others and then hearing reports later of what has changed in their work or personal life. Sometimes, people don't even believe their own experience! One now-enthusiastic Brain Gym supporter shares:

> When my school principal scheduled Kathy Brown for an in-service workshop on Brain Gym, I listened and participated skeptically, not sure that this program had anything special to offer. So many "great new ideas" had come and gone in my two decades of teaching; I was sure this was just one more. And I'd always done movement activities with my students, so I already knew what movement offered.
>
> However, that year my special-needs pre-Kindergarten class was particularly challenging. One Monday, out of desperation to create more calmness in the classroom, I pulled out my notes and had the children do all the PACE activities I'd learned. Everyone got a drink of water, then we spent some time finding our Brain Buttons and rubbing them. Doing the Cross Crawl was really revealing—so many children couldn't manage this at all! Then I had them sit in Hook-ups for a while.
>
> And the most amazing thing happened—my students became calm, focused, and attentive! I was astonished! And still skeptical; it had to be a coincidence. So on Tuesday, I led them in other activities. We danced the Hokey-Pokey, did some stretching, lots of whole-body games—and the kids were "off the wall" again. Intrigued, on Wednesday I went back to including Brain Gym, and we had another lovely day. On Thursday, we did just other physical activities again, and the children were back to their challenging behaviors.
>
> After several more days like this, it finally sank in: these Brain Gym activities really do make a difference. It wasn't just *movement*, it was the *kind of movement* we were doing. I eventually started combining all types of activities together, but I was always sure to include Brain Gym. I'd finally realized how big a difference it makes.
>
> Months later I helped organize the summer Early Learning Institute for my school district and invited Kathy to do a presentation there. I laughingly told my "skeptical" story as I introduced her, sharing my enthusiasm and appreciation for what Brain Gym movements have to offer! I love seeing other teachers realize this same thing.

Reorganizing for coordination

PACE is a remarkable process: a mind-body power-boost that helps us to gain access to our potential. One recent story illustrates this quite powerfully. Kelly is a physical therapist in schools, where her job is to assess children's abilities and help prepare them to be physically capable of participating in all aspects of a school day. Her young clients have a wide variety of profound challenges, from Down syndrome to cerebral palsy. She shared:

One day I arrived at a new school to assess Simon, a child diagnosed with Asperger's syndrome, a form of autism. He could walk and sit with only minor balance issues, and I wondered how well he would do when asked to perform more challenging movements. This room happened to have a large, colorful carpet that included a hopscotch pattern, so I had Simon jump on one or two feet from square to square. His arms flailed through the air as he attempted to keep his balance, and his legs seemed unable to support him dependably. Several times, he came close to falling.

I had never met Simon before, and had no idea what modalities had worked with him in the past. Then a thought occurred to me: I wonder if doing PACE would make any difference? We visited the drinking fountain, and I led him in Brain Buttons, the Cross Crawl, and Hook-ups. Each activity took a bit of coaching.

When we returned to the carpet, his hopscotch movement was accurate and balanced! He was stable landing on one or two feet, and his arms coordinated perfectly with the rest of his body.

I don't know how, but just doing PACE had clearly helped Simon organize his body systems more effectively.

Truly surprising results

Using the PACE movements makes a difference; using them over time makes a cumulative difference. And every time I think I understand all the benefits of PACE, something comes around the bend to surprise and impress me even more.

A woman named Tina scheduled a Brain Gym session to address some personal issues that she felt were preventing her from moving forward in her business life. She said she was also interested in learning more about the program because she had a feeling it would help her seven-year-old son, James, who had cerebral palsy. We completed her session, and I didn't hear from her again until almost a year later, when she called to register for a Brain Gym® 101 course I would be teaching soon. I inquired about her business and heard that her session had produced great results: she was right where she wanted to be professionally.

Then I asked about James. She said, "Well, you know, I've been doing Brain Gym with him for a year, and he's so much better. His speech was a terrible issue. I was the only one who could understand him, and that's after four years of speech therapy. A year ago, he got on the wrong bus at school and couldn't tell the bus driver his name or phone number. I was terrified it would happen again. Also, he couldn't walk at all without braces on his legs. He hated physical education class, and running was out of the question.

"So I started doing Brain Gym with him, and I couldn't believe the changes I started seeing. First, his speech improved—dramatically. He's not perfect by any means, but now anyone can understand him. He's answering the phone at home! A few months later, the doctor said we could take James' leg braces off and go with just orthotic devices in his shoes. Finally, we could even remove the orthotics. He's wearing regular shoes now. He's much more confident physically, and his teacher says he's really participating in physical education class. He's actually running. And at home, he's riding a bike! With training wheels, but he's riding a bike!"

I was stunned by this story. Mentally scrambling to remember my session with Tina a year before, I tried to recall if I had taught her some Brain Gym balance processes to use with James, and what books she might have bought. What had she done that made such a big difference? So I asked, "Um, what Brain Gym did you do with James over this year?" And she replied, "You know, those four things."

Those four things. "Those four things" are the PACE process, one element of which is simply drinking water!

At this point, I was even more stunned. "Just PACE?" I asked. "How many times a day?" "Just once, on the days I'd remember and have time, maybe four or five times a week." She went on to describe how she had begun by "motoring" James through the movements, moving his arms and legs herself, because his muscles were too stiff for him to be able to do it on his own. At a certain point, his body seemed to relax, allowing him to move more fluidly. Now he can do the movements easily on his own.

She said, "It's like all the work we've put into his health—all the therapies, all the help—has just blossomed all at once. He's a different boy. I never dreamed that he might someday ride a bike. I'm just amazed."

Believe me, so am I.

"Just" PACE. It works wonders. Little wonders and, sometimes, big wonders. James had had years of different therapies, and his progress had been so slow. The only explanation I have for this rapid shift is that the lessons from those skilled therapists had been stored—somehow, somewhere—in his mind-body system, and became available once integrating movement built a structure through which they could emerge and come together.

How often do you recommend doing PACE?

I like to do PACE first thing in the morning and then periodically throughout my day—especially after a meeting or running errands, shifting gears in my office, or before the umpteenth pass at editing a certain chapter. I may add in other Brain Gym movements that I feel inspired to do, perhaps depending on what tasks lie ahead for me, usually saving Hook-ups for last, since it's so calming. It's fine to do PACE as often as you like.

And you don't always have to do all four steps. It's wonderful to learn to notice what specific movement you're drawn to in any moment. Some people tell me that just doing the Cross Crawl makes all the difference in their day. Or just doing Hook-ups or rubbing their Brain Buttons. Or just making sure they drink more water. But when we combine all four elements and do them in sequence, we're really giving ourselves a power-boost.

Now that you know the movements, it won't take long to do PACE. As you take a drink of water, you can rub your Brain Buttons for thirty seconds or so. Follow this by perhaps a minute of the Cross Crawl and then another minute of Hook-ups. Before long, you'll be noticing how much of each movement feels right; what's optimal one day may not be enough the next. And of course, one day you may actually have more time to spend, or less time, so you simply adjust.

When people ask me how long to do certain Brain Gym movements, my standard reply is a question: "How long do you cook vegetables?" The person smiles as she realizes there's no real rule for vegetables, except this: "You cook them until they're done." It's exactly the same with Brain Gym. You do the movements until you can tell you've made the shift you were looking for.

Do you need to do the PACE movements in this order?

No, but if you do, you may find it helpful. Beginning by drinking water makes sense, so we can energize our body and get ready for new input. Ending with Hook-ups is a nice way to settle into a calm state before we move on to whatever comes next in our day. Actually, this order for PACE came out of Paul Dennison's own experience with clients over many years. He once told the story this way:

> We found that people's reading improved once they could manage doing Hook-ups while standing up. But some people couldn't do that—until they'd done the Cross Crawl. And some people couldn't manage to Cross Crawl until they'd rubbed their Brain Buttons. And some people got nothing at all out of rubbing their Brain Buttons until they'd had water.[6]

PACE: Water, Brain Buttons, the Cross Crawl, Hook-ups. That's how this warm-up evolved, in this form and this order. In four short sentences, Paul Dennison described the outcome of years of exploring the benefits of various movements with challenged learners. And that's the essence of Brain Gym.

Is PACE enough for everyone?

Many children make big improvements with just PACE, especially when used consistently over time. Others have much more significant perceptual or coordination issues that need to be addressed with additional tools.

Tracing Lazy 8s

Brenda, a second-grade teacher, began using PACE daily with her students. A few children were able to Cross Crawl from the outset (she recognized that these children were the classroom "achievers"), and most others improved gradually. Weeks later, almost all the children in her class could now Cross Crawl easily, and she saw quite a difference in their reading (more fluid) and handwriting (significantly fewer reversals and more accurate letter spacing and formation).

One child, Carlos, continued to do poorly. Brenda had never been able to read his handwriting, and even Carlos often couldn't read his own writing. Brenda eventually added Lazy 8s to their daily practice, because she had learned that this was very helpful patterning for correct letter formation.

One day, after all the children had done their Lazy 8s in preparation for handwriting practice, Brenda looked up and saw a group of Carlos's classmates standing around his desk, and they were cheering: "Wow, Carlos! We can read what you're writing! Keep going!" Carlos was thrilled with his own improvement and delighted to experience such reinforcement from his friends.

> The Lazy 8s activity encourages smooth, coordinated movement of both hand and eye across the midline, and helps to build the spatial orientation required for proper handwriting.

Many schools and agencies employ occupational therapists (OTs) to help children and adults who have coordination problems, especially with fine-motor skills such as handwriting. I frequently hear back from OTs who've taken a Brain Gym course. One woman's comment seems to sum up their feedback: "We just do a little PACE, and all of a sudden people are able to do things we've been trying for months to get them to do."

Another OT wrote to say, "I think the biggest "aha" for me in this course was having the brain-body connection reinforced in such a practical manner. I have always believed that there is a strong link between the two, but I guess I had never found a tool to utilize and enhance it until now. I have a bachelor's degree in psychology, plus my master's in occupational therapy. Both fields discuss the brain-body connection, but on a more abstract and theoretical level. This was just—WOW!"

A bit more than PACE

Many adults find that just using PACE is perfect for them, too. Others experience PACE as a good beginning, and they'd like a bit more. These people may add other Brain Gym activities throughout their day, since certain movements are very helpful in preparing us for specific tasks. Or they may do what I call "PACE Plus." They begin with Sipping Water, Brain Buttons, and the Cross Crawl; then they do a few of their other favorite movements and conclude with Hook-ups. It's fun (even for us grown-ups) to put on some music and get into PACE!

Yet, PACE is just the beginning. Beyond this warm-up lie the rest of the incredibly effective Brain Gym movements and the transformative Edu-K five-step balance process. We'll learn about that in Chapter 12, "Make Lasting Change with Brain Gym Balancing."

Let us send you a page showing the PACE movements! Visit www.EducateYourBrain.com and click on "Free Tools."

To fully understand the balance process, it will help to know more about some of the supporting concepts of Brain Gym, which I discuss in the next chapters of this book. Let's begin with a bit about how we can literally *move into learning.*

Foundational Concepts

Helpful background information
in this section falls into
two main categories:

- aspects of how *physical movement*
is understood in child development
and learning

- specific theories and practices
that are unique to the
Brain Gym®/Edu-K program

Chapter 7
Move into Learning

What an incredible journey it is to discover how integrating activity allows us to be more physically comfortable, mentally refreshed, and ready to participate in life! I continue to be amazed at how movement draws out our best.

In this chapter, we'll explore some of the ways in which movement contributes to our ability to focus, read, control our actions with precision and coordination, and "anchor" what we learn. We'll learn about how some of our most subtle sensory systems are developed through physical activity. And I'll offer my own perspective on how we can bring more joy to life through movement.

This chapter title refers to "learning," so it might be logical to think it pertains only to young children and the classroom. I invite you to keep in mind that we are always learning as we go through life, and to take this opportunity to reflect on your own experience.

Movement and focus

How often have you found yourself spontaneously tapping a foot, doodling, or rocking in your chair? That's your body's way of waking up your brain so you can focus and pay attention.

> "When we don't move and activate the vestibular system, we are not taking in information from the environment." [1]
> ~ Carla Hannaford
> *Smart Moves*

Our capacity for attention is regulated by a small but mighty mechanism in the brain stem, the Reticular Activating System (RAS), whose job it is to pick up sensory signals around us and determine the relative importance of each one. For priority signals (flashing light, sudden sound, touch, or shift in body position), it sends a special wake-up message to our brain's cerebral cortex: "Incoming information!" However, when what we see or hear doesn't engage us (a droning voice, lifeless visual presentation), there's less to keep our RAS stimulated, and our sense of attention fades.

In addition, the sensory filter of the RAS doesn't work as effectively as it might in some people and fails to bring in important signals. A person in this condition who wants greater focus may spontaneously begin moving, to stimulate the RAS in a different way. This is why a child who hears his teacher saying, "Pay attention! This is very important!" might start rocking or tapping to rev up his RAS. This child's impulse to move is not necessarily disobedience, but a sign of interest and a desire to learn; he may need this movement to help him become alert.

> Alternatively, the RAS may allow too much information to come through, leaving the learner reacting to every sight, sound, or touch in his environment (and often on ADHD medication). In either case, such individuals may be evaluated and labeled with "sensory integration" issues—which can be addressed through Edu-K balancing.

The challenge occurs when we must keep from moving, yet still remain attentive to the teacher in the classroom (or the presenter in the boardroom). Perceptive teachers will prepare their students for listening by taking movement breaks to refresh their ability to focus. Otherwise, children who are told simply to "sit still and pay attention" may be able to do only *one or the other*.

> A fourth-grade teacher told me she "couldn't understand where all the extra time was coming from" in her classroom. Then she realized that since she'd been doing Brain Gym® movements with her students throughout the day, she hadn't had to repeat her instructions over and over. "After doing the Calf Pump, they're so much more focused, and after the Thinking Cap, they listen so much better. Now they hear me the first time, because they're really ready to listen. When we take time for movement, we get so much done. And we're all so much happier! It's a great investment in time."

Here's an opportunity to experience these movements and see what happens for you.

First, a pre-check: Notice your level of focus and comprehension as you read these words. Does your mind feel clear, or are you distracted by other thoughts, or activity in the room around you? Listen to the sounds that are nearby and notice how fully you hear each one. Stand for a moment, and see what you notice in your body's posture or balance.

When we're under stress, the muscles on the back of the body tighten up, which inhibits our ability to focus and comprehend. To alleviate this tension, we can do the Calf Pump, which you may have seen or experienced as a typical jogger's or dancer's warm-up.

▶ Standing, take a long step forward with one foot. (You may want to stabilize your position by holding on to a wall, chair, or table.) With both feet pointing forward, bend your front knee until you feel the muscles just begin to lengthen in your back leg, causing that heel to rise up a bit. If your front knee extends past your toes, take a longer stride, to keep your knee safely over your ankle. Remember that your front foot stays flat and stationary throughout.

The Calf Pump

Now you are in position to begin. Gently allow the heel of your back foot to lower toward the floor, creating a lengthening of the calf muscle. Hold for a moment, then lift your heel again; repeat several times. Remember to breathe as you move. When this release feels complete, switch foot positions and lengthen the muscles in the other leg.

The Calf Pump releases tension in the muscles of the lower legs and feet, which tighten when we're under stress (from a "freeze-response" involved in what's called *tendon guard reflex*). Releasing tension may help to discharge this fear reflex, allowing a return to normal muscle tone in our legs, supporting a more natural stride.[2]

Take a moment and observe: What do you notice now about your posture or balance? Anything else?

Our second activity is the Thinking Cap. Begin by noticing: How clear and crisp are the sounds of the room round you? How ready do you feel to hear them?

The Thinking Cap

Using your thumb and fingertips, gently "straighten out" the rolled edges of your ears. Start at the top and work your way around, finishing at the earlobe. You can "unroll" both ears simultaneously; repeat three or more times.

This activity may enhance auditory processing, short-term memory, listening comprehension, and thinking skills.[3]

> Using the Thinking Cap has been shown to increase beta waves in the brain, as shown on an EEG machine, indicating a state of *focus*.[4]

For the final post-check: Listen again to the sounds around you; how fully do you hear each one? Is there any difference in how loud or clear they sound? What do you notice about your level of focus or comprehension as you read these words? Has anything shifted in your ability to filter out distractions?

Stand and take a moment to settle into your posture. Now notice your body's alignment and sense of stability. The state you're experiencing is very likely one that is more "organized" for listening and focus.

I frequently call on these movements to refresh my own focus, especially as I write. I consider them some of my "best friends for productivity"! And I know of schools where the principal asks all students to "unroll their ears" before an assembly begins, and sometimes again halfway through. Teachers share that this greatly alleviates children's wiggliness and distractability during these presentations.

Movement and reading

Every moment of the day, as we move, sit, lie down, or stand, the experience of gravity activates a special sensory apparatus in our inner ear: the *vestibular system*. This body-balance mechanism helps us to always know where *up* is, so we can maintain equilibrium as we shift from one position to the next.

An important aspect of the vestibular system is that it's always communicating with our eyes, sending the information they need to maintain a steady view of the world even when we're moving. When our vestibular system is well developed, our eyes are happy to track across a line of print as we read and work together for other tasks. Without good vestibular development, eye-teaming and tracking, and therefore reading, can be challenging—or exhausting.

Effective vestibular training comes from the kinds of whole-body movement that should be common in childhood: running, hopping, dancing, tumbling. If children aren't inclined (or allowed) to do those things, next best would be playing on merry-go-rounds and teeter-totters—except for the fact that this equipment has vanished from our playgrounds. Children who are uncoordinated, overweight, or otherwise disinclined to run and play have lost these more passive means of vestibular training.

The only remaining opportunity for passive vestibular stimulation on most playgrounds today is on the swings. Children with the very natural desire to tightly twist up the swing so they can experience the vestibular activation of rapid untwisting are often reprimanded: "That's not what swings are for! Swing straight!" Maybe we should be lining kids up to twist on the swings.

Vestibular activation is one of the reasons we encourage people to Cross Crawl slowly (s-l-o-w-l-y!), because it leaves them balancing on one foot so much of the time. Doing Hook-ups while standing is another vestibular challenge, with big benefits:

A teacher I know invited her first-grade students to decide when they were ready to "graduate" from doing Hook-ups sitting to doing it standing—and then to standing *with their eyes closed*. They loved the vestibular challenge, and she was astounded at the difference it made in their

> If communication between the vestibular system and the eyes is disrupted, the result may be motion sickness.

> "With merry-go-rounds and swings disappearing from parks and playgrounds as fast as liability costs go up, there's a new worry: more learning disabilities." [5]
> ~ Eric Jensen
> *Teaching with the Brain in Mind*

> "The vestibular system is already visible in a two-month-old embryo. There is much activation of the head as the fetus moves in the amniotic fluid, then as the child goes from early movements and crawling to walking and running. The stimulation from these movements is crucial to brain processing." [6]
> ~ Carla Hannaford
> *Smart Moves*

Hook-ups with eyes closed

learning. She said, "As soon as a child could stand in Hook-ups with eyes closed, he or she made rapid growth in reading and overall ability to focus and attend. I never knew a healthy body-balance system was so necessary for learning."

How's your body-balance?

You can check yourself by following this teacher's suggestion: stand in Hook-ups and then *close your eyes*. What do you notice about your balance?

▶ Now you can experience a Brain Gym movement that supports your physical balance: the Balance Buttons. Rest one hand over your navel; place the fingertips of the other hand right behind your earlobe on the indentation at the edge of your skull. After thirty seconds or so, switch hand positions to cover behind the opposite ear.

Check your standing Hook-ups again—and then with eyes closed, if you like. Do you notice a difference? Your fingertips were covering the area of your *vestibular system*, the body-balance mechanism in your inner ear; your hand over the navel called attention to your center of gravity.

Balance Buttons

Of course, the best way to improve vestibular development is through a regular practice of whole-body physical movement. But it's lovely to have an activity like Balance Buttons to provide a boost when needed!

Movement and physical coordination

How is it that we develop the ability to move our body with skill and accuracy? *Proprioceptors* are special nerve cells found in muscle tissue, tendons, and joints. Their job is to constantly gather information on the status of each muscle or tendon (Is it flexed or extended? To what degree?) and send it back to the brain.

> Actually, our most important proprioceptors are found in the inner ear, as part of our vestibular (body-balance) system. Their first, exceedingly important job is to notice that we're experiencing the pull of gravity and automatically trigger our muscles to engage and *tone* so they hold our structure erect.

The brain combines this input with that of other systems (vision, touch, vestibular), makes an instantaneous evaluation (Did I move enough? Too much?), and issues a command to maintain or adjust the activity of each individual muscle or tendon. The result is an elegant—and very busy—feed-forward/feed-back process that is going on underneath our awareness, every millisecond, for every muscle or tendon in our body.

As we grow and learn, this amazing system allows us to refine our control. Feedback from our proprioceptive system is what teaches us how to hold a pencil firmly enough to make a solid mark but not break the lead, and then eventually form the curves and lines of our written language. This process continues throughout our life, with every new physical skill we learn.

Our proprioceptive system develops only through *movement itself:* both large-motor (as we run, walk, skip, crawl, roll, dance, carry objects and set them down) and fine-motor (as we manipulate puzzle pieces, build with blocks, dig in sand, draw, model with clay). These activities are not just idle play: they're vital for developing a well-tuned mind-body system that will then be able to execute more and more sophisticated physical commands with skill and accuracy.

Now let's experience an activity that helps us to refine proprioception for both large- and fine-motor coordination.

▶ Arm Activation is one of the Brain Gym Lengthening Activities, which have as their goal, releasing tension in the back of the body. This specific movement unlocks stress held in the shoulders, so we can have easier use of the arms and hands. Here's a way to experience this activity:

First, a pre-check: Write your name, and then a sentence or two. Notice the formation of your letters and words, and how your hand and arm feel as you write.

Position your right arm straight up overhead (or at any comfortable angle in front of you). Place your left hand on what's now the front of your right arm, near the elbow. Hold steady with your left hand as you press gently against it with your right arm. Use only twenty percent of your push power; in this activity, muscles and tendons seem to respond best to a gentle release.

Arm Activation

Pressing to the front   Pulling to the back   Toward your ear   Away from your ear

Continue holding for about eight seconds (or until you feel a slight melting of shoulder tension) and then relax. Now bring your fingers around to the "back" of your arm and exert pressure against them. Repeat in the remaining two directions, pressing against your hand, "in" toward your ear, and then "away" from your ear.

Lower both arms, then let them hang at your sides. Do you notice a difference in how they feel? Does your released arm seem "longer" than the other? You're experiencing how your arm feels when there's less tension in your shoulder. Now—activate the other arm!

When this is complete, write your name and a few sentences again, as a post-check. How do your arm and hand feel as you write? Is there a difference in the words and sentences themselves?

During my years as a teacher, I observed that many students had small, cramped handwriting, despite repeated lessons about proper letter formation. Now I realize that this contracted handwriting may be caused by shoulder tension that results in a vise-like grip on the pencil. Once children (or adults) release this tension, I often see their letter formation spontaneously become more graceful and flowing. The Dennisons say, "Lengthening refreshes proprioception that has been confounded by excessive sitting or immobility. It restores muscles to their full range of motion so they can properly contract, as required for an accurate match of muscle movement to visual or auditory input."[8]

Movement and visual ease

Our brain keeps us physically balanced through combined feedback from our vestibular system, our proprioceptive system—and our eyes. If we don't have good vestibular and proprioceptive functioning, our eyes may need to do more than their fair share of the work. Do you recall your experience of standing in Hook-ups with your eyes closed? It's possible you were a bit wobbly, partly due to the *vision* connection.

When we over-rely on our visual system to do the work of physical balance, it has less energy left for such things as reading, guiding the movement of a pencil, or simply enjoying beautiful scenery. It also creates a tendency for our eyes to "grab" at objects we see, creating a hard focus that ends up being uncomfortable and sapping energy. It's almost like the way we may physically grab at a handrail as we go down a staircase. As we improve physical balance and the awareness of our body position in space, our eyes relax and function as intended.

The Brain Gym Double Doodle movement is particularly good at helping us overcome this visual "grabbing" tendency. You can Double Doodle by drawing simple lines and shapes in mirror image, on paper or in the air, with both hands simultaneously.

> Gail Dennison, co-founder of Brain Gym, developed the course "Double Doodle Play," which offers rich opportunities to use our vision in new ways.

When we draw in this way, our eyes cannot hold a hard focus on the activity of both hands simultaneously. We then begin to relax and shift into soft-focus, which is very soothing to our visual system.

> ▶ Take a moment to experience the Double Doodle! And to see just what this movement has to offer, I suggest doing a pre-check first. Holding your head still, move just your eyes—up to the ceiling, down to the floor, then from side to side. Do your eyes feel free to move, or are they a bit resistant? Look around and notice: How easily do you see the forms and colors of the objects that surround you? Become aware of any stress in your body, especially in the muscles around your eyes, or in your forehead and the rest of your face.
>
> Now for the Double Doodle. You may want to warm up by doing a bit of this activity in the air, but for the actual exercise, I suggest doing it on a whiteboard or flipchart pad, or on a table with your paper taped down.
>
> Now, take up a pencil, pen, or marker in either hand and begin drawing mirror-image swirls, circles, or patterns of any kind. Take your time and spend several leisurely minutes on this activity, perhaps with some soothing music playing in the background. Allow yourself simply to be playful with your sense of movement. Do you notice yourself releasing the tendency for "hard focus" that's typical when we draw conventionally?
>
> Now the post-check: How do your eyes feel when you move them up-down-left-right? Do you notice a difference in the muscles of your face or any other part of your body? Does anything seem different in your perception of the room around you?

Double Doodling in the air

A Double Doodle pattern

> "Amazingly, the part of the brain that processes movement is the same part of the brain that's processing learning." [9]
> ~ Eric Jensen
> *Teaching with the Brain in Mind*

Movement anchors learning

For any learning to be complete, we must create a strong personal connection with it: this is often referred to as "anchoring" learning. Some of the most effective ways to do this involve activities that allow the learner not just to receive information passively, but to actively participate in making the knowledge his own.

Physical movement helps us to store new information in a whole-brain way. For example, we can take learning a new spelling word (typically a rote, left-hemisphere activity focusing on the symbols of our letter system) and create a whole-body/whole-brain kinesthetic experience around it. Singing the letters, modeling them out of clay, whispering them into a friend's ear, forming your body into each of the letters, or doing some Cross Crawl as you repeat them, all improve our ability to recall them later.

Movement for other kinds of learning can take the form of discussing, writing, acting out, or drawing a picture to illustrate a point in the story. Some learners remember more fully when doodling odd shapes or patterns.

Brain Gym movements are a fun way to anchor what we've learned. Many teachers trained in Brain Gym now say things such as: "Great! You figured that out! Now let's do some Cross Crawl to anchor it, so you'll really remember." In this way, the "aha!" moment transcends the purely mental act of learning something and brings the experience and memory of it into the body itself.

Building access to potential

When learners of any age are given enjoyable and appropriate opportunities to move, they gain access to the experience of their own innate abilities, and they (along with their educators and parents) begin to perceive the potential that's been waiting to be tapped.

I recently returned to a school where I'd taught a one-day workshop. The teachers had enthusiastically begun using a variety of Brain Gym activities with their students. In every classroom I visited, the response was the same: "The kids are suddenly so capable! They listen and follow directions, and even their reading and writing have improved. And they're so much more cooperative and interested in learning. How could just a few movements be doing so much?"

Just a few movements. Yes, that's what it seems like! However, as I explain to these teachers, Brain Gym activities are helping their students *build a body that is capable of learning* by improving postural control, shoulder girdle stability and neck relaxation, visual skills, spatial orientation, ability to cross the midline, eye-hand coordination, listening skills, focus, and more.

Who wouldn't have better reading and writing with all these abilities strengthened? And when students are truly capable, their sense of achievement naturally carries over into positive behavior.

We learn not to move

Various kinds of movement should occur naturally throughout everyone's day. Children benefit greatly from moving their bodies through games, rhythmic marching, gymnastics, dance, and joyful running and playing. They develop vital fine motor skills through manipulating toys, balls, blocks, clay, paints, and scissors—more than just a pencil, computer mouse, or videogame controller. Older students and adult learners benefit from discussing, writing, doodling, dancing, doing athletics, creating art projects, and performing skits that relate to their area of study.

"Optimally, in the first year of life an infant will have ample three-dimensional experiences of moving his body in space, without the constraint of infant seats or walkers, so that all of his 620-plus muscles will develop in balance." [10]
~ Paul and Gail Dennison

Unfortunately, many children are prevented from experiencing the joy of free movement—starting in infancy. With the overuse of playpens and roller-walkers, too much time spent in portable car seats, and practices that keep them from being down on the floor enough—especially on their tummies—some babies fail to progress appropriately through key developmental movement stages, most notably the crawling process. (You'll learn more about these developmental stages in the upcoming chapter, "Wired for Ability.") And children can be "helped" too much. Infants and toddlers need to discover for themselves the joy of initiating, practicing, and mastering the skills of moving, sitting, standing, and walking—*on their own* and *on their own timeline*.

Once children are older and want to run and play, some fearful parents may require that they remain in the house or under close supervision. This may be an appropriate concern, or it may be an overreaction to the onslaught of media sensationalism about child safety. In any case, few children today have the same freedom to play outdoors that was common a generation ago.

Pre-teen and teen years are often filled with self-consciousness that inhibits free physical expression. These children may participate in team sports where they learn to equate exercise with stress, over-efforting, and fear of failure.

And as adults, it's easy to let the pressure of a demanding day override our desire to take a walk, ride a bike, go to the gym or dance class, or just simply stretch from time to time. At work, we may see the need to move as an inconvenience to be avoided if at all possible. Unfortunately, this is less than optimal for our health in general, and it's certainly less than helpful for cognitive functioning.

It takes conscious effort to break this pattern. I intentionally put some office supplies I use frequently in a hallway closet adjacent to my office. This requires that I get up and move periodically when I'm working. These "inconveniences" are actually beneficial movement breaks; the result is that I'm more productive in the long run.

How many of us "tough it out" and make ourselves sit and sit, waiting for that good idea? Even in writing this book, I'd find myself writing more and more slowly, deleting and changing text in endless circles, and then realize I had been sitting for more than an hour. I'd get up and do a quick round of PACE, pet the cat, get some fresh air on the patio—even take a quick walk or put on some music and move to the beat—perhaps five minutes in all. Then I'd sit back down and the right words would just flow. Amazing.

Adults aren't the only ones who sit for hours. A school day now involves more and more sitting and less and less movement, even in the youngest grades—often to devote more time to reading instruction in order to raise literacy!

Some schools have eliminated physical education class and, believe it or not, are starting to do away with recess even for the youngest children.[13,14,15] Unfortunately, the less we move, the less well our brain works.

One of the best reasons to move is because it's *fun*

Our bodies are meant to be active, and we're meant to have a good time in the process! Joyful movement is done just for the fun of it. How often do we (adults or children) take time to enjoy movement outside of sports leagues or other competitive environments? When we test our abilities against an unrealistic model, we're just creating another form of stress!

What would happen if we found ourselves comfortable enough to cross the boundaries of what's typical for our "role" in life, and did what was really *fun*? Corporations invest heavily in workshops and consultants to teach employees how to be creative. Yet amazing things happen when a person just does a few Brain Gym movements and then approaches his daily activities with a mind-body system that has released stress. My experience is that when we "move out of our brain stem" and into an integrated state, we're naturally more creative, comfortable, and happy.

> I recall with great joy a day years ago when I took my pre-teen students out to play kickball. A cohesive group, they chose teams and played with great enthusiasm. As we walked back in from the field, I asked one boy which team had won. He turned to me in surprise and said, "Gee, we were having so much fun we forgot to keep score!"

A closing thought on movement

In his book *A User's Guide to the Brain*, John J. Ratey, M.D. offers this gem:

> Movement is fundamental to the very existence of a brain. . . . A tiny marine creature known as the sea squirt illustrates the point. In the early part of its life, the sea squirt swims about like a tadpole. It has a brain and a nerve cord to control its movements. However, when it matures, it attaches itself permanently to a rock. From that moment on, the brain and the nerve cord are gradually absorbed and digested. The sea squirt consumes its own brain because it is not needed anymore.[16]

Is our brain going to be absorbed if our body doesn't move? Of course not. But the point is certainly telling: movement develops the brain and its myriad abilities, and it brings joy to life. Adding appropriate, integrating movement makes any task or project much more enjoyable, and learning easier as well.

Chapter 8
Wired for Ability

During my twenty-three years as a classroom teacher, I was mystified by certain students' behaviors. I'd see them slouching over their desks or sliding down in their chairs with legs stretched out—that is, if they weren't continually popping out of their seats to stand or walk around. Some would position their work to one side of midline or the other, and then have to assume an odd arm or head angle to read or write. Some would hold their pencils in a fist-like grip or chew on their shirt collars. Students would do their best to sit or work "correctly" when I reminded them—and then drift right back into their old patterns.

Then there were the learning challenges: reversing letters and words (confusing "d" for "b," for example, or reading "saw" for "was"), poor comprehension, lack of focus, and the inability to write with proper spacing or copy from the board.

Students struggled, and I struggled as well, wishing my professional toolkit held more solutions. When I came across the Brain Gym®/Edu-K program, however, I found what I'd been missing: a means of not only supporting children in learning more easily, but of understanding the core challenges that left them feeling so stuck in the first place—the "issues behind the issues." This changed my view of learning in two ways:

> While I learned much about movement and cognitive processing in my initial Brain Gym®/Edu-K training, my greatest knowledge of reflexes and associated concepts was gained through upper-level Edu-K courses and supplemental reading. Please see the Appendix for these resources.

- I began to understand the physical, developmental reasons for many of these behaviors and learning challenges.

- And I came to appreciate how improving physical coordination could help systems of "internal wiring" to mature from the inside out, and that, through this maturation process, many of these behaviors diminish mildly or significantly—or even resolve completely.

So, in the spirit of sharing some of the biggest *aha!* moments of my career as an educator, I'd like to explore with you the world of internal wiring.

The process and purpose of internal wiring

It was my journey through the Edu-K curriculum that opened up a whole new world of inquiry for me: How is it that we end up with our most basic skills—the ability to move our body or focus our attention, selectively and accurately? How do we start out as infants, with small bodies and little motor control, and end up so coordinated and capable?

"Children's entire orientation to the world develops through movement."[1]
~ Clare Cherry
Creative Play for the Developing Child

Through my coursework I began learning about a series of developmental stages we are all designed to go through that lay the groundwork for accurate, intentional movement. Once these patterns are integrated within the body, we are able to easily perform all types of physical activity. And this physical structure also builds our capacity to focus, comprehend, and learn.

Without mature wiring, we're likely to live our life constantly struggling, and the result can be some pretty bewildering behaviors, as I mentioned above. I know now that these children's actions were not conscious or intentional. Sitting, reading, or writing in any other way felt unnatural to them and was impossible to maintain for long. Now that I understand the way our wiring system develops, it's easier for me to see certain behaviors as *compensations*: ingenious means of accomplishing a goal when internal resources are limited.

If this overall stage of infant reflex patterning is left incomplete, it can affect our ability to learn—because we're limited in how we can *move*.

This struggle with limited resources often leaves children feeling exhausted. Even simple daily life activities can take more energy than others might think possible. Such children are also likely to be slower than their peers in acquiring key coordination and academic skills; in some, this is significant enough to be identified as "developmental delay." Other children may exhibit milder challenges but still require assistance and intervention. In either case, it's a matter of internal wiring—which needs to be in place in order to learn and grow.

Infant reflexes: nature's patterning program

If you've spent time with a newborn child, you may have experienced her infant reflexes at work—perhaps without even knowing what they were. Put your finger in the baby's hand and she grips very tightly. When she turns her head to one side, the arm and leg on that side extend, and the other arm and leg pull in toward her body. Stroke one side of her back and that hip spontaneously rises.

These *primitive reflexes* are automatic movements that the infant is neurologically prompted to make—for a very specific reason. Some reflexive movements are for survival, such as the Root-and-Suck Reflex, without which the newborn would not be able to take in nourishment. Others are designed to develop patterns of wiring—through repeated actions the infant is prompted to make—so that she can effortlessly achieve postural stability and motor control.

Each postural reflex refines a single, specific element of coordination. Once the infant acquires sufficient patterning from each reflex, the sensory stimulus that has been triggering it will no longer do so. At this point, the intended bit of "wiring" will blend seamlessly into the overall movement patterns in the body, and the reflex is said to be "inhibited" or "integrated," depending on the language used in your resource material. Then, the child is able to freely call on that pattern when it's needed, rather than being driven by involuntary reactions; she now has *volitional control.*

A wide variety of books have been written about the infant reflex continuum. A detailed description of infant reflexes is offered by Sally Goddard in her book *Reflexes, Learning and Behavior: A Window Into the Child's Mind.* Helpful online resources also are available, many with video links that allow you to see various infant reflexes in action. An excellent primer on this subject is also included in *Does Your Baby Have Autism?: Detecting the Earliest Signs of Autism* by Osnat Teitelbaum and Philip Teitelbaum, Ph.D., who introduce reflexes to explain how autistic babies' movement patterns differ from the norm even in the earliest months of life.

A vital time span

Each of the many infant reflexes has a fairly predictable period during which it will begin to emerge and be fully experienced. Most reflexes overlap others on this timeline. Some appear before birth or during and just after the birthing process. The majority are active during the infant's first year; and the final reflex, Tonic Labyrinthine, fully integrates at about three years of age. Doctors gauge a child's development by the orderly progression of these reflexes.

Depending on the source information you find, infant reflexes may be named and described slightly differently, and some listings are more complete than others. Here, I address several key reflexes; many more exist.

If all this patterning is unimpeded, the result is fluid, accurate movement: we can activate selected parts of our body without reflexively moving others as well. We've developed both physical and cognitive agility, which means we're now essentially "wired for ability."

At this point, I must share a concern about the modern practice of keeping infants in car seats—outside of the car. Laura Sobell, an authority on infant development and care in Santa Barbara, California, cautions parents about the overuse of infant car seats because they hold babies' bodies and heads in one position. She states, "I can tell just by looking at a baby if she's spent a lot of time in a car seat or infant seat. Babies like this have no rotation in their body; when I pick them up, their backs are stiff." She explains that when infants spend excessive time in car seats, their normal movement is inhibited. They do not go through the beneficial challenge of dealing with their body in relation to gravity, to move fully in the space around them, to learn and maintain balance. Sobell describes how infants kept immobilized in this way become listless and may skip important stages, such as rolling, crawling, and sitting—and how missing these steps may lead to learning challenges. You can find out more about her recommendations in her book *Save Your Baby—Throw Out Your Equipment,* and at her website, www.calmbaby.com [2]

The "invisible puppeteer"

However, this progression of infant reflexes can be interrupted by a variety of circumstances. The fetus in utero may experience his mother's prolonged or sudden stress: financial or marriage difficulties, a car accident, a death in the family, exposure to chemicals or drugs, surgery, or illness. Difficult or

Difficult or Caesarian births or neonatal surgery can result in trauma to the infant as well. It's believed that any such event can cause him to "pause" in his current developmental stage. Vital reflexes may not fully integrate, and vestiges of them may remain throughout his lifetime.

Then, he may live his life at the mercy of what I call the "invisible puppeteer," who pulls him this way and that—completely outside his awareness. Countering the pull of these puppet strings takes first call on his energy reserves, leaving little for other tasks of life and learning. This is true for children in school and equally true for adults who retain these patterns.

Recognizing a retained infant reflex

Each infant reflex movement is triggered by a sensory stimulus of some kind: touch, sound, change of position, etc. If that trigger still produces involuntary action in the older child or adult, it's said the reflex is "retained," either mildly or strongly. As a result, various behaviors are very likely to show up.

In the following paragraphs, I discuss several key reflexes, some of their associated characteristics, and a few of the ways they may manifest in older children, teens, and adults when the reflex is still present in the body.

Root-and-Suck Reflex: Stroking the infant's cheek will prompt her to turn her head to that side and begin a sucking action. Root-and-Suck Reflex emerges at 24-28 weeks in utero (present at birth); should integrate by age 3–4 months.

My primary resource for this infant reflex information is the seminal work on this topic, Sally Goddard's *Reflexes, Learning and Behavior: A Window Into the Child's Mind*, which I highly recommend if this subject interests you. While many books describe infant reflexes, this is the best I have found for a complete description of behaviors caused by retained reflexes in older children.

Note: Some children with a retained reflex will exhibit only a few of the behaviors that may be associated with it.

Donna has a hard time articulating words, and chews and bites objects like her pencil, toys, or shirt collar while concentrating. She displays labored, noisy chewing, is overly sensitive to touch on her cheek or mouth, and is prone to immature emotional reactions.

Moro Reflex: An unexpected occurrence of any kind (noise, pain, sudden light or movement in his visual field, change in temperature or head position) will cause the infant to throw his arms out and take in a quick gasp of air (often followed by a loud wail) then slowly draw his arms back in toward his body. Moro Reflex emerges at 9 weeks in utero (present at birth); should integrate by age 2–4 months.

Jahan startles at just about anything. He overreacts to fears (some children underreact). He has difficulty with near-to-far vision and often loses his place when copying from the board in school. He is prone to digestive issues and is physically timid in unfamiliar surroundings.

Palmar Reflex: A touch to the inside of the infant's hand causes her to grip very hard, curling fingers around that object: perhaps your finger, hair, or necklace. A neurological loop between the mouth and the palms of the hands (sometimes active when nursing) may cause the mouth or tongue to move when manipulating objects, drawing, etc. Palmar Reflex emerges at 11 weeks in utero (present at birth); should integrate by age 2–3 months.

Birgitta has poor manual dexterity and holds her pencil in a tense, fist-like grip. She has speech articulation issues and moves her mouth or tongue while writing.

Asymmetrical Tonic Neck Reflex (ATNR): When the infant turns his head, his arms and legs automatically assume specific positions. Head to the right—right arm and leg extend and left arm and leg draw in toward the body. Head to the left—the opposite limb movements occur. This reflex builds the ability to move one side of the body while the other side is still. ATNR emerges at 18 weeks in utero (present at birth); should integrate by age 6 months.

Rafael struggles to concentrate and has challenges with reading and writing. Unable to fully combine input from both eyes, he avoids working in the midfield, so he often positions his book or paper off to one side. He has a history of coordination challenges, from tying shoes to balancing and ball-catching. He's learned to stare straight ahead when riding his bike because if he turns his head, his hands jiggle the handlebars and he risks steering into a parked car—or oncoming traffic.

Infant in ATNR position.

Tonic Labyrinthine Reflex (TLR): a reaction to changes picked up by the vestibular system, the body-balance mechanism within the inner ear. Forward movement of the head (relative to the spine) immediately causes her arms and legs to bend; backward movement of the head causes her arms and legs to extend. When fully integrated, this response becomes the muscle tone that allows us to automatically hold our body upright in opposition to gravity. TLR emerges in utero (present at birth); should integrate at about age 4 months.

Akemi has low muscle tone, or hypotonus. *(Other children may have high muscle tone, or* hypertonus.*) She assumes a multitude of peculiar sitting postures including slouching and propping up her head on her hand. She struggles with sequencing, organizational skills, short-term memory, and sense of time. She experiences difficulty focusing near to far (copying from the board in the classroom) or accurately perceiving figure-ground (seeing the words in a sentence rather than being distracted by the white space around them).*

Spinal Galant Reflex: A touch to the infant's side near the waist triggers an immediate pulling up of the hip on that side. It's thought that Spinal Galant helps in the birthing process: As one side of the low back is stimulated and contracts, the other side comes in firmer contact with the birth canal; then the other side contracts. The result is a back-and-forth wriggling motion. In my experience, children who are delivered by Caesarian section, or whose birthing was very quick, frequently have this reflex retained—I suspect because it's still waiting to be "used." Spinal Galant emerges at 20 weeks in utero (present at birth); should integrate by age 3–9 months.

> *Sheldon fidgets and can't sit still for any length of time. He instinctively takes unusual seated postures so his low back doesn't rest against his chair, especially if it has lumbar support. He dislikes elastic waistbands or tight clothing, and may wet or soil himself.*

Fear Paralysis Reflex: the tendency to retreat from anything the least bit threatening. This reflex is unique in that it is supposed to be fully integrated by the time the baby is born. However, in my experience, many people still hold vestiges of this reflex (some quite strongly), which may appear as "elective mutism" in children, or as "social phobia" in adults.

> *Opal is extremely shy and avoids eye contact. Her body is always on "red alert," so she dislikes change or surprise and is prone to panic disorders. She is hypersensitive, complaining that people "hit" her, when the truth is they only brush by as they pass in a crowded hallway or make other casual contact. She is very uncomfortable in tight clothing or in sleeping bags.*

Symmetrical Tonic Neck Reflex (STNR): Backward movement of the head (relative to the spine) causes the arms to straighten and hips and legs to bend; forward movement of the head causes the arms to bend and the legs to straighten. This reflex aids the infant in rising off his tummy and, eventually, into an all-fours crawling position, but when retained, may be responsible for some of the odd seated postures or hyperactive behaviors a child may exhibit. STNR emerges 6 to 9 months after birth; should integrate by about age 9–11 months.

> *Alex has great difficulty focusing in school. He's constantly wiggling in his chair and finds every excuse to be out of his seat. He can hardly stand still and is always bumping into those near him in line.*

More on a specific reflex: STNR

Because Symmetrical Tonic Neck Reflex is at the core of so many behaviors that teachers and parents end up trying to correct, I'll describe it in more detail here. We'll learn about the nature and purpose of this reflex and why it so profoundly affects learning and behavior.

The role of the STNR is to help the infant rise up off the floor onto hands and knees and maintain a solid "all-fours" posture in preparation for crawling.

Here's how this occurs:

At about one month of age, the infant on his tummy will start raising his head. Soon after, he will bring his hands under his shoulders and use them to stabilize his view. However, starting at about six months of age, the STNR engages, and this same head-raising now triggers a dynamic movement sequence: his arms automatically straighten and his hips and knees bend. This lifts his upper torso off the floor as he sits back, lower legs folded under him, leaning forward on his hands. Some call this the "cat-sit" position.

Just prior to this photo, this infant was tummy-down and raising her head. This triggered the STNR, causing her arms to straighten, and her hips and legs to bend.

When he then lowers his head, the opposite actions will be triggered: his arms reflexively bend and his legs straighten, leaving his hips elevated and his head down toward the floor.

After eight to ten weeks of this reflexive patterning practice, the baby's limbs are strengthened and balance is improved, and the "rocking" forward and back that he's done in the sitting-up position will have helped to integrate the STNR reflex. He can now elevate his upper and lower torso at the same time, and he's off the floor in a stable all-fours position.

When the raising or lowering of his head no longer triggers the impulse to bend or straighten his limbs, it's said that the STNR is now *integrated*, or resolved. The infant is now free to crawl, looking up or down, unencumbered by tugging from the "invisible puppeteer."

However, if a child remains "stuck" in the STNR stage, crawling may be fraught with challenges. If he should want to look at something interesting straight in front of him, he'll raise his head—and automatically sit back as his hips and knees bend and his arms straighten. Or he may tilt his head down toward some fascinating object on the floor—and find himself taking a nose-dive toward it as his arms collapse under him and his legs straighten.

As mentioned in other chapters, infant crawling is a key means of developing cross-lateral patterning necessary for many aspects of cognitive processing. Therefore, children who skip the crawling stage may be at higher risk for learning challenges.

This is not a very satisfying or safe way for him to move across a room or explore the world around him, so he may find creative ways of "crawling," such as sideways, backwards, or scooting on his bottom; or he may skip the crawling stage altogether and simply sit, until the urge to move pulls him up on his feet to walk.

Effects later on in life

As a child with retained STNR continues to grow, the reflexive pull of this movement pattern may act up without his being aware of it.

Sitting at a desk with his legs bent, he'll feel agitated unless his arms are straight, so he'll hold his book or pencil with arms extended out in front of him, perhaps leaning far forward so he can see what he's doing. Made to sit back with arms in a more typical (bent) position, he'll feel agitated unless his legs are straight, so he'll find something to put his feet up on or slide forward on his chair until his legs extend out in front of him. He may consistently

Seated postures that relieve the STNR impulse

find reasons to stand, sit on the floor, or even lie down, all in an unconscious attempt to straighten his legs.

Yet, even standing can be a challenge, especially in the "soldier" position, which leaves his legs *and* his arms straight—triggering the unconscious need to bend one or the other. This is the source of much agitation as such a child tries to stand for very long, even unintentionally "poking" or "tickling" others as he reflexively bends his arms. Such a child would do much better with his hands resting on opposite elbows or clasping his hands near his waist.

The book *Stopping Hyperactivity: A New Solution* by O'Dell and Cook describes retained STNR as a significant root cause of ADHD diagnosis in children.

Of course, these behaviors are not the child's fault: they're the direct result of delayed integration of this basic reflex. The effort required to maintain a "proper" seated or standing position may drain him of energy needed for focus, resulting in all sorts of behaviors that may be categorized as hyperactivity. In this case, a child may end up being medicated to control impulses that are part of a retained reflex.

Edu-K courses addressing infant reflexes are available as part of the Edu-K curriculum. Please see Appendix A and the course listings at www.braingym.org.

Calling on Edu-K balancing to resolve reflex issues

One of the things I appreciate most about the Brain Gym/Edu-K program is that it offers a means of resolving core issues behind learning challenges. Through various upper-level courses, those trained in Edu-K can learn to address retained reflexes through the five-step balance process.

Here's an example of how this process was of use in supporting a student who simply couldn't sit still and focus:

I recently worked with Ronny, a very bright, likable boy, whose teacher was amazed (and frustrated) by how agitated he was when sitting and how poor his focus was. Now in eighth grade, Ronny was still struggling to achieve academically. I had seen him several times over the past few months, and after each session, he showed progress but still lacked the ability to sit quietly, and he was not reading at grade level.

Smarter standing up

Throughout the course of our sessions, perhaps as a direct result of the way Brain Gym processes foster inner noticing, Ronny became a very good observer of his own state. One day he commented, "You know, I think I'm smarter standing up." What a revelation! I asked for more details and he continued:

"When I sit down, I can't focus at all. I do my homework standing, using the ironing board as a desk, and that works great!" It was clear: *Ronny had found the perfect physical posture—standing with arms bent—to relieve himself of the pull of the invisible puppeteer.*

We created a goal for his balance, which was to "sit comfortably while I focus and learn." Not surprisingly, out of all the choices available on my Brain Gym/Edu-K learning menu, Ronny was drawn to one that addresses Symmetrical Tonic Neck Reflex.

Noticing the strings of the invisible puppeteer

I led Ronny through some pre-checks to determine if STNR was present. One involved seeing if he experienced stress while sitting or standing. When seated (legs bent) he was stress-free only with his arms straight; when standing (legs straight), he was stress-free only with his arms bent. He was bound to feel agitated in a typical seated posture.

The process Ronny selected was Total Core Repatterning, a specialized kinesiology technique (and course) developed by Paul Dennison. When this was complete, taking about 45 minutes in all, I rechecked Ronny for postural stress. Although the reflex issue was not completely resolved, there was great improvement.

Following this session, I explained the STNR reflex to Ronny's teacher. She immediately created a standing workspace for him by placing an inverted box on top of a table and gave him permission to move there whenever he needed to.

Finally: comfortable sitting

Two weeks later, Ronny was excited to report all the positive changes he'd experienced since our last session. He didn't always need to stand at his workspace, because sitting was more comfortable than ever before. He also said that he had much better reading comprehension and had just earned 100% on a social studies test.

We definitely celebrated all these changes! Delighted, Ronny said he wanted to improve even more, and again he was drawn to Total Core Repatterning. This time when we were finished, he showed no stress at all, whether sitting or standing, with his arms straight or bent.

Three weeks later, Ronny's teacher reported that he was much more able to sit still in the classroom, and his schoolwork had improved as

> You've seen mentions of the Edu-K Five-Step Balance Process in previous chapters, and an upcoming chapter includes a more in-depth explanation.
>
> For now, these two client stories offer a glimpse at the possibilities this process holds.

> For these pre-checks, I used the Applied Kinesiology process of "muscle checking," which challenges the ability of a muscle to "hold" in certain positions, revealing aspects of systemic stress.

> You'll find several courses within the Edu-K curriculum that address infant reflexes. In this particular case, Ronny chose Total Core Repatterning. On another day, he might have been drawn to a different process and seen similar gains.

well. Ronny told me that he was now perfectly comfortable studying at a table; he no longer felt the need to stand or move around in order to concentrate.

Ronny will still benefit from additional sessions to address other areas of learning challenge, but this STNR shift will certainly go a long way toward providing a new, more integrated foundation for all his future changes.

Simpler interventions

Not all children (or adults) need lengthy intervention to resolve retained reflexes. Some reflexes are mildly retained and respond quickly to simpler balance techniques.

I worked with Hector, a seventh-grader who was plagued by his lack of ability to focus in class. He was slow to begin his work and late in completing it. A pre-check of his ability to focus showed how easily distracted he was by noises nearby.

Hector's balance called for addressing Symmetrical Tonic Neck Reflex. Just like with Ronny (above), I checked the level of stress produced by sitting and standing, with his arms flexed or bent. And (again, just like Ronny) he couldn't comfortably maintain a seated working posture.

These were Hector's unique choices; another child in the same circumstance would very likely choose something else.

For his balance, Hector selected from my menu a combination of on-the-floor crawling patterns, homolateral and then cross-lateral, taking perhaps six or seven minutes in all. When this process was complete, he was able to sit comfortably, with his arms in any position, and focus despite the noises nearby.

Then I asked Hector if he was noticing anything else. He got an amused look on his face and said, "Yeah, my arms and hands feel different—more relaxed." After completing a handwriting sample, he said, "This may sound weird, but I feel like the pen is smaller and thinner. My writing is better, not sloppy. I have better control."

Why was extensive intervention required for Ronny to move through the STNR process when Hector's STNR was resolved so quickly? I can only assume that Ronny had a more firmly retained reflexive pattern than Hector, one that was embedded more deeply in his mind-body system. Perhaps Hector's early childhood had provided more of the movement experiences he needed to move through this pattern, and he was more ready to complete the process.

However, regardless of what route we take to eventual integration, Hector and Ronny's stories illustrate the profound effect of retained reflexes on the activities of daily living; life is so much easier when reflexes are resolved.

My own reflex-release story

So far I've described how retained reflexes affect children, but some of us have lived with these challenges our entire lives— most likely without even knowing it. We're never too old to benefit from reflex-release work.

Note: Reflex patterns have been known to "spring back to life" following a physical or emotional trauma. And as we age, we may lose the energy we've been putting into compensations, and our reflexive impulses may become more evident.

Over the years, I've had the good fortune to learn several different methods of addressing reflexes, in courses developed and taught by gifted Edu-K instructors. One of the benefits of these learning opportunities is that course participants practice the techniques by balancing each other, so we have our own personal experiences of the shifts that are possible.

In the first course I took, as each reflex was addressed, I noticed an improvement in something significant: the ease with which I could walk or sit, move or remain still, focus or think. But it wasn't until I made a trip to my massage therapist that I got a different perspective on the changes I'd made; she was astounded at the new level of flexibility and movement in my back.

I'd always felt embarrassed by the chronic tension in my body, rather like it was a character flaw that showed how challenged I was at handling stress: mind affecting body. What I came to realize was that my level of muscular stress was due in large part to how my body spontaneously held itself to counter the pull of specific reflexes: body affecting mind. Once I began to release these retained-reflex tensions (a process that continues to this day), I began to have more fluid movement patterns— and a more easeful life.

Resolving reflexes through playful activity

The examples above illustrate addressing reflexes using the Edu-K five-step balance process. Many people also find that, even without using the balance process, consistent use of the Brain Gym movements over time may help in resolving mildly retained reflexes. By rekindling the maturation process of their inner wiring, many children will develop the ability to sit, learn, and move more easily and calmly, as their sensory processing becomes more integrated and available.

A vivid example of the benefits of this kind of whole-body movement is coming up shortly in Chapter 10, "Cultivating Natural Focus."

Why dedicate an entire chapter to exploring infant reflex issues? Because if a child has not fully developed these foundational movement patterns, he will very likely end up with unconscious compensations that sap time and energy, leaving him less able to read, write, and learn. Even as adults, we may "bump into" reflex-oriented behaviors that prevent us from accomplishing various physical and learning tasks with freedom and ease.

Using the Brain Gym activities can help us, both children and adults, naturally overcome many retained reflexes, and Edu-K balancing can help resolve reflex-driven coordination or learning issues even more deeply and completely. In this way, we can use these rich resources to support ourselves and others in developing patterns that allow free, joyful movement and, therefore, a greater ability to think, learn, and grow.

At www.EducateYourBrain.com, you'll find updated information about the latest programs, books, and courses on the topic of infant reflexes.

Chapter 9

Brain Gym: Theory in Action

- *Whole-Brain Processing*
- *The Balance of Balance: The Three Dimensions*
- *Honoring the Learner's Noticing*
- *Integrated Low Gear, the Missing Piece in Learning*
- *Brain Gym as a Behavioral Model*

When Paul and Gail Dennison began working with challenged learners in the early 1970s, they couldn't have foreseen that the processes they were developing would one day become a profound system whose principles and practices would span the globe.

Their introduction of physical movement into the learning process seemed to hold keys to achievement and inspired them to delve even more deeply into both brain science and learning theory. Eventually, their inquiry evolved into an extensive body of knowledge about the relationship between movement and learning, now known as Educational Kinesiology.

In this chapter, we will explore some of Edu-K's unique contributions to the study of mind-body integration and how we can enhance our experience of life through movement. Together, these concepts form some of the language and philosophy that make Brain Gym® and Edu-K so uniquely geared toward the learner's ability to release stress and access the potential of the whole brain.

We'll begin by taking a look at the left and right hemispheres to then see how they operate, both individually and as a pair.

Whole-Brain Processing

What does it mean to have "whole-brain processing"? How can what we often think of as a single structure—the brain—not be used in its entirety, all the time? It could be looked at as a matter of hemispheres, a brain bridge, and stress.

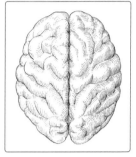

The cerebrum's two hemispheres

The *cerebrum*, the largest part of the human brain, is the location of what is commonly called our *intellect*. It is divided into two hemispheres, which are linked by the *corpus callosum*, a thick bundle of nerve fibers that connect almost every part of one side of the brain to its corresponding part in the other. When we have full communication across this "brain bridge," we can easily perform tasks that call mainly on one hemisphere or the other, or use them both together. For example, our right brain imagines the story we want to write, and our left brain helps us retrieve the spelling of specific words; to fluidly compose the paragraphs, though, we need our whole brain, so we can spell as we write.

To provide a foundation for deeper understanding of the dynamic relationship between our two hemispheres, let's look at what current research has revealed on this topic.

Left Brain	Right Brain
temporal	global
processing over time	processing over space
linear, sequential	simultaneous
symbolic, verbal	spatial, intuitive
two-dimensional	multi-dimensional
starts with pieces first	starts by seeing the entirety
technique	inspiration
future-oriented	present moment
sees differences	sees similarities
routine, predictability	novelty
analytical	imaginative
deliberate	spontaneous
expressive	receptive
effort	flow

The right brain is commonly called the "gestalt" hemisphere. This word is derived from the German language and is often translated as "unified whole"; it refers to "a set of elements considered as a whole and regarded as amounting to more than the sum of its parts."

Axons in the right hemisphere are actually longer than in the left. That may be why this hemisphere can call on more different areas of the brain at the same time.[1]

Left brain, right brain

The left hemisphere is the expressive area of the brain, and its main mode is to *process over time* in a linear, logical way. It handles the symbolic, language-oriented aspects of the information it receives, such as numbers, math symbols, and letters of the alphabet; it's good at rote learning and happiest with routine or predictable events. This hemisphere first recognizes separate parts as opposed to a whole: when viewing a forest, the left hemisphere is adept at perceiving and analyzing one tree at a time, or even the bark of one tree.

The right hemisphere perceives the world as one cohesive unit, or "gestalt," rather than as diverse elements that may somehow be connected. This hemisphere views and understands a topic in its most global sense. It will automatically see the forest as including not only trees, but shrubs, vines, and lichen; streams and lakes; deer, birds, insects—and people—all as one complete, interrelated ecosystem. As partner to the left (expressive) hemisphere, this half of the cerebrum is only receptive; its main mode is to *process over space*, producing our kinesthetic and spatial awareness. Other key attributes of this hemisphere include imagination, spontaneity, and recognition of novelty.

However, what we think of as left-brain or right-brain functions may overlap. For example, while the brains of most men are organized in this typical left-right fashion, many women access aspects of their language ability through both hemispheres of the brain.[2] In addition, territory in either hemisphere can "learn" tasks thought to be the exclusive province of the other; this is often how skills are regained following brain damage through accident, brain surgery, or stroke.

While most tasks require simultaneous use of both hemispheres, we may call more predominantly on one or the other for specific activities. We want to be able to fluidly shift back and forth between processing linear, detail-oriented (left-brain) tasks and those that are more spatial and imaginative (right brain).

All of these diverse capacities of both hemispheres are important, and we need to be able to combine them easily as we work, play, learn, and move. However, if we find ourselves in an unintegrated, "stuck" state, we are left without the balance provided by access to both brains simultaneously, and a variety of less-than-helpful qualities are likely to emerge. Our left brain, so good at linear, logical thinking, could leave us adrift with only tense, mechanical reactions; we may use lots of effort but without results, comprehension, feeling, or understanding. And the benefits of spontaneity and imagination of our right brain may evolve into daydreaming, hyperactivity, and disorganization; we may feel overwhelmed and act without thinking, often appearing angry, frustrated, or depressed. As always, *movement* is the key to maintaining an integrated, whole-brain state!

> The brains of very young children are not specialized in this way. Until about the age of four, both hemispheres contain all attributes; then, bursts of dendrite growth occur, first in one hemisphere and then in the other. The right hemisphere is the first to begin this specialization process, between ages four and seven. The left hemisphere begins to specialize somewhere between age seven and nine. This specialization process is complete by about age twelve. [3]

Left Brain Under Stress	Right Brain Under Stress
rigid	chaotic
inflexible	dreamer
mechanical	hyperactive
rule-dominated	no perception of time
tunnel vision	oversensitive
ideas blocked	disorganized

> "When we use the cerebral, thinking part of the brain to the exclusion of our feelings, we often bounce from the analysis of the left brain to a state of judgment that can derive from the right frontal lobes, and we then feel stuck and unable to make decisions. This cycle often leads to frustration, anger, and depression. Yet, when we honor our feelings, the right frontal lobes access associated memories and movement experiences that provide neural connections to the left frontal lobes and our sense of possibility, giving us that euphoric "Aha," not just of making a choice, but of having a choice choose us." [4]
> ~ Paul E. Dennison

"Lead" hemisphere

In every person, one hemisphere—the right or the left—will develop as the one he most easily calls on, and that sets the overall tone for his favored mode of learning and operating in life. Rather than the terms "dominant" or "non-dominant," Edu-K has adopted the terms "lead" or "non-lead," reflecting the cooperative relationship between the two hemispheres.

Since I lead with my right brain, my natural mode is to see any concept in its entirety first and then move to the component parts as needed. For example, when I got my new digital camera, I simply played with it to see what it would do and read the directions only when stumped on how to accomplish something. My left-brained husband, however, starts with the details: he loves reading the manual for any new equipment he buys!

Building—and refreshing—your brain bridge

The ability to call freely on the attributes of either hemisphere, or both hemispheres together, is called *lateral integration* and occurs only when messages can flow back and forth across the brain bridge. As with all other information pathways in our body, the more we use this inter-hemisphere highway, the more readily its neural fibers will develop an insulating layer of *myelin*. This makes communication across the brain bridge quicker—and therefore more efficient—so it's easier to coordinate our use of both hemispheres. This may explain why people who participate in cross-lateral activity over time (starting with infant crawling) tend to learn and process easily.

So this is how the brain bridge is formed and refined in the first place. But once we've achieved a certain state of integration, why would we continue to need integrating movement? Do Brain Gym activities in some way refresh the communication between our two hemispheres? If so, why would that communication become diminished in the first place?

"Switching off" and "switching on"

The answer may be *stress*. No matter how integrated we may typically be, a stress reaction to situations around us can cause us to shift in an instant from feeling "ready" to feeling "stuck." When I think of those words, a memory of high school comes quickly to mind. I loved English class; with that material, I felt capable, intelligent, and in charge of my learning. Chemistry, however, was challenging for me, and I can easily recall the anxiety and sense of brain-fade that accompanied me as I walked through the door to that classroom. What happened to me in the hallway between these two classes?

In the world of Edu-K, the playful term "switching off" is used to describe that "stuck" condition. We all know that there is no switch and there is no *off*, but this phrase certainly describes my experience, then and now: the feeling of ability and confidence can simply vanish when I go to do something that activates a learned stress pattern.

However, I also experience how Brain Gym movements and the Edu-K balance process have a dynamic effect on this "switched off" state. When I notice myself feeling stuck or resistant (recent example: cleaning out the garage) and choose to do Brain Gym movements, my reluctance diminishes or vanishes

Many people think that, to be creative, one must be "right-brained." Perhaps they're confusing "creativity" with the right-brain attribute of "imagination." It's true that a creative person will need access to the aspects of the right/gestalt hemisphere. However, it's equally true that he'll need access to the linear, logical, and detail-oriented left hemisphere in order to execute his ideas with skill and refined technique. The truly creative person has easy access to both hemispheres to write the story, form the sculpture, or compose the music.

The concept of "switching off" under stress was more fully explained in Chapter 4, "The Cross Crawl: Power Up Your Hemispheres."

altogether, and I can easily approach and finish my task; I now feel "switched on" for tackling the garage clutter!

Stress and our brain's hemispheres

The Dennisons have recognized for decades that people who strongly favor the processing style of one hemisphere over the other may experience their *non-lead* hemisphere as being even less available when they're under stress.

I experience this regularly in my own life. When I'm feeling relaxed, I can switch easily between the big picture and the details of any topic. But when I am tired or feeling overwhelmed, I function easily only with the big picture; activities that require intense left-brain processing (math calculation or following complex printed directions) take much more effort. I feel as if my non-lead (left) hemisphere is "switched off."

Again, this is a playful term, not a literal one! Certainly, an entire side of my brain does not truly "switch off," but I can attest to feeling as if this is the case. And my body behaves as if it's true: I'm suddenly less able to coordinate my left and right sides, as if the communication between them is failing. For example, at the end of a long, tiring day, I may go to Cross Crawl and find myself bringing my right elbow down to my right knee—a very homolateral pattern—even though I've done this movement daily for years.

Yet, just as with my "switched-off for cleaning out the garage" experience, above, a bit of movement refreshes my integrated state, and then I'm able to Cross Crawl easily. And once I'm back in lateral balance, I can deal with both the big picture *and* the details, since both brains are now participating—and I can more easily achieve my goals.

Networks and patterns

When I first heard the term "brain organization," I couldn't quite imagine what it meant; how could a brain be *organized?*

In essence, it's this: only certain portions of the brain are required for any given task, so we link up those portions in a network that gets triggered when it's time for that task. Every moment of the day, our brain will be re-organizing so we're ready to handle the next situation in which we find ourselves: chopping vegetables, reading a novel, computing how much tip to leave for the dinner we just ate.

Modern science now uses technology to observe these networks in action. MRI scans reveal that activity rises and falls in certain brain regions depending on what the person is doing. Researchers assume that these regions are working together and so must be linked in some way.

To envision this linking, we could imagine a network, or web, that runs throughout the brain. When we engage in a specific task, only the portions of the network that are needed are activated. This could be called a brain organization pattern. An "optimal" brain organization pattern would be one that provides easy access to brain regions needed for that task or movement, allowing for expression of our gifts and abilities: an "integrated" state. However, any given organization pattern we develop may include elements of compensation that require extra energy and drain our internal resources, perhaps leading to the feeling of being "stuck."

And any brain organization pattern may also involve an emotional component. For example, when we learn through joyful experiences, we feel good when we repeat what we learned. Conversely, when we experience distress or trauma as we're learning, that state is what emerges when we remember the content involved.

The outcome of the Edu-K five-step balance process is often experienced as a shift from stress and compensation to greater efficiency and a more positive emotional state. This shift is described as a change in functional patterns of "brain organization" as we move from a one-sided to more whole-brain processing.

The concept of "brain organization profiles" is fully explored in the Edu-K course "Optimal Brain Organization" and in the book *The Dominance Factor*, by Carla Hannaford, Ph.D.

In Edu-K, the term "brain organization profile" is also used. This refers to the pattern formed by a person's leading (or dominant) eye, ear, hand, foot, and brain hemisphere. These elements combine to make certain capacities more available (or less available) when the person is learning, or under stress.

Whole-brain organization, "lead," and "switching off": These concepts revolutionized my understanding of how and why certain learning challenges persist in the classroom (and in one's life) and why such simple Brain Gym movements have the capacity to improve skills so quickly.

The Balance of Balance: The Three Dimensions

Scientists have known for decades that certain kinds of movements help to develop a foundation for cognitive functioning. As Paul and Gail Dennison worked with clients over time, they noticed correlations between specific movements and the emergence of specific cognitive abilities, and theorized about which brain structures might be involved.

Paul Dennison explains, "When we do Brain Gym activities, we reconnect with our concrete, three-dimensional experience. From my studies in the field of brain research, I hypothesize that Brain Gym works by establishing neural learning pathways in the three-dimensional body."[5]

Learning in three dimensions

Out of this inquiry, the Dennisons developed their concept of the Three Dimensions of Whole-Brain Learning: Laterality Dimension (involving communication between right and left hemispheres), Centering Dimension (cerebral cortex and limbic system), and Focus Dimension (brain stem and frontal lobes).

In his book *Brain Gym® and Me*, Paul Dennison further describes his theory this way:

> When these dimensions of intelligence—Laterality, Centering, and Focus—are available to us, we have a sense of purpose and a feeling of comfort in moving toward objectives. We feel our emotions deeply, are organized, and are relaxed in our bodies so that we can think rationally in the present moment. We're able to process information laterally with ease, from left to right, right to left, or beginning to end, in a temporal, linear fashion. The full integration of these three aspects creates whole-brain organization and integration of the body and heart.[6]

How can we notice our ability to function in these three dimensions? The everyday experience of how fluidly we stand, sit, and walk can provide clues; however, when we're in motion, we're not always able to notice the subtleties. The Dennisons developed standing "postural checks" (checks of actual physical balance), which they identified as a reliable means of noticing our level of integration in these three dimensions.

Effects of stress on movement and learning

I was surprised to realize that our actual physical balance changes when we're under stress. And the postural checks can help us "read" our own state of integration and, therefore, readiness for cognitive functioning. I'll illustrate the principles involved, using my own experience as an example:

Laterality Dimension: When I check my "side-to-side" balance (gently shifting my weight from one foot to the other, noticing differences in balance or stability on either foot), I'm essentially seeing how integrated my Laterality Dimension is. Being "off" in this dimension might affect such things as:

- how ready I am to call on the attributes of both brain hemispheres

- how fully I can engage paired body systems, such as both eyes for reading, both ears for hearing, or both hands or feet for balanced motor coordination

- how fluid my eye-hand coordination is

- whether I am confused or clear in response to the question, "What am I thinking?"

Centering Dimension: By checking my "up-and-down" balance (gently rising onto my toes and then bending my knees just a bit, observing my balance and whether this movement feels fluid or awkward), I'm seeing how integrated my Centering Dimension is. Challenges here might affect such things as:

- how physically grounded I feel

- how well I can organize my thoughts and belongings, and orient myself in the world around me

- how connected I feel to myself and others

- how easily I can harmonize emotion with rational thought

- whether I can easily notice, "What am I feeling?"

Focus Dimension: By checking my "front-to-back" balance (lightly shifting my weight between the balls of my feet and my heels, noticing if I catch myself by locking my knees or fall off balance, ready to pitch forward), I'm seeing how integrated my Focus Dimension is. Stress showing up here might affect such things as:

- how attentive I am

- how fully I can comprehend

- how able I am to shift between details and the big picture, and back again

- how inclined I feel to participate

- whether I can easily discern, "What am I sensing in my body?"

The Three Dimensions in daily life

I love the way these postural checks can offer a reference point for noticing inner shifts as we add integrating movement. Here's an example. Have you ever felt resistant about accomplishing something? Me, too:

I had a huge pile of papers to organize for my taxes. When I recognized how unready I felt to approach this task (I didn't want to even look at the pile), I stood and noticed my physical balance. As I shifted my weight from side to side, I felt less steady on one foot than the other. Rising onto my toes left me feeling tippy, and as I bent my knees just a bit, I felt heavy; my transition from bent knees to toes felt jerky and awkward. As I shifted my weight from the balls of my feet to my heels, I felt my knees lock and tension rise rigidly up my spine; as I moved front-to-back, I lost any capacity I previously had for feeling safe. My breathing became shallow, and I felt no ability to focus—especially on taxes.

Then I began doing Brain Gym movements—the first ones that came to mind. By the time I had done only three activities, my balance was much more stable, my movement was more fluid, and my sense of focus and easy breathing had returned. Not only that, but as soon as my body showed me that I was now physically balanced, I could also tell the difference in my mental state: I felt ready to tackle those tax papers—and I did!

It had been clear to me as I began that I was not ready to do that paperwork. With these postural checks as an inner balance meter, I could notice just which elements of inner integration were "off" and track my own internal shifts as I chose from my learning menu of movements. This is a very empowering way to make personal change.

The very act of becoming aware of changes in the mind-body system leads us to the next aspect of theory: the fine art of noticing. I find this to be the most profound illustration of how Edu-K processes are truly directed by the learner.

Honoring the Learner's Noticing

One of the hallmarks of the Edu-K program is that of self-observation, or *noticing*. Gail Dennison describes her experience of noticing this way:

> Every time I notice my patterns of movement or behavior—my mental, emotional, or sensory experience—I'm using my front brain to observe the postural, sensory, or movement patterns based in the brain stem, and I invite integration between these two areas of the brain.[7]

This kind of noticing helps us to become aware of things we may tend to overlook about our physical, mental, and emotional state, so we can come to understand ourselves more fully and make choices that are in our best interest.

For example, when a child finally recognizes that his first reaction to frustration is hitting, an opening exists for him to change that pattern. This opening does not exist when he's simply corrected by others; *he can change only after he sees his own behavior*. This capacity for self-reflection is a function of the frontal lobes and can take time to develop.

Chapter 16, "Brain Gym in Education," offers suggestions for introducing the concept of inner noticing to young children.

When I began as a student of the Brain Gym program, my sense of internal noticing was limited. It took time and coaching from a facilitator to go more deeply into my experience of how and where I felt blocked. Now, with years of Edu-K balancing and coursework behind me, I have a much greater vocabulary for this kind of noticing, and my sense of when I'm "off" or "on" is more available. Becoming adept at this kind of inner awareness is definitely a process, and cannot be rushed. It's important to honor every stage of a person's ability to notice his inner state.

Noticing and the learning process

Many people are familiar with the concept that certain exercises are "good" for the body. It's a common occurrence to go to a physical trainer and have him or her observe our physical condition and prescribe activities that will help build muscle.

With the learning process, however, the dynamic changes. While it's true that certain movements help develop specific skills (practicing the Lazy 8s pattern is very helpful in developing correct letter formation, for example), when a learner feels stuck, the most important movement to do is *the one he is drawn to*.

Following a Brain Gym workshop, Carson, a special-needs teacher, couldn't wait to include the Brain Gym movements in his work with children. He opened each student session with the PACE warm-up and found that his students were suddenly more ready to learn; it seemed to him that they began benefiting even more deeply from his other techniques—the ones he'd been doing all along with them.

Arm Activation

But his biggest surprise came when he began allowing students to choose their own path to achievement. He and the child would identify the skill to work on that day, and then Carson would offer the child a list of perhaps ten therapy activities—always including Brain Gym—and allow the child to choose. Carson could not believe how quickly his young students began improving in core skills, as they selected one activity after another, essentially directing their own learning.

Carson wrote, "One day I was working with Jonathan, age ten, who wanted to improve his handwriting. He said that writing was exhausting, and it took him a long time to complete his assignments. The sample he wrote for me had small, cramped letters, reflecting perfectly the way his elbow was compressed to his side and his hand gripped on his pencil. Tension radiated from his shoulder down to his fingertips.

"I showed Jonathan a poster with all twenty-six Brain Gym movements on it and invited him to choose the one that would be 'best for him right now.' Out of all those movements, he chose Arm Activation, an isometric activity that releases tension from the shoulders.

"After Arm Activation, Jonathan's writing sample was very different; his letters were larger, and his handwriting overall was more fluid. His arm was relaxed, and his hand had a lighter grip on the pencil. He said, 'That was easier! Can I do this every day?'"

Later, Carson told me, "When I looked closely at myself, I realized that, on some level, I had always been focused on figuring out what was 'wrong' with kids and 'fixing' them. My biggest 'aha' moment was realizing that every child arrives at my door ready to show me what he can most benefit from—that day. When I support the child in noticing and choosing, and follow his lead, amazing things happen."

Following the learner's lead

When we hold the inner posture of meeting the learner's needs, even actions that could seem small and insignificant can open the door to self-noticing in a very big way:

Varsha, an occupational therapist, took the Brain Gym® 101 course to learn new techniques to blend into her work with children who have learning challenges. During the course, we explored the Lazy 8s movement, experiencing this pattern in many ways, including tracing it on each other's backs.

Back at work the next day, Varsha's schedule included working with Tanlia, whose many challenges included being almost completely nonverbal. Nine years old, she had never spoken in school, hardly spoke at home, and found written expression all but impossible. Varsha had been working with her for months using all the techniques of her training and had seen very little improvement.

Lazy 8s on the back

When Varsha arrived to pick up Tanlia for that day's session, she was sitting on the floor with her classmates, already involved in a whole-group language activity the teacher was leading. Varsha decided to sit on the floor as well, right behind her. Then Varsha wondered, "How can I bring a little Brain Gym into this moment?"

Remembering what we'd done in class, she was inspired to begin tracing Lazy 8s on Tanlia's back. Gently and slowly, with one hand and then the other, she kept up this activity. After a few minutes, Varsha grew a bit tired and dropped her hands into her lap—at which point Tanlia turned around and said, "I need more."

Stunned that this girl had actually spoken, Varsha continued tracing Lazy 8s on her back for another few minutes until the class activity was over, then together they left for Varsha's office. On the way, Tanlia spotted the playground equipment and declared, "I need to swing!" She spent a few minutes in earnest swinging; then she played on the climbing bars; and then she bounced on the mini-trampoline. She had never just taken herself to the playground in this way.

Finally in Varsha's office, they began the day's lesson: handwriting. Varsha suggested that Tanlia describe what she had just done. She had never written a complete sentence on her own, but that day she took up her pencil and wrote: "I played on the swing, on the bars, and on the trampoline." Varsha helped only with spelling; the thoughts and determination to finish were entirely Tanlia's.

> "Children with sensory integrative dysfunctions are often able to choose exactly the kind of activity that produces the sensory input and makes the motor demand that helps the child organize that input." [8]
> ~ A. Jean Ayres
> *Sensory Integration and the Child*

Varsha could hardly wait to tell me about this amazing event, and together we pieced together what may have prompted this new learning:

- Varsha had wondered "How can I bring a bit of Brain Gym into this moment?" and offered Tanlia the movement experience that presented itself; she followed Tanlia's lead and continued with this activity.

- Tracing the Lazy 8 on Tanlia's back activated both sides of her sensory cortex, providing lateral integration and (probably much-needed) tactile stimulation at the same time.

- The front-to-back action of swinging stimulated the Focus Dimension, enhancing her ability to comprehend and participate, along with her vestibular system, benefiting eye-teaming.

- Hanging on the climbing apparatus had a lengthening effect on the muscles and ligaments of her arms and shoulders. (This action is similar to that of Arm Activation, the Brain Gym movement that helps release *tendon guard reflex*, which tightens the back of the body in response to any perceived threat and inhibits language expression.)

- Bouncing on the mini-trampoline stimulated her vestibular system again and perhaps even helped to integrate her Centering Dimension, improving internal organization.

With all these pieces in place, Tanlia had more access to her innate ability to express herself and was primed for writing. And all this occurred simply because Varsha followed Tanlia's lead in getting the movement that brought access to her potential.

Varsha now uses Brain Gym on a regular basis with all of the children with whom she works, offering them the opportunity to choose their "best" movements for that day. She says, "Once we do Brain Gym, my students are so much more capable. I can't believe how much more they're learning since we began using these deceptively simple activities."

New tools for noticing

As a student of Edu-K, and through the process of sharing these tools and techniques with others, I have had the opportunity to experience many aspects of noticing. It's always an adventure to see just what opportunities present themselves.

One day, I was working with a client, Edward, whose balance session called for doing some Lazy 8s. At first, his eyes resisted moving smoothly with the flow of this pattern. In particular, when he followed his thumb to the upper right, his eyes jumped away.

Finally, that experience of visual "speed-bumps" started to even out, and his eyes began moving a bit more smoothly. When he finally stopped, I asked, "Did you get everything you need from that movement?" He replied, "Yes. . . no. . . I can't tell." He had uncertainty written all over his face.

I had a strong sense that Edward's mind-body system was asking for just a bit more of this movement. If that were indeed so, I wanted the impulse to continue to come from him. What means of noticing could I offer that would help him connect more to his inner knowing?

Lazy 8s

Then I remembered Tanlia and her heartfelt declaration of "I need more." I explained to Edward that the way we say something often reflects how we feel about it. I invited him to repeat Tanlia's phrase, and its opposite: "This is complete" and "I need more."

Edward took his time. After saying "This is complete," he sounded hesitant, as if his words had a question mark after them. When he said, "I need more," his voice was lower and firmer and carried the strength of conviction. Edward said, "I was hoping to be finished, because this was not an easy exercise for me, but I can tell that I would really benefit from more of it." He continued with Lazy 8s, and after just two or three more circuits of the pattern, his eyes began following the flow much more naturally. Even then, he continued with his Lazy 8s, enjoying what it felt like to be at ease with the sense of visual relaxation and flow. When he concluded, he repeated, "This is complete. . . I need more," and nodded his head with confidence. "This is complete. I can really tell."

> Sometimes the word "need" evokes a state of powerlessness. In this case, however, I believe the phrase "I need more" reflects an authentic recognition of our inner yearning, a vital aspect of our desire to grow and change.

This is complete. . . I need more. When I use these phrases as a form of noticing, I am aware of the difference in the volume, timbre, and resonance of my voice—the sense of truth with which I speak. These simple statements become a bridge to deeper awareness, through which I can become more attuned to the feelings that want to make themselves known.

Integrated Low Gear: The Missing Piece in Learning

Do you remember your first attempts at something that required a lot of focus or coordination? Perhaps it was riding a bike: your first wobbly trials at simultaneous pedaling, steering, and balancing. Then, one day you found yourself simply riding down the road, thinking about something else entirely. You had mastered the skill of bike-riding and it didn't require your focused attention anymore.

Anything we do easily, we do automatically, without having to think about it. The Brain Gym program identifies this state as "integrated high gear," which means that we can move and think about something else at the same time. Into this category fall all kinds of effortless actions, like signing our name, brushing our teeth, or driving the route home from work. We could think of this as "cruising on autopilot."

When we learn something new, however, we must slow down, so we can take time to explore the details of it at our own pace. The Brain Gym program calls this state "integrated low gear," where we can stop and think when we need to. Into this category fall all kinds of learning, from figuring out how to multiply fractions, to operating a complex computer program, to making your first soufflé. We could think of this as "safely slowing down to explore."

A gear for slowing down

I like to illustrate the ability to shift between integrated high gear and integrated low gear by thinking about traveling on holiday. Imagine you are driving through a part of the world you've always wanted to explore. You're on the freeway (cruising) and you spot a little village in the distance, which you decide to visit. You certainly can't cruise through it at freeway speed, so you exit on the appropriate off-ramp and find your way into town. You drive slowly, exploring all the charming buildings and shops. Perhaps you even park the car so you can get out and walk about on foot, to find that lovely café for lunch or afternoon tea, and purchase a remembrance or two. When you're all finished with your exploration, you get back into your car and return to cruising on the freeway again, taking with you all that you learned about that picturesque place.

This is the way true learning works: the learner moves seamlessly between integrated high gear and integrated low gear as needed. When reading, he can pause to figure out the meaning of a word and then return fluidly to the story. When learning a new mathematical algorithm, she can instantly call on the math facts she knows while taking time to figure out which numbers go where. This kind of processing calls on many different parts of the brain, which need to be ready to communicate with each other.

What happens when a child (or an adult) is not operating in an integrated state? He may end up moving compulsively: "Help! I can't slow down!" This learner may miss details and produce poor or incomplete work, acting thoughtlessly and creating havoc in her surroundings.

Or the learner may end up sitting listlessly: "Help! I can't get moving!" He may start late and need prodding to finish; he may blend into the background or stare off into space.

When these behaviors occur to a mild degree, they simply get in our way a bit, and we learn to manage them with compensations. But in the extreme, these are the very behaviors that could end up being labeled as ADHD (Attention Deficit Hyperactive Disorder) or ADD (Attention Deficit Disorder).

It's very important to be able to move effortlessly between integrated high gear and integrated low gear. Yes, it's lovely to do things quickly—*but integrated low gear is the only state where we can learn something new.*

Hitting the pause button in order to learn

How often do we give children time to thoroughly play with a newly acquired skill before we ask them to use it in a more complex way? Okay, you've learned your numbers; quick—time for addition! Ah, you can write words! Oops—you've spelled them wrong. Too much of this prevents children from experiencing the satisfaction of accomplishment, since they're forced to hurry to the next skill level before they've rested in this one. As adults who have taken on this pattern, we may pressure ourselves for instant achievement. (Oh, I'm learning guitar chords—Why can't I play a real song yet?)

Without integrated low gear, we may career anxiously through life "trying" to do things. In this state, we can't slow down enough to do them thoroughly or accurately; we never have the satisfaction derived from small moments of accomplishment.

An emerging state of balance

Integrated low gear is a state that ideally emerges in childhood through the joy of discovery at our own pace. This kind of exploration occurs only in the absence of stress. It feels playful, emerges from curiosity, and is internally directed. Through it, we develop the qualities required for focus and sustained concentration.

However, I believe that, when our initial exposure to a concept is stressful, we develop a fear-based reaction to it, leaving us unable to access our most integrated brain organization patterns. The Edu-K balance process offers us myriad possibilities for taking on new patterns of thought and movement. You may be relieved to know (as I was) that we can develop this internal pattern for integrated low gear (and its companion, integrated high gear) at any age, through Brain Gym balancing.

Elsewhere in this book are stories of clients who were able to take on an entirely new pattern of thought or behavior as the result of a balance session. For example, there's the story of Alexa, who couldn't focus on the details of English grammar enough to study for a crucial exam. Once she had balanced to "easily understand and study English grammar," she could focus on those details—and even found them interesting!

You can read Alexa's entire story in Chapter 12, "Make Lasting Change with Edu-K Balancing."

Of all the elements of the Brain Gym program, I find that Dennison Laterality Repatterning (DLR) and Three Dimension Repatterning (3DR) are the most effective at supporting learners in developing both an integrated low gear and integrated high gear. These balance processes, developed by Paul Dennison, are what I call "the crown jewels of Brain Gym." They can open the door to new possibilities in a most profound way.

Both DLR and 3DR are learned in the Brain Gym® 101 course.

A hurricane in tennis shoes

Meet Parker, a young client who was simply a small hurricane in tennis shoes. He was five years old and developmentally delayed, having missed a number of important neurological milestones. His mother, a physical therapist, had described to me some of his behavior and processing challenges, but nothing had quite prepared me for the way Parker hurtled into my office and set about seeing and touching everything. I began working very quickly and intuitively, and said, "Hey, Parker! Come lie down here on the carpet!" Parker's mother, Cristy, had just taken the Brain Gym® 101 course, and I found myself saying, "Cristy, I think it's time for a DLR with Parker!" She sat down with me to help with this process.

There are five main steps of DLR, which involve various combinations of arm and leg movement, eye direction, and other elements in a specific sequence. Parker was able to do the first step fairly easily: it included the Cross Crawl, which Cristy had been helping him learn to do. This part of the repatterning process develops the integrated high-gear state of automatic movement. However, when it was time for Parker to do the second step, which included raising and lowering his same-side arm and leg simultaneously, he simply could not do it. This part of the repatterning process helps develop the integrated low-gear state: the ability to stop, think, and safely explore.

Then it struck me—Parker was a whirlwind of activity, and he could not do this movement; it seemed he had no integrated low gear at all. *He was incapable of slowing down!* What would happen once this repatterning was complete? What would Parker be able to learn once he felt safe enough to explore at his own pace?

Cristy and I carried on by "motoring" Parker through this movement; she'd raise his left arm and left leg together and lower them, then I'd raise his right arm and right leg together and lower them, back and forth, back and forth. Finally, Parker began participating in the process and started moving his arms and legs in that pattern on his own, first awkwardly and out of sync, then more fluidly. We completed the rest of the repatterning process in this same very simplified way, taking about fifteen minutes in all.

When the process was complete, Parker rolled onto his side and curled up, very content. A feeling of serenity filled the air. My sense was that Parker's body was absorbing this new experience of integration, and Cristy said that this was the longest she'd ever seen Parker be still when he wasn't asleep.

In addition, some other remarkable things were occurring. I mentioned above that Parker had struggled to achieve many basic infant skills, and one of them was nursing properly. As he lay there, he spontaneously began sucking motions with his mouth (which continued off and on for the next several days). Also, his next bathroom visit, a few minutes later, produced the first authentic, complete bowel movement of his life; Cristy said he'd never used the core muscles of his lower torso in that way before. These very basic steps are huge milestones in the life of a developmentally delayed child, and indicate that Parker had made several very important shifts through that very quick and spontaneous repatterning process.

From hurricane to happy observer

The next day, Parker went with his father to the shopping mall. Ordinarily, he would be "everywhere at once," but on that day he stayed right by his father's side, calmly looking at the things around him, despite the noise and distraction. This child, who had been stuck in the "Help! I can't stop!" state, was now stopping, thinking, and choosing. After that one DLR, Parker was no longer living a life of such compulsive action, and he was finally able to process at his own pace.

Since that time, Parker has continued to grow and change, making improvements in language expression, chewing, acceptance of new foods, tolerance of noise and disruption, auditory discrimination, and the ability to dress himself. He has also returned to some earlier developmental behaviors (the "clingy" stage of two-year-olds, for example). Cristy and I agree that he is spontaneously "backing up to move forward," this time completing each step more fully. Parker will certainly benefit from more sessions, but this beginning to his journey with Brain Gym balancing created a powerful foundation for future changes.

> "Back up to move forward" is the succinct phrase from Paul Dennison that inspired Cecilia Freeman Koester in her Brain Gym work with multiply challenged, medically fragile children. She describes her techniques in her book *I Am the Child: Using Brain Gym® with Children Who Have Special Needs.* 9

Honoring the time to explore

Not every child has Parker's extreme challenge with integrated low gear, but many children (and many adults) have this challenge to different degrees. Teachers describe with dismay the increasing number of children with impulsive behaviors, for whom it takes tremendous effort to sit still or keep their hands to themselves; prescriptions for ADHD medication are at an all-time high.

As teachers and parents, it's our responsibility to support learners in taking time to playfully explore so they can make the elements of any new concept their own. We validate slowing down by providing time for it and resisting the need to press for mastery right away. We also validate it by allowing *ourselves* to slow down, to enjoy the exploration, and model this for others as well.

Articles abound on the speed of life today, reporting that many adults feel they are "spinning out of control." How many of us are struggling in life and wish we could feel safe enough to simply pause and think? Brain Gym balancing is a wonderful support for anyone who wants to make this kind of change.

Once we experience integrated low gear, we begin to know the joy (and relief!) of working at our own pace. Then our world offers new richness, new possibilities, and, most of all, *choice*. We can actually pause when appropriate and reconsider. This allows us to freely create and recreate how we move through our day—and our life.

> You will learn in the next chapter, "Cultivating Natural Focus," that Paul Dennison describes the state of *integrated high gear* as "ambient attention" and *integrated low gear* as "focal attention."

Brain Gym as a Behavioral Model

I marvel at the ability of physical movement to draw forth the state of integration that is inherent in each of us.

Yet, as much experience as I have with this process, I still wonder just how these shifts occur—what systems are at work for the mind and body to communicate in this way. I believe I share the Dennisons' curiosity about which biological functions are operating as we experience changes such as this, and I search for scientific explanations. It's amazing to realize how much we know, and yet how much more there is to know, about the dynamics of the mind-body system. Certainly, the process must entail a complex, subtle, and elegant interplay between the brain and a multitude of functions in the rest of the body.

Scientists continue to develop new concepts of brain function in their search to unravel its mysteries. Each new model emerges and then eventually is replaced, in part or in its entirety, as more is learned; each has something to offer in our ongoing search to understand the human mind-body system.

Through Brain Gym and Educational Kinesiology, a new model is emerging—one based entirely on observable behavior. We who use and experience this dynamic discipline may strive to explain our observations through currently available scientific models of brain and body function, but the validity of Edu-K itself actually does not rest on the validity of any current model. We see every day that it works, especially when it is implemented consistently and by those who have training in the process.

Science may eventually reveal and explain the systems at work in Edu-K. In the meantime, we can use it, explore it, and add to the knowledge base that will support future scientific findings. These findings are certain to be interesting but are actually not the point of Brain Gym. As Paul Dennison so eloquently states, "Our purpose is not to understand the brain. Our purpose is to help people to better understand their lives."

Chapter 10
Cultivating Natural Focus

When I offer Brain Gym® workshops in schools, I often begin by eliciting teachers' priority issues. I say, "Fill in this blank: *If only my students could* _____." Invariably, "pay attention" is high on the list, right after "sit still."

Teachers are often surprised to discover that *physical movement* is actually the key to developing both of these abilities. As they experience Brain Gym activities in the workshop, they find themselves more mentally present and able to focus and listen. And when they bring these activities into the classroom, they see these same changes in their students.

> The *ability to focus* is a topic of much interest in many realms, none more so than education. After all, focus makes or breaks a learner: those who have it *achieve*.

Then, an even greater shift occurs: After including Brain Gym movements in the daily schedule for several weeks, teachers tell me their students are able to actually sustain attention—listening to lessons, participating in discussions, doing written work—over longer and longer periods of time.

I am continually impressed by the power of Brain Gym activities to refresh focus and concentration—and yet I am compelled to wonder just how this shift to sustained attention happens: What is the difference between *refreshing our focus* and *developing the capacity to focus in the first place?* Paul Dennison states, "Attention needs an organizing principle."[1] What does this mean?

In reflecting on these questions, I found myself reviewing various aspects of child development, learning theory, and the body's sensory systems. I knew each piece was significant—and I wanted to understand how they interrelated. When I attended the 2009 Brain Gym® International Conference

The Waldkindergarten day begins by walking a half-mile to school.

The teacher leads the students in a playful language activity during learning circle time.

The children are free to create their own activities out of the natural materials at hand.

in Kirchzarten, Germany, however, two pivotal experiences combined to provide that exciting new perspective.

Natural exploration

While in Kirchzarten, I had the opportunity to visit the local Waldkindergarten, or "forest preschool," an innovative learning environment where nature itself is the classroom.

In this school, the "curriculum" is simple: sun, rain, or snow, the children—age three to six—dress for the weather and spend the day *outdoors*. The adults are nearby but do not hover or direct, as the children create their own activities out of whatever is at hand. In this way, they learn independence, responsibility, and collaboration while developing skilled, coordinated movement. The teacher brings them together daily to practice language and movement skills through music and play, but most of their time is spent independently or in small groups.

I began to realize how extraordinary this day would be when I chatted with the lead teacher as we all—adults and children—leisurely walked the half-mile from the meet-up point to the kindergarten location in the woods. He said, "The children may behave a little differently today. It's the first day back after a week of holiday, and when they're at home, they don't get enough movement."

What had I heard? These children get more movement at school than they do at home? He also described to me one of the benefits of using the forest as a playground. He said, "When children have to collaborate and create games out of what they find around them, they use more language with each other and so develop these skills very naturally."

After depositing their backpacks filled with morning snacks in the cozy kindergarten cabin, the children dispersed to climb and play, creating activities on the edge of the forest surrounding them. They decided where to go exploring, which logs to climb or branches to haul, which sticks and stones to assemble, order, stack, or turn into the elements of a game or project.

I was impressed with the children's ability to collaborate, cooperate, and move with confidence in the world around them. And while I saw an abundance of enthusiasm and joy, I never once saw a child move thoughtlessly or hyperactively. They spoke kindly to each other, and they were respectful of their environment and compassionate toward the creatures in it. As a group, they were significantly different from children of that age that I'd seen anywhere else.

This child is engrossed in his activity.

I became even more impressed when the teacher responded to my questions about how these students do when they go on to elementary school. He said, "They learn very well, and as they move on through the grades, they continue to excel. But what really sets them apart in first grade is that *they can sit still*."

Again, I was surprised: first graders who can sit still? What elements of their Waldkindergarten experience helped build this extraordinary capacity for sitting still and learning? I had a feeling that a key element was movement itself.

Organized for attention

You may recall elements of Chapter 7, "Move into Learning," where we explored the Reticular Activating System (RAS). This tiny structure in our brain stem plays a vital role in focus and attention: movement (as well as other sensory feedback) stimulates the RAS, which in turn immediately alerts us to watch for something new in our surroundings. This is why intentional movement (or even unconscious activity, such as tapping our foot) can help us rekindle a more attentive state—again and again—when we feel sluggish or distracted.

In that chapter, we also discussed aspects of how physical movement builds our vestibular and proprioceptive systems. When we can accurately perceive and process sensory information, we can skillfully execute commands for all types of coordinated physical action. And in Chapter 8, "Wired for Ability," we explored how important it is to integrate all of our infant reflexes into more mature movement patterns. This allows for effortless physical posture and coordination, which help build a structure for cognitive processing.

The first outdoor kindergarten was created in Germany over 100 years ago. The concept then appeared in Denmark and Sweden, where it expanded and grew; it has now spread to many other countries. The Waldkindergarten program in Germany is a growing, state-supported educational model, and more than 700 now exist there. Many are currently being organized in the United States, as well. [2]

An additional, unquantifiable factor may be exposure to nature itself. You may be interested in Richard Louv's book on this subject, *Last Child in the Woods: Saving Our Children from Nature-Deficit Disorder*.

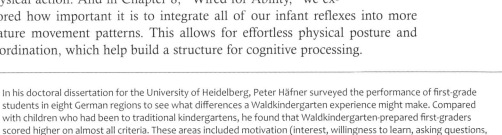

In his doctoral dissertation for the University of Heidelberg, Peter Häfner surveyed the performance of first-grade students in eight German regions to see what differences a Waldkindergarten experience might make. Compared with children who had been to traditional kindergartens, he found that Waldkindergarten-prepared first-graders scored higher on almost all criteria. These areas included motivation (interest, willingness to learn, asking questions, independent thinking), academic performance (language expression, reading, math, and aptitude for learning the English language), social skills (cooperation, compassion, fair play, conflict management, lack of aggression), physical development (sports performance, physical fitness), creativity and use of imagination, and—of high importance to this conversation—self-control (ability to sit still, impulse control) and focus (ability to sustain concentration, perseverance at school tasks). [3]

I already knew that when these systems are functioning well, we are able to freely, intentionally, and accurately move in space: our body, our pencil on a page, our eyes across a line of print—the actions of daily living that we take so for granted. The realization was growing that these systems actually combine forces to do even more: create the capacity to focus. And all of this happens through movement.

This could explain why Paul Dennison says, "When children haven't moved enough and played enough, they are easily distracted by, instead of being comfortable in, their surroundings."[4]

The foundation of attention

At this same conference in Germany, the final piece fell into place for me when Paul Dennison gave a keynote presentation that introduced us to the concepts of *ambient* and *focal attention*. He described ambient attention as essentially a "map," or background awareness, woven out of information from auditory, visual, kinesthetic, tactile, and vestibular feedback, and focal attention as the ability to purposefully select appealing stimuli to stand out against all other awareness.[5]

Paul Dennison notes that these concepts build on those of Dr. A. M. Skeffington and Dr. Christof Koch. [6]

"Through movement, infants build an internal map by which they orient themselves, connect with the world, and self-teach." [7]
~ Paul and Gail Dennison

Some people "stuck" in the state of under-focus may develop a fear-based compensation of over-focusing on tasks. [8]

Paul Dennison offered his theory on why physical movement—and being comfortable in one's surroundings—are essential for learning to occur: they help to build the structure for ambient attention, out of which focal attention spontaneously emerges. Once we have natural focal attention, he said, it's possible to *sustain attention*; then the *ability to concentrate* simply manifests. When we can concentrate, we can actually learn.

Even once developed, though, this ambient state may not be constant; it can be interrupted by stressful life events, which shut down our higher cortical centers. Again, Paul Dennison notes,

> This kind of stress breaks down the ambient structure. It is the antithesis of both learning and play, activities that require a safe and familiar structure.... Without such stress, the brain stem can code new, learned patterns of movement; the limbic system can engage in social activities and experience emotions of love and caring for others, organizing the brain to play; the neocortex can engage in language, logic, and reasoning; and the frontal cortex can plan, imagine, and create.[9]

And yet the greatest gift of focus may be that it allows us to feel a rich sense of accomplishment and reward from total immersion in a chosen task. As Dr. Maria Montessori has eloquently stated, "The child who concentrates is immensely happy."[10]

The power of purposeful movement

In the Waldkindergarten, I believe I was watching children becoming internally organized for focus and concentration. Through continually putting their whole bodies to intentional use, they were moving easily through the stages of reflex development and maturing the inner networks necessary to process and organize sensory input. This left them receptive to (rather than disturbed by) their sensory surroundings: the sights, sounds, textures, temperatures, and scents of the world around them. They were able to create a rich, complete internal "map" of ambient attention, out of which focal attention—and the ability to concentrate—spontaneously emerged. *Through movement, they were building the capacity to learn.*

> These rich sensory experiences build the *sensory integration* skills that occupational therapists may help a child in gaining, if he is late in achieving developmental milestones.

Beyond attention to connection

My thoughts on this topic go even beyond learning, however, as I continue to reflect on one more aspect of my Waldkindergarten observations: how self-confident the children were, and how compassionately they behaved toward each other and the world around them. I contrast this with other children I've known, whose sensory-defensiveness (or sensory under-responsiveness) left them anywhere from irritable and frantic to vacant and withdrawn.

I believe that, as we develop this rich map of ambient awareness, we begin to operate within a state of internal safety, out of which we authentically recognize who we are, and where we are, and feel comfortable within our own being. This translates naturally into being open to and respectful of others and the world around us. What a wonderful basis for joyful learning and thoughtful participation in our family, society, and world.

Supporting natural development

Is it possible for children to develop natural ambient and focal attention without an outdoor classroom experience? I would say the answer is yes—if their home life and preschool or kindergarten offer abundant opportunities for purposeful, whole-body activities so they can literally *move* through all their developmental stages.

> The Brain Gym program would be an excellent component of such a learning environment.

Through appropriate activities at any age, we can move gently through incomplete or "stuck" aspects of earlier developmental stages. Once we are free of the pull of retained infant reflexes, once we're comfortably receptive to our sensory surroundings, we are able to develop a more complete ambient awareness—and spontaneous access to the ability to focus, learn, connect with others, and feel good about ourselves. This is the ultimate accomplishment of integrating movement.

Chapter 11
Ready for Reading

If someone is good at reading, it may seem to be an instantaneous process of making sense out of squiggles on a page. However, reading is actually a complex, sophisticated series of events.

Consider what needs to take place: The eyes must be able to accomplish the initial physical skills, such as teaming and left-right tracking, through which we bring symbols off the page and to the brain in the right order, and the brain's structures must then be able to receive, perceive, interpret, respond to, and communicate about those letters, words, and phrases in order to create meaning.

With practice (and whole-brain integration) these steps happen so quickly as to seem simultaneous. Yet, without the proper internal organization, any of these steps can turn into a stumbling block and limit success. Such learners may find reading to be fatiguing or frustrating; in the extreme, they may be labeled "learning disabled" or even "dyslexic." How many of these children have a simple "wiring" problem as their true, underlying challenge, one that could be easily remedied?

Let's explore how to overcome obstacles such as these, and thrive as a reader.

Our brain holds no centers for *reading*, as there are for such abilities as smell, touch, and hearing. In his book *Reading in the Brain*, cognitive neuroscientist Stanislaus Dehaene describes how our brain draws on diverse neural networks to accomplish the many stages of reading: "Are these letters? What do they look like? Are they a word? What does it sound like? How is it pronounced? What does it mean?" [1]

Paul Dennison shares, "The act of encoding and decoding symbols requires the integration of the auditory, visual, kinesthetic, and tactile areas of the brain, and the ability to interpret such received information as meaningful, relating such to one's own experiences." [2]

Wired for Whole-Brain Reading

What does it take to be ready for reading? An important component is *movement*.

Our earliest movement experiences help to "wire" us, not only for a lifetime of physical coordination, but also for efficient cognitive functioning, so we can focus, think, and learn.

For example, one outcome of an infancy and childhood filled with cross-lateral activities (creeping, crawling, running) is that our two hemispheres learn to work in concert. This lateral communication within the brain is vital for the process of reading. First, our two hemispheres must coordinate the movement of both eyes to pick up images accurately and in the correct order. Then, the distinct contributions of both hemispheres must easily combine in order to create *meaning* out of the symbols on the page.

As a licensed Brain Gym® consultant, I am an educator, not a vision therapist; however, I've learned that knowing the basics of the vision system can vastly improve one's understanding of many learning issues and explain why these simple Brain Gym® interventions are so effective in improving reading ability.

As an educator, coming to know what's actually involved in the process of *learning to read* was a major revelation to me, as it explained why so many of my students had struggled in school. And when I recalled that many of these same children had also been physically awkward or uncoordinated, I wondered: had they missed these all-important early movement experiences?

Now, as a Brain Gym® consultant, I still work regularly with children who have learning challenges. And, finally, I not only understand the nature of many of their blocks to reading, I have tools that almost universally help them to succeed at it.

In this chapter I will share the elements of Paul Dennison's theories about reading that have most profoundly changed my work with readers of all ages. Each of these could be a chapter of its own; here we'll cover the simplified basics of each topic as we explore the following:

- why reading is actually not a visual process, even though specific vision skills are involved

- why it's important to know which eye a person leads with (his dominant eye), and how to determine whether it's his right or left

- why those who lead with their left eye may be prone to reading challenges

- why eye-teaming is important for easily following (tracking) a line of print

- how stress prevents fluid left-right tracking and, ultimately, comprehension

- how our two hemispheres contribute unique qualities to the reading process

- why auditory processing ("inner speech") is a vital part of learning to read

- why whole-brain integration is necessary for reading to develop as a spontaneous, natural skill.

You'll journey through these concepts and more, experiencing the power of whole-brain integration *through physical movement* to revolutionize the experience of reading.

Consciously noticing our reading process

Because this chapter is about a single topic—reading—I thought I'd include opportunities for you to personally explore the benefits that Brain Gym movements can bring to this one essential skill. Let's begin with a before-and-after experiment using the Cross Crawl.

Start by observing your "before" state now, as you read this sample text:

▶ **Notice as you read**

The basic, physical skills of reading are accomplished by the two eyes, which need to focus together and track smoothly in order to perceive symbols accurately and bring them in correct sequence to the brain. Ideally, the two eyes work comfortably in the midfield and can track together, both left-to-right and right-to-left.

While our two eyes function identically in almost all other regards, there are very subtle differences. The right eye is more "tuned" to left-brain aspects, such as identifying phonetic symbols, and the left eye helps us with the more right-brain skills of spatial orientation and building a complete picture out of the details. Skilled readers use both eyes fluidly together, allowing the brain to receive and interpret the symbols and construct internal images of the meaning. However, Paul Dennison finds that "at-risk" readers often favor one eye and inhibit the other, in essence preventing the capacity for either *phonetic analysis* or *comprehension* from fully developing.

> "The midfield, where input from the left and right visual fields overlaps, is the domain of all manipulative skills involved in the symbolic processes needed for communication, information processing, and most of the activities that call upon short-term memory." [3]
> ~ Paul and Gail Dennison

What did you notice as you read this paragraph?

- Were your eyes tracking smoothly left-to-right, or did they want to jump around the page?

- Did the material make sense the first time, or was it "just words"?

- How quickly did you read?

- Did you need to repeat some lines?

- Did you feel engaged with the content?

- Were you distracted by anything in your environment or on the page?

- Was there any tension in your body (especially shoulders, neck, eyes, face) as you read?

Take a mental picture of this "before" state, and set it aside.

The Cross Crawl

▶ Shifting into a whole-brain state

Now let's see what the Cross Crawl has to offer! Stand (or sit) comfortably; slowly raise one knee and bring its opposite elbow or hand to it; lower that leg and raise your other knee, to connect with its opposite elbow or hand. Continue in this way for a minute or so. Notice your ability to balance on one foot while the other is raised as well as your overall level of coordination; both will likely improve as you continue this activity! Cross Crawl for a minute or so, perhaps to some music.

Now that you've "buffed up" your state of whole-brain integration, I invite you to read once again. This time, the selection is a bit longer.

> Even though our language flows only left-to-right, it's important for our eyes to be able to track easily in both directions. This is an indicator of an integrated state and lack of stress. And, of course, vision overall happens in "the real world," where tracking in both directions is necessary.

> "Reading is first and foremost an auditory process. Vision is incidental to reading [as evidenced by those who read Braille with their fingertips] and has to be so stress-free and automatic (integrated high gear) that the auditory-language processes are not inhibited and can lead, not follow, the process." [4]
> ~ Paul E. Dennison

▶ Notice as you read

The basic, physical skills of reading are accomplished by the two eyes, which need to focus together and track smoothly in order to perceive symbols accurately and bring them in correct sequence to the brain. Ideally, the two eyes work comfortably in the midfield and can track together, both left-to-right and right-to-left.

While our two eyes function identically in almost all other regards, there are very subtle differences. The right eye is more "tuned" to left-brain aspects, such as identifying phonetic symbols, and the left eye helps us with the more right-brain skills of spatial orientation and building a complete picture out of the details. Skilled readers use both eyes fluidly together, allowing the brain to receive and interpret the symbols and construct internal images of the meaning. However, Paul Dennison finds that "at-risk" readers favor one eye and inhibit the other, in essence preventing the capacity for either *phonetic analysis* or *comprehension* from fully developing.

Reading requires auditory processing. Do you hear your own internal voice as you're reading these words? And do you recall how children initially read out loud? Hearing themselves verbally expressing written words is the most important aspect of *learning to read*. With enough practice and sufficient integration, they naturally graduate to a silent, inner reading voice. Paul Dennison describes this as a shift from left-brain "decoding" to the right-brain capacity for fluidly absorbing meaning from the page ("gestalting" the ideas). Only at this point do they have true comprehension.

All of these concepts will be more fully explained later in this chapter. For now, simply reflect on your experience of reading this time. Did anything change in regard to the following:

> The term "gestalting" refers to the ability to instantaneously perceive a complete picture (idea, mental image) from the details (letters, words). 5

- your eyes moving across the lines of print

- the material making sense

- the need to re-read

- your reading speed

- your feeling of engagement

- your ability to ignore distractions

- tension in your shoulders, neck, eyes, or face?

When I take workshop participants through this exercise, they are often amazed at how much more easily they read after doing Brain Gym activities, and report improvements in everything from physical comfort and clearer focus on the text itself, to speed and comprehension.

One participant shared, "I got it so easily this time! I thought at first it was because I was reading the same paragraph. Then I went on to the next paragraph, and the meaning still seemed to jump off the page and turn into pictures in my mind. What an incredible experience!"

Following a comment like this, I often ask, "Would you wish this for your children or students?" The response is always a resounding "Yes!" and participants share their strategies for using this simple PACE warm-up in their classroom or at home. So let's investigate why *integrating physical activity* is such a powerful and necessary component of the reading package.

Eye Lead: Which Eye, Which Way?

Because we have two eyes, we might naturally assume that we use them both equally. I know I did. However, our two eyes actually function somewhat differently. One develops as our dominant, or "leading," eye. Its job is to be the main "lookout," pointing at whatever is most important in our environment: the object of our focus. The other becomes our non-dominant, "blending" eye, offering

> The concept of "left-eye lead" is an aspect of Brain Organization Profiles, taught in the Edu-K course "Optimal Brain Organization" and explained in the book *The Dominance Factor* by Carla Hannaford, Ph.D.

In the Brain Gym/Edu-K program, the terms "dominant" and "lead" are often used interchangeably.

additional visual input from its unique perspective, creating depth perception, and more. Think of it as similar to hand dominance: We may unscrew the bottle cap with our dominant hand, but we hold the bottle steady with the other. They're both needed, and they play different roles.

The right eye most naturally tracks left-to-right

The left eye most naturally tracks right-to-left

Our right and left eyes have opposite tracking preferences. On its own, the right eye prefers to scan left-to-right, the same direction as written languages of the western world. The left eye, however, most naturally scans right-to-left. This would come in handy if you're learning Hebrew or Arabic; it's less helpful for English.

About seventy percent of people are right-eyed; thirty percent are left-eyed.[6] However, in my experience, left-eye lead is incredibly common among children in special-education classes. During a day of consulting at one school, I was asked to work with nine children who were being assessed for special help. *Eight of them were left-eyed.* I can only assume that the left eye's tracking preference (combined with lack of integration) is at the root of many "learning disabilities."

This boy's dominant left eye wants to keep jumping "backwards" along the line of print.

The importance of teamwork

Regardless of which eye we lead with, our two eyes are meant to work together. This is called "eye-teaming" and can happen only if both brain hemispheres are easily sharing information.

A left-eye-dominant reader whose eyes are not teaming will almost certainly struggle in school. He may look at the word "dog" and, scanning right-to-left, start by saying the sound *guh.* Children who lead with their left eye may end up straining to track the line of print, since their eyes tend to jerk back to the left, again and again, sometimes even jumping to a different line. It's all but impossible to comprehend material read this way. A little reading like this is tiring; a lot is exhausting.

When both hemispheres are communicating, both eyes team and track easily.

Whole-brain integration is the key

So, is a left-eye-dominant child destined to a life of reading failure? Not at all. If a child's two brain hemispheres are sharing information effectively, his two eyes will be able to communicate as well. For many left-eye-dominant folks, patterning for this kind of communication happens naturally in childhood, through crawling and other cross-lateral movement. Many highly skilled and academically proficient people I know have been surprised to recognize that they are left-eyed; they were fluent readers from the start. "In fact," Paul

Dennison states, "the left-eyed reader, once integrated, often becomes the gifted reader and may be able to skim, scan, and master the art of speed reading, skills their right-eye-dominant friends may find less available." [7]

If a reader does struggle, however, I find that once he's done sufficient cross-lateral activity (such as the Cross Crawl, Lazy 8s, or—especially—the specific Edu-K balance process known as Dennison Laterality Repatterning), he very often reads left-to-right quite easily. In essence, his right eye is now able to communicate with his left, and says, "Hey, friend, I know which way to go—follow me." And together they will track left-to-right, transforming both his ability and his attitude about reading.

Researchers who study vision and reading have developed these concepts: *fixation* (eyes focusing on a specific symbol or group of symbols), *saccades* (movements of the eyes from one point of fixation to another), and *regression* (the tendency of the eyes to return to previously scanned material). Expert readers tend to have fewer fixations, longer saccades, and fewer regressions (perhaps as they "gestalt" entire words and phrases into meaning, a right-brain capacity). Readers identified as dyslexic have been found to have significantly more fixations, shorter saccades, and more regressions compared to non-dyslexic readers. [8]

True *dyslexia* is a multi-faceted challenge that causes the inability to process written language. It often includes significant auditory-processing issues (leading the child to confuse certain letters—for example, "d" and "b"—because he cannot accurately *hear* the frequencies needed to discriminate between them) [9] as well as visual issues that also cause letter-identification confusion. However, the term *dyslexia* has come into common use to describe many reading difficulties, especially a more typical "tendency to reversals," which is common with children in their early years of learning to read and write, and for some, persists long into their school years—and beyond. It would be more accurate to describe such reversal challenges as *midline issues*, which stem from confusion between right and left sides of the body and inability to fluidly "cross the midline."

▶ Time out for movement

Before we move on, let's pause to refresh our whole-brain state with a little integrating physical activity. Notice: How comfortable are your eyes right now, as you read? Is there any stress in your face or eyes? You can check for visual stress this way: Look away from the page, and holding your head still, allow *just your eyes* to look up, down, left, and right, then track back and forth, left to right. Do you notice a feeling of fluidity or of discomfort? Are you able to move just your eyes, or does your head want to move as well? (If your eyes aren't comfortable moving, you'll instinctively move your head instead, so the muscles of your eyes don't have to work.)

Take a moment and rub your Brain Buttons—first with one hand, then with the other—while the opposite hand rests over your navel. Breathe deeply, releasing any tension that may be present. Allow

Brain Buttons

your eyes to track side to side a few times as you do this, about a minute in all.

Now, as you return to reading, notice any changes in your ability to follow the words on the page or absorb their meaning.

Eye lead at work

When I began to understand the concept of eye lead and the different preferred direction of tracking for right and left eyes, it was like having x-ray vision into many learning challenges and provided new insights in my work with clients.

"Kaley just hates to read. She's in the sixth grade, but she's reading at only the third-grade level. I make sure her assignments are easy enough, but it still takes her forever to do any work." These words from Kaley's teacher presented a very common scenario and set the stage for my day as a visiting Brain Gym consultant at her school.

As I began my session with Kaley, we chatted about school. Eventually, she shared that reading made her feel uncomfortable. She said, "It gives me a headache, and I get kind of dizzy." I asked what it was like moving her eyes across the page, and she admitted, "It takes real work, and when I get to the end of a line, I've forgotten what I read. I have to read everything at least twice." When I invited her to read out loud, she chose a simple storybook and used her finger to guide her eyes slowly and hesitantly across the lines of text.

I suspected that Kaley was reading primarily with her left eye, so I took her through the steps of a simple check and determined she was indeed left-eyed. At this point, I drew her a little diagram illustrating what happens when someone tries to read with her left eye without help from her right eye. I emphasized that this is a wiring challenge that most likely developed very early in her childhood, and she was not to blame for it; in fact, it had nothing at all to do with how much she cared, or how hard she tried.

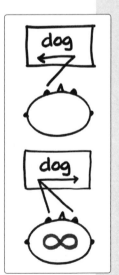

I also drew the companion diagram to show how we want our eyes to work: as the two sides of our brain share information, our eyes are more able to team and, therefore, to track the right way across the page.

As Kaley learned all this, her eyes filled with tears. I told her she was a champion simply for coming to school each day and doing her best when reading was so difficult for her. Then I asked if she'd like to do something that would very likely help her to read more easily and offered her a list—or learning menu—of Brain Gym movements and processes from which to choose.

I was not surprised to find that Kaley was drawn to Dennison Laterality Repatterning (DLR), since this process has a profound effect on our ability to use both hemispheres (and therefore both eyes) together.

A pre-check for this process showed that Kaley was very awkward in doing the Cross Crawl: her first impulse was to bring her elbow to her same-side knee. She self-corrected, but still was less than fluid, and held a look of concentration on her face as she continued this movement. However, when the DLR was complete, she could easily Cross Crawl; her body looked relaxed and she was smiling.

> Every child may have a unique mix of challenges. For a child with relatively straightforward midline issues, it's not at all uncommon to see immediate changes along the lines of those Kaley experienced. For others with more extensive underlying challenges, a series of sessions over time may be called for.

At this point, Kaley picked up her book again. She read paragraph after paragraph fluently and with expression, not struggling at all. I watched her eyes track smoothly from left to right. When she set down the book, she said, "Wow! Reading can really flow! And the words all mean something now! This is cool!"

Kaley has gone on to become an enthusiastic reader. Now that she's able to absorb content from written words, her academic career has flourished as well.

Which eye is leading?

Right about now you're probably wondering which eye you lead with! Here's a quick lesson in how to check yourself and then someone else.

▶ Check for your leading eye

Overlap your hands, leaving a small space between the crooks of your thumbs. Hold them out directly in front of you, with elbows straight, in line with your midline. *With both eyes open*, look through the space you've made, and focus on something specific across the room. Close one eye; open it and close the other.

This woman sees the object with her right eye only. Her left eye essentially "switches off" so as not to provide confusing input to her brain.

What was your experience? Did the object seem to suddenly vanish? Which eye did you have open at that point?

When you close one eye and still see your target, you're very likely using your dominant eye. When you look with the other eye, and the target seems to have moved, that's most likely your non-dominant eye.

How does this eye-check work? If we're looking through a small hole in this way, our eyes are converging right at that point and *crossing* beyond it. This means that, even with both eyes open, only one can actually align with the target. For most people, this is their right eye; for others, it's their left.

Checking another person

Left-eyed girl   Right-eyed boy

Just noticing which eye you close first may be a clue to eye dominance. Most people are inclined to close (or wink) their non-dominant eye. This would leave their dominant eye more consistently open.

Some people (especially young children) cannot easily check themselves, perhaps because they have a challenge closing one eye or the other. In this case, I do the check a bit differently. I have the person assume the very same position (hands overlapped, elbows straight, both eyes open, looking through the space between their hands). But instead of looking across the room at an object, I stand a distance away and have him look *at my nose*. Then I can look through that space, directly at the only eye that's truly aimed at me: his dominant eye. In the case of this girl, you can see only her left eye, which is spotting the camera used to photograph her. The boy, in contrast, is spotting with his right eye.

After following these instructions, some parents or teachers say, "I realize now that my child (or student) leads with her left eye. *How do I fix that?*" There is nothing to "fix" about being left-eyed, any more than we need to "fix" being left-handed. Remember, many fine readers are left-eyed! Balance is the key. If a child (or adult) has sufficient cross-lateral integration, it doesn't matter which eye she leads with, since both eyes are working fluidly together.

These are very simple eye-check techniques, and we humans are complex. For example, some people lead with one eye for near vision and the other for distance. Other people may learn stress-based compensations and appear to be right-eyed when, indeed, they're left-eyed. It can take time and training to learn all the ins and outs of this topic. For now, I invite you simply to notice the vision-related challenges you experience (or those of the children, students, or clients in your care) and see what happens when you introduce movement!

The Stress Connection

Even when we're wired for efficient eye-teaming, we may not have full access to this ability for an entirely different reason: stress. This is true even for right-eye-dominant readers like me.

Survival takes first call on our body's resources, and the main job of our dominant eye is to scan for danger. When I'm under stress, my dominant eye ends up looking *out there somewhere* rather than at the words I need to read or write.[10] Eye-teaming vanishes, and I end up struggling with just my left eye, which tends to "swim upstream" against the flow of the written page. The result? Reversals and choppy reading.

Our dominant eye's first job is to be on the lookout for danger. This right-eyed girl, under stress, will tend to read with her left eye.

Similarly, a left-eye-dominant reader under stress may have only his right eye available. This could sound beneficial (knowing what we do about the right eye's natural scanning direction), but it isn't. Without true eye-teaming (which really means hemisphere teaming), he will still experience challenges; he may be able to track left-to-right to decode the symbols and fluently pronounce the words, but he won't understand what he's reading.

One of the key reasons that Brain Gym activities are so useful in preparing us to read is that they help us experience a state of safety. We simply cannot learn until our mind-body system relaxes out of a vigilant survival state. When we are no longer automatically scanning the periphery for danger, our eyes are free to focus together in the midfield, at near-point.

Integrating movement for learning

What does it take to develop—or re-establish—our state of whole-brain readiness for reading? *Physical movement.* The Brain Gym activities are a rich source of whole-brain integration, and the Edu-K balance process can support us in going deeper, making lasting changes that improve how we learn, move, and process.

If your child is having reading challenges—no matter which eye she leads with—it may be appropriate to explore various Brain Gym movements with her and see in what way she benefits. Or you may wish to schedule sessions with a Licensed Brain Gym® Instructor/Consultant who is experienced in facilitating the Edu-K balance process.

> ### ▶ Now a vision refresher
>
> At this point, let's pause again and bring a bit of movement back into the picture with some Lazy 8s. Start with your thumb out in front of you at the level of your nose, elbow slightly bent. Keeping your head still, begin tracing the Lazy 8 with your hand, and follow your thumb with just your eyes: up and around to the left, up and around to the right—completing this pattern several times. Trace the Lazy 8 with your right hand, left hand, and then with joined hands.
>
> What do you notice? Are you holding your breath? If so, remember to breathe, and do some Lazy 8s again. Now—are your eyes able to comfortably follow your thumb? Is it easier to track one hand than the other? Do you notice points at which your eyes resist focusing, or feel like "skipping"? As you continue your Lazy 8s, or repeat this movement over time, these "glitches" will very likely lessen.

Keep in mind that we react to all kinds of stresses as if they're *physical* threats. We may scan for "danger" even if we're stressed over financial worries, divorce, etc.

"Though access to both skills is theoretically available through each eye, in practice, one eye must lead as the other eye blends. Stress in learning the tasks of focusing and blending for reading may cause visual disorientation." [11]
~ Paul and Gail Dennison

"The increased emphasis on early reading is all right for those who have the neural organization to cope with it. However, many children don't have this degree of integration at age five, so they experience early failure and a loss of self-confidence." [12]
~ A. Jean Ayres, *Sensory Integration and the Child*

Lazy 8s

Now, as you return to reading, what do you notice about your ability to track the lines of print and absorb meaning from the words?

Note: Children are born *farsighted*, and it may take some time before they can *comfortably* sustain focus at near -point. Until children are about 7 1/2 or 8 years old, they should do their Lazy 8s some distance from their face: out at arm's length in the air, on a whiteboard or a tabletop, etc.

Diving deeper into the reading process

We've covered two physical skills involved in reading—eye-teaming and tracking—which allow our eyes to pick up printed symbols in the right order. Now, let's revisit what happens once these skills are fluid and automatic.

The phenomenon of *reading* actually happens within the brain itself, as an auditory/linguistic/cognitive process. It's an internal ballet of information routing, sorting, and communication. When flawlessly executed, it results in true reading comprehension: we understand the information, the instructions, or the story. Involved in this ballet are our two brain hemispheres, two eyes, and (as we'll explore shortly) our two ears.

Two Eyes, Two Different Jobs

For readers who are blind, input arrives in the brain through the fingertips, as they pick up Braille symbols.

Our left and right brain hemispheres contribute unique elements to the process of reading. The left brain is more ready to handle the "symbolic, detail" aspects; the right brain is best at accomplishing the "big-picture, spatial" elements. How does information arrive at those portions of the brain? For most of us, it's through our eyes.

Better at seeing the details, sound/symbol analysis (phonics), and visual memory

Better at perceiving *meaning* as you see the words, and spatial awareness of words on the page

The right eye takes in more "left-brain" visual information

The left eye takes in more "right-brain" visual information

Our *right eye* is more involved in bringing in information that our *left brain* deals with: letter shape and sequence, the sound each symbol represents, and visual memory. This is the hemisphere that "does phonics."

Conversely, our *left eye* is more tuned to pick up information for our *right brain*: spatial awareness of the page and the "entirety" of anything we see, allowing us to instantly absorb meaning from whole words and phrases.

Each element is important—and we need them both in order to actually *read*.

> Roger Sperry was awarded a Nobel Prize in 1981 for his discoveries in the field of right-left brain science. His experiments in the 1960s were with people who had severe epilepsy and whose corpus callosum (structure through which left and right hemispheres communicate) had been surgically severed to eliminate their debilitating seizures. These people ended up with "odd behaviors," which Sperry explored in depth through various cognitive-task experiments; each hemisphere functioned but was unaware of the presence of the other, and he was able to associate specific cognitive abilities with either the right or left hemisphere. [13]

How stress affects reading

When we are able to read and comprehend easily, it's a sign that we've achieved a reliable state of whole-brain communication: our eyes team and track correctly, information is routed appropriately to the brain's internal structures, and we simply absorb meaning from the page. Yet, on occasion, we may find ourselves reading less than fluidly. What could be happening?

Earlier in this chapter, I mentioned how stress impedes proper eye-teaming and, as a result, comprehension. Using myself as an example, I described how "eye-teaming vanishes, and I end up struggling with just my left eye, essentially 'swimming upstream' against the flow of the written page." Now, we'll bring what we know about our two hemispheres into the picture, to explain how this might occur. When my dominant right eye is scanning for danger, I end up reading with mainly my left eye, *which knows how to hold (right-brain) spatial orientation but is not tuned to the (left-brain) ability to decode symbols or pick up detail.* When I'm slightly stressed, I can often simply re-read and "get it," though it takes more effort; when I'm in a high-stress state, the text becomes a "foggy mush" of visual information and re-reading barely helps.

I'm already an expert reader (thank goodness), so when I notice this happening, I can always alleviate my "foggy mush" condition by using a few Brain Gym movements. Children, however, are just learning to read. If a child is under constant stress and his dominant right eye is always busy scanning for danger, it won't be available to track correctly and provide symbol recognition—the most basic of reading skills. He'll very likely struggle and, to varying degrees, simply fail to learn to read.

As described previously, the left-eye-dominant reader may have difficulties as well. Under stress, his dominant *left* eye may be scanning for danger, rather than doing its (right-brain) job of keeping track of where the words are on the page, so he can follow them in the right order. Again, a child

> "When the eyes work together, without stress, as a binocular team, providing access to the whole brain, the reading challenges disappear." [14]
> ~ Paul E. Dennison

> Remember that the brain registers "danger" in anything unpleasant or alarming. For a child, this could include being called on in class, taking a test, or realizing she's forgotten her homework. The body's response is the same as to physical danger: the irrepressible impulse to be on the lookout for it. And "danger" is always "out there" somewhere, not on the page.

struggling for this reason may fail to learn to read—despite any creative compensations he may come up with, like the one I'm about to share with you.

A compensation with consequences

A left-eyed reader may learn to inhibit his left eye (and therefore his right brain) in order to track left-to-right with his right eye.

> "When we don't have integration, we have compensation with stress." [15]
> ~ Paul E. Dennison

A left-eye-dominant reader who struggles may eventually stumble upon the awareness that, if he inhibits his *left* eye, his *right* eye will take over and lead him left-to-right more easily. What a clever compensation! Unfortunately, if he's switching off his left eye, he's also (essentially) switching off his right brain. Without full access to right-brain capacities, his spatial awareness of the page will vanish and he'll get lost in a jumble of symbols; he'll have no way to turn the symbols into words, and the words into meaning.

The anxiety of failure may cause additional challenges, as the stress itself causes his (dominant) left eye to stay on alert (as explained above). Of course, he scans for danger on the periphery—it's never on the page itself—and he'll lose centralized focus.

If he returns to a sense of safety, he may regain access to both hemispheres—and therefore, both eyes—and return to easier reading. However, in some people, this "switched-off" compensation pattern becomes chronic, requiring considerable relearning to alleviate it.

Listening *is the Key*

We're about to explore the role of our auditory system in the reading process, so let's take another movement break—this time, for a Brain Gym activity that will help tune up our listening ability.

▶ A listening boost

The Owl

First, notice any sounds in the room around you. How distinct and clear are they? Do a range-of-motion check: How far can you comfortably turn your head to the left and then to the right?

Now, experience the Owl. With your left hand, firmly grasp the top of your right shoulder. Find the tense spots in the muscles there and apply a bit of pressure. Turn your head to look over that shoulder and exhale fully; then look over the opposite shoulder, again breathing out. Continue back and forth this way until tension seems diminished; then drop your head as you exhale toward the floor, releasing stress in your neck and upper back. Repeat this process, using the right hand to grasp the left shoulder. As you exhale, you can playfully "hoot" like an owl (or make any other sound) to add to the auditory experience of this movement.

What do you observe now about how fully you hear sounds in the room around you? And how far you can you comfortably turn your head?

Now, let's move into the world of *listening* as a vital part of *reading*.

> "When we can't relax and turn our head, we're unable to access certain neural pathways of the temporal lobe that are critical to the functions of memory and speech." [16]
> ~ Paul E. Dennison

The power of "inner speech"

One of the most intriguing aspects of learning to read is that *listening* is required. Paul Dennison has extensively studied how the auditory, linguistic process known as *inner speech* (hearing our own voice saying words and sentences) helps us build meaning. However, this capacity doesn't always automatically develop. Without the whole-brain integration required, a child may fail to develop as a true *reader*.

> Paul Dennison's doctoral dissertation was on the relationship of covert speech (thinking skills) to the acquisition of beginning reading skills, for which he was honored with the Phi Delta Kappa Research Award at the University of Southern California.

Jamaal had struggled with reading for years. Now fourteen years old and in the eighth grade, he faced going on to high school without the skills he needed for success. He told me that he hated reading because it was embarrassing: he had to read everything out loud or he couldn't understand it at all. I asked if he'd ever heard his own inner voice while reading, and he clearly had no idea what I was talking about.

Together, we set the goal for his balance: "I hear the story while I read." I had him do two pre-checks: First, I had him read out loud from his current fiction book; after four short paragraphs, I asked him a few questions about the text, which he was able to answer accurately. Then, I had him read the next few paragraphs silently. I watched him squirm in his seat while he did his best to focus on the words, his mouth moving silently the entire time. Even with this effort, he reported not understanding what he'd read.

Jamaal's balance called for Three Dimension Repatterning, after which I asked him to take up his book and read silently again. He sat still and his mouth did not move as he read paragraph after paragraph. When he stopped, he looked at me, eyes wide with astonishment, and said, "It's like someone is reading to me! The words become a story I hear in my head!" We celebrated with a jubilant "high-five."

Jamaal's teacher later told me that his behavior in class was "transformed." He was able to sit and read with focus, and his attitude was improving along with his grades.

How could Jamaal suddenly hear his own inner voice? I can make a guess based on the changes I observed in his movement patterns. As Jamaal began his repatterning process, he was awkward in doing the Cross Crawl movement, which would indicate that he was not able to fully access both brain hemispheres at the same time. By the time his repatterning was complete, however, Jamaal's Cross Crawl was fluid and easy.

As you'll learn shortly, it's just this kind of integration that's required to shift from sounding out words and phrases to fluidly hearing them in your head as you read. Here's a bit about why.

> I notice this concept regularly in my life. I'll spontaneously hold the phone to my right ear if I'm listening to (left-brain) details, and find myself switching to my left ear if the subject turns to a story with vivid language and emotion (right-brain).

Two ears, two different jobs

Again, let's recall that each ear is tuned to the attributes of its opposite brain hemisphere. The right ear is better at listening for the (left-brain) details and literal meaning of language. The left ear more easily picks up the (right-brain) elements of emotion, tone, and inflection, as well as the melody of language.

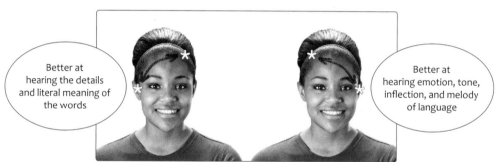

The right ear takes in more "left-brain" auditory information

The left ear takes in more "right-brain" auditory information

Better at hearing the details and literal meaning of the words

Better at hearing emotion, tone, inflection, and melody of language

> Paul Dennison explains that the right hemisphere is vital for fluidly knowing how to read. In Chapter 9, "Theory in Action," you learned that, in Edu-K, this is called the "I've got it!" state of integrated high gear. However, as we're learning how to read, we're primarily in the slowed-down "I'm getting it" state of the left hemisphere, which Edu-K calls integrated low gear. The concept of integrated high and low gear was introduced in Chapter 9, "Theory In Action."

In a "switched-off state" (whether through stress or lack of initial integration), both sides of our auditory-processing equipment will not be equally available, compromising our ability to fully "hear our inner voice" as we read.

Children initially read out loud as they're making their way through decoding symbols, "sounding out" the words as they're *learning how to read* (denoting that it's an effort-based activity, primarily using the left brain). However, once they shift to *knowing how to read*, their voice becomes internal (indicating an automatic, stress-free activity taking place in the right brain). When they finally arrive as "right-brain readers," they will effortlessly absorb the meaning held by the words.

For this shift to occur, the right eye must focus and track left-to-right, as the right ear (left brain) *hears* the language pattern from beginning to end. The left ear (right brain) comes into the act a second later, as soon as it recognizes the auditory pattern (the sounds that make up the words) and creates *meaning*.[17] Without whole-brain integration, we won't have all these capabilities available and will fail to develop as readers. So how do we achieve and maintain this all-important state?

The Movement Connection

Coordinated physical movement is the key to successful reading. Through integrating activity at any age, we can overcome a past that didn't provide enough movement of the right kind or at the right time and enhance communication between both eyes, both ears, and both brain hemispheres.

Once this whole-brain pattern is developed and integrated, *it's available*. Then, when stress arises and our abilities seem to fade, a few simple Brain Gym movements are all it takes to return to easier reading and comprehension. Perhaps you've experienced this yourself, as you've done the exercises in this chapter. And here's yet another opportunity: a whole-brain boost before our concluding text sample.

During my years as a teacher, the pendulum of reading-instruction practice has swung back and forth between programs that are more phonics-based (with extensive drill in sound-symbol associations so children can learn to decode unfamiliar words) or whole-language- or sight-based (emphasizing recognition of whole words and phrases). I realize now that the *integrated brain* spontaneously does both: the child notices and internally organizes the patterns of written language he's exposed to, which become identified as whole words—and their meaning. Our job as educators is to ensure that the child is integrated enough to operate easily with both the details and the big picture for accessing written language: then, he'll be able to benefit from any type of reading instruction.

▶ One final movement break

This time, let's do the Calf Pump, a Lengthening Activity, to release stress and make our *ability to focus* more available. Stand and stabilize your position by holding on to a wall, chair, or table, and take a long step forward with one foot. With both feet pointing forward, bend your front knee until you feel the muscles just begin to lengthen in your back leg, causing your back heel to rise up a bit. (If your front knee extends past your toes, take a longer stride to keep your knee safely over your ankle.) Now you are in position to begin. Gently allow the heel of your back foot to move toward the floor, creating a lengthening of the calf muscle. Hold for a moment, then rise again onto the toes of your back foot; repeat several times. Remember to breathe as you move. When this release feels complete, switch foot positions and lengthen the muscles in the other leg.

The Calf Pump

> "Learning reading is an auditory, linguistic process (not visual) that moves to the right [hemisphere] when the left hemisphere, right ear, and right eye are synchronized with the left eye and left ear. Without this ability to move to the right easily, the language experience is compromised." [18]
> ~ Paul E. Dennison

Now that you've "buffed up" your whole-brain integration one last time, I invite you to read once again. In this final selection, Paul Dennison brings together all the topics of this chapter:

▶ Notice as you read

As soon as the left-eyed student does Brain Gym movements, such as Brain Buttons, the Cross Crawl, and Lazy 8s, both eyes begin to function as a team on the midfield, the left eye now holding the visual space and "gestalting" the words and phrases in ever larger chunks, while the left brain processes symbols as language through the right eye. The two eyes track effortlessly back and forth as one system across the midline of the page, the left eye comfortable enough with the visual physical skills that the right eye's language focal skills can develop and integrate and flourish! [19]

This is a complex passage filled with profound concepts. What did you notice about your experience of tracking the lines of print, hearing your own internal reading voice, and comprehending the ideas those words contain?

Back to the basics—and to movement

This chapter has been quite a journey through core reading concepts! Happily, we don't need to fully understand every element of the reading process; however, a bit of knowledge certainly helps us to appreciate the shifts we may experience. The most important thing to remember is that reading requires whole-brain integration, and for that, we need movement.

You can observe this for yourself in the days and weeks to come. Notice when you (or your students or children) are not reading well, and then see what happens after a few minutes of whole-body activity, perhaps including the Cross Crawl. This is often enough to help us shift into processing language much more easily, transforming our experience of reading from stress and effort to ease and enjoyment.

Balancing for reading success

And as helpful as Brain Gym movements are on their own, you may find that you'd like to make deeper or more rapid change. At this point, Edu-K balancing might be an appropriate next step, and you might choose to contact a local Brain Gym consultant.

In my own practice, I work regularly with clients of all ages who want to address reading issues. Many adults have struggled their whole lives with these challenges, and their outcomes from balancing may be life-altering. And the same changes can turn around a child's experience of school, and of life, as well.

When I work with youngsters, I always have the parent on hand to observe and participate. It's often a real eye-opener for a parent to see how much difficulty her child may have with the Cross Crawl, for example, especially once I explain the correlation between lack of coordination and academic challenges. And if we discover that he leads with his left eye, or has other eye-teaming issues, it puts a whole new perspective on the battles over reading she may have had with him, for example.

The concepts of dominant eye and eye-teaming are explained in Chapter 9, "Theory In Action."

Then the parent is amazed to see how easily the child may be Cross Crawling after his session, and how his reading improves. She is in a perfect position to appreciate changes in her child's academic performance and attitude in the days that follow and to do Brain Gym movements with him at home.

A very concerned grandmother brought Clark, age eight, for a Brain Gym balance session. Nightly reading practice had become quite a battle at his house. His parents said they could hardly get him to sit and read at all. So I turned to Clark and asked, "Why don't you like to read?" Clark told me it made his stomach and head hurt.

When I asked Clark to read out loud from a very simple storybook, he read haltingly, miscalling several simple words and completely ignoring the punctuation. He was extremely awkward in the Cross Crawl portion of PACE, and almost fell down as he did it.

At the end of his balance (which included Dennison Laterality Repatterning and a few additional Brain Gym movements), perhaps forty minutes later, Clark picked up the book again and read without hesitation, and without stumbling over the words. He even read with inflection, pausing or stopping at the appropriate punctuation—indicators of true comprehension.

I heard later from the grandmother that when Clark came home that night he had his nose in his book until bedtime, and the next day he enthusiastically read thirty more pages! A note from the grandmother concluded, "His self-esteem is so much higher now. I have never seen such a turnaround in my life. I am a very enthusiastic believer in Brain Gym. Thank you for giving Clark so much hope and help."

I love telling this story for several reasons. First of all, it shows the profound effects that one Brain Gym balance can have.

Secondly, this is a perfect example to share with teachers. When I finish telling this story, I often mention, "I did no reading practice with Clark; he did no comprehension worksheets. We simply did Brain Gym movements and processes after Clark *set his goal* to improve *his reading*. The reading ability and comprehension were waiting to emerge, once his mind-body system was truly prepared.

"It's been my experience as an educator that, until people are able to make their own choices or set goals from their own unique needs, no true learning takes place." [20]
~ Paul E. Dennison

Lastly, and most importantly for me, this story illustrates the belief I strongly hold: all children really do want to learn, do well, and get along in school. Think of Clark's headache and stomachache when he tried to read. Of course he avoided it—wouldn't you? How many of us sign up to do things that make us feel ill? I would certainly be surprised if someone with motion sickness said, "Oh, boy! We have a long driving trip coming up. I think I'll sit in the middle of the back seat!" We'd think that person was crazy. But if a child avoids something, we may call him "contrary" and just make him do more of it, because it's so "good" for him. Perhaps not. Perhaps it's time to look at *why* he's avoiding it and do something about that.

Exactly what shifted for Clark?

It's impossible to know for sure, but I can certainly make a guess or two based on what Clark told me, what I know about learning challenges, and what I observed in his session.

If someone's eyes aren't teaming properly, he can feel uncomfortable (stomachache, headache) trying to bring them to focus on a specific object, like a letter or word. Trying to follow a line of print that seems to move around on him would be extremely disorienting. Think: vertigo.

If the two sides of his brain aren't sharing information easily, it's hard for him to create *meaning* out of words on the page. Attempts at this would require a tremendous amount of effort, leaving him frustrated, confused, exhausted, and with a tendency to avoid it at any cost.

With Clark's two hemispheres now sharing information more fully, his eyes would find it much easier to cooperate with each other. His right eye would be a stronger lead, or a strong blending partner, and focusing with both eyes would be much more comfortable and require less energy. The "squiggles" of written language would automatically become the meaning of the story.

Just like that, reading can be so much easier. And what's easy is often fun or rewarding, so we end up doing lots of it. Sometimes, it's actually just that simple.

So imagine this scenario: you're the student who simply can't read (or comprehend, or understand math—and on and on) when others all around you can. How long will your good nature hold before you stop trying and start doing something that's easy for you? So you begin to draw (or play with your shoelace, or fidget, or find patterns in the ceiling tiles—anything!) and you get into trouble—again, and again, and again. And you keep getting farther and farther behind. Your self-esteem is in shreds, but your energy has to go somewhere; you end up acting out and reap the consequences.

Before long, you begin to think that you really aren't intelligent, that all the negative messages you've received over time must be true, that the wonderful confidence, imagination, joy, and dreams you had as a young child must be false. Years of this create students who end up in alternative schools or juvenile detention, on drugs or alcohol, or pregnant. What career choices does life hold for them? Only the most unusual of students are able to rise above these circumstances.

Now imagine this scenario: again, you're the student who simply can't read, when others all around you can. Your teacher recognizes your struggle and introduces integrating movements that help you build the inner capacity to make sense of what's on the page in front of you. As your ability grows, so does your sense of accomplishment, and you see yourself as someone who can overcome challenges and confidently pursue your studies. Now what's available to you? A whole world filled with career choices and the means for a happier, more fulfilling life.

The "aha!"

Perhaps now you see why I was so incredibly excited to learn about all the elements that comprise reading and, especially, learning to read. Once I understood the elegant complexity of the systems involved, I had a greater appreciation for where so many learning challenges originate, and I valued the Brain Gym movements and Edu-K balance process even more.

Now, when I explain these concepts during workshops, I love seeing the "aha!" on participants' faces as they begin to realize just why some of their students or children are having such difficulties. I'm happy knowing that this new perspective will change forever how they view these learners and the issues they're struggling with, holding the door open for greater patience and compassion in working with them.

I hope your new awareness of these key concepts will inspire you to use simple Brain Gym techniques to begin addressing the source of reading challenges. I look forward to the day when all children read easily—and naturally—because integrating movement has prepared them for learning and achievement.

Chapter 12
Make Lasting Change through Edu-K Balancing

The 26 Brain Gym® movements are an effective daily boost to comfort, ease, and productivity. When they're used in the context of the Edu-K's *Five Steps to Easy Learning*, also known as the "balance" process, they can offer even greater possibilities for change. The balance process is truly the heart of Edu-K.

The Edu-K five-step balance process is a means of addressing any aspect of life that takes more time, energy, focus, or effort than you think it should. For example, you can use it to eliminate a self-defeating habit, develop a potential within yourself, gain (or regain) a specific skill, or add a new level of enjoyment to something you already do well. The key elements of this process can be endlessly varied to meet the needs of any learner, but it always begins by setting a clear *intention* for change.

Here are a few academic, professional, or personal goals that clients have balanced for:

I confidently move on to college.

I fluently use the Spanish I've learned.

I skate with balance and coordination.

I easily organize and complete my résumé.

I relax and let things flow in my life.

I'm calm at test time and keep my cool.

> Brain Gym movements and Edu-K balancing have often been found to be an excellent support to those who are recovering from brain injury or stroke, helping them re-learn lost skills. Scientists describe the "plastic" nature of the brain, which allows one region of the brain to take on functions previously operated by a damaged region.

> "In Edu-K, we have a process of bringing an intention, also called a goal, into an accessible movement pattern. We call this process a 'balance.'" [1]
> ~ Paul E. Dennison

I effortlessly keep my work area organized.

Math makes sense to me.

I clearly communicate what I'm feeling.

I read easily.

I remember the details of what I read.

I find the right keys when I type.

I appreciate my learning pace and process.

I comfortably coexist with my next-door neighbor.

I confidently ask my boss for a raise.

I easily learn to operate my new cell phone.

Sometimes a client nonverbally sets an "action goal" by simply performing an activity that's currently challenging. She might:

Kick or catch a ball.

Play the piano or type on a keyboard.

Do a certain math problem.

Write in cursive.

Perform a dance movement.

Simply put, setting an intention "gets the ball rolling" in making a change. Then, integrating activity leaves behind a preferred brain organization pattern that's available to call on in that situation.

Can't I just use "mind over matter" about things like these?

It's certainly great if you can. There are lots of wonderful books and workshops about the power of positive thinking. Often, however, a client will share how he's listened to inspirational speakers, journaled, or repeated affirmations in an effort to change; and things may have shifted a bit, or for a while, but he never made the leap he was looking for—until he found Edu-K balancing. This is where this process is so helpful: it goes to the core of the blocks we're experiencing. One of my clients said it this way: "Edu-K balance sessions empower my intention to change."

If you're like I was, you've lived a lifetime believing that making personal change is hard work and takes a lot of effort. Perhaps it's time to let go of that thought.

How do we get so stuck in the first place?

As explained in the "Wired for Ability" chapter, a person may experience challenges because her childhood didn't include enough integrating movement for her to develop key aspects of internal "wiring." For someone like this, it's possible that no amount of "mind over matter" will have the desired effect over the long haul. Working with incomplete patterning often requires sustained energy and effort that would exhaust the best of us.

Many people who are skilled in academics can't fathom the challenges in reading and writing that some children experience—even as they do their best, day after day. For these children, simply sitting up straight and writing without reversals may require an immense expenditure of energy. This leaves little energy for other tasks such as listening to the teacher or spelling correctly, making academic progress excruciatingly slow. Children with these challenges can end up with labels that follow them into adulthood.

And other blocks may develop as well. Sometimes the basic wiring is in place, but an event in our life leaves behind a reaction pattern that served a purpose then, but is not so helpful now. This is most likely the case when a sudden, fearful incident occurs which we experience as trauma. Here's an example of how this can happen:

I was driving west on the I-10 freeway near my home in Phoenix, Arizona, and wanted to exit at Seventh Street. A lot of other people wanted to exit at Seventh Street, too, and the traffic was backed up all the way to the freeway. I found myself at almost a standstill in the far right lane, with cars in the other lanes traveling by at full speed.

The person in the car behind me must not have seen that our lane was stopping. I heard the sickening squeal of brakes behind me and then came the sound—and feel—of impact as I was thrown forward against my seat belt. Fortunately, that other driver had already slowed considerably, and I was left with only minor damage to the car and a nice project for my chiropractor. It could have been a lot worse.

But there was other damage that wasn't so easy to see, and I didn't notice it until I was traveling west on that freeway again. I was driving confidently and comfortably when I found I was holding my breath, my body quite rigid. I actually broke out in a cold sweat as fear ran through me. I realized that I was nearing the Seventh Street exit again, and I was preparing myself for the impact of another rear-end collision.

That event had done a very good job of teaching my mind-body system that this part of the freeway was dangerous. I now found myself reacting to conditioning that I certainly didn't consciously choose. I could tell myself that I was in no danger, but every time I passed that "dreaded exit," I reacted as if I was about to be rear-ended. It took some time, and many safe passes through that area, for the reaction to fade.

> This accident occurred before I learned about Edu-K balancing. If something like this happened now, I'd have excellent tools for releasing the trauma of the event so it wouldn't hang on as a reaction pattern.

I get it. You couldn't just choose to react differently.

That's right. As we travel through the countryside of our lives, we learn many different lessons about what's dangerous to us. Bumping my bicycle's handlebar on a post as I tried to zip through a small space taught me to slow down in places like that or I could fall. I expect that lesson will be valuable for a lifetime. And there's the childhood classic "touching a hot stove." We do that only once.

Other lessons are helpful during the period when we learned them but are less helpful as time goes on. During childhood, ridicule may teach us that standing out or speaking up isn't worth the risk. When Mother says, "*Of course you love your Auntie—now give her a kiss!*" we may learn to deny our truest feelings. A bad fall may teach us to move forward (physically or metaphorically) only with caution. If we grow up with parents who fight or aim verbal abuse at us, we may learn to block out hearing the world around us or become hyper-alert to criticism. These are all forms of self-preservation, a means of coping with painful circumstances we have no power to change.

Then, each trauma holds its own specific set of reactions that emerge in any similar (sometimes even just vaguely similar) situation. Only now they're not so helpful. Learning not to hear your abusive parent's critical words can result in a more universal block to hearing that continues to affect your life in other ways: you're at school and don't hear your teacher; you're at work and don't hear your boss; your spouse keeps asking, "Did you hear what I said?" Behaviors like these are a reaction pattern, the result of the survival tactics we learned long ago.

It's important to recognize that most of the emotion-based blocks we experience in life were first developed as perfect compensations—very creative means of coping with difficult circumstances. We don't identify most current issues as compensations, however. We simply see that in some situation we are fearful, nervous, frustrated, or stuck. When we recognize this pattern of behavior and see how much it's getting in the way, we have arrived at the perfect moment to resolve it.

Andrew works in commissioned sales for a large communication systems provider. He was considered quite a "hot shot" in closing contracts; in fact, he typically led his team in sales each month. That is, until he was promoted. Once he began selling much larger systems—to much larger companies for much larger commissions—his productivity took an extreme downturn. Regardless of how many pep-talks he gave himself, he couldn't seem to shake a sense of disorientation and frustration. With a bit of support, Andrew set his goal to "confidently sell large communications systems," and then asked, "How will this change anything?" I replied, "Let's just see what happens."

Well into our balance session, while Andrew was sitting quietly in Hook-ups, a memory from his school years flooded vividly into his mind. He said, "You know, in eighth grade I was on top of the world. I was an honor student, and I had a reputation for excellence with both the teachers and my classmates. Everybody knew me, and everybody liked me. Then I went on to high school, and I was lost. Suddenly I was on a new campus, with a whole new mix of kids and all new teachers. I had to start at the bottom and build my reputation all over again."

Andrew continued sitting, still in Hook-ups, and suddenly a thought struck him: "My new job is in a new building, with a whole new mix of co-workers and all new supervisors. Nobody knows me. I'm having to build my reputation from the ground up. It's exactly the same. No wonder I'm disoriented—it's high school all over again."

A wave of sadness swept over Andrew for the years of hard work it took, so long ago, to regain his sense of who he was. I watched his body finally relax as years of tension and regret were released.

A few days later, Andrew reported that he felt like "himself" again. His self-confidence was returning and so was his outstanding commission performance. He was surprised by what a strong hold such an old memory had on his attitudes and actions—a memory that had no active part in his daily conscious thought. He was also amazed (and relieved!) that a single balance session could make such significant change.

Andrew hadn't thought about that high-school situation in years, yet the memory had emerged when he was ready to release the pain of it. This happened as he sat quietly in Hook-ups, but the stage had been set for this shift by beginning with a very clear intention to return to his old level of sales confidence. This intention shone what I call a "subtle light" on the original block itself, which was buried deep within. Talking about this memory as it emerged helped Andrew appreciate the depth of this old pain and the significance of the shift he was making.

> During the process of a balance, the release of old memories may not always occur, or it may not be evident. The Edu-K balance will be equally effective in either case.

"Artifacts" become today's issues

I think of issues like Andrew's as the "artifacts" of our prior years. If the distress we experience is not resolved when it occurs, it becomes buried and we forget it's there. But as years go by and the layers of earth erode a bit, we may find a corner of this artifact sticking up above the surface—just enough to catch our toe. We naturally associate this frustrating experience with our life's current events when, in fact, it may be that we're really reacting to something that occurred long ago.

Some emotional artifacts can even result in fears and phobias, ranging from inconvenient to debilitating. I've worked with people who were afflicted with varying degrees of claustrophobia, fear of flying or driving, fear of water and swimming, social phobia, and more. My experience is that issues such as these respond very quickly to the Edu-K balance process.

> "When behavior doesn't change, it is often because we haven't connected mental and emotional experience to the physical body, but have only calmed the superficial areas of the mind. Unless we get into the body, we can't modify automatic behaviors operating at the deepest levels. In our Brain Gym classes, we teach that 'Learning is changed behavior.' Until new behavior is available in the impressionable and ever-growing brain, there will be no new learning, only words, feelings, and information." [2]
> ~ Paul E. Dennison

Penny had an extreme fear of heights. She kept far away from any balcony railings, and glass elevators sent her into a true panic. Unfortunately, the Phoenix Public Library has both of these things, and Penny needed to go there regularly. All five stories are built around a large central atrium. On the fifth floor, where Penny spent most of her research time, only a waist-high transparent railing kept patrons safe from the atrium opening.

Penny said, "This may sound odd, but anytime I'm near that railing, I have to fight the urge to get down on my hands and knees, for fear that I'll somehow be pulled right over the edge. I've caught myself actually holding on to the ends of the bookcases near that opening as I pass by, as if I had to anchor myself to them to stay safe. And don't even ask me about the glass elevators." Just saying this, her breathing froze, and a look of panic appeared on her face.

We began addressing her goal of "comfortably managing heights" through a variety of Edu-K balance elements, each one doing its bit to leave behind an integrated state. At the end of her session, I asked Penny to imagine again that she was on the fifth floor of the library. She stood there, her body and face quite relaxed, and said, "Now wait a minute. . . . I feel just fine about this! Where did my panic go?"

As it turned out, Penny's next stop following her balance session was actually the Phoenix Public Library. That evening, she called to say that her experience there had been "amazing." She said, "It's like heights have lost their 'charge.' I felt absolutely normal, except for the odd feeling that long ago I was afraid of such things. I experienced for the first time what I can only describe as 'healthy fear'—the feeling that simple, logical caution will keep me safe. If I don't lean over the railing, how could I possibly fall?"

"I believe that, no matter how many times we repeat a 'learned' task, if a better way is presented and the whole mind-body system experiences the ease and joy of that better way, all former patterns can be released. This, for me, is true learning." [3]
~ Paul E. Dennison

This story illustrates what happens so frequently following a balance: the learner is so at home in her new way of operating, it seems like that's the way she has always been. I believe this is an indication of the depth of change being made, perhaps because this change comes from a release of conditioned reactions, revealing who we really are, and have been all along.

What does an Edu-K balance look like?

As mentioned earlier in this chapter, an Edu-K balance is a sequence of steps designed to facilitate the change we want to make. We begin by getting clear on what our issue really is and how it affects us. Then we do movements and processes that help us create a more integrated mind-body pattern—which automatically becomes linked to the issue we're balancing about. The result is greater access to new behaviors, skills, or attitudes that help us feel more comfortable or perform more competently in that target situation. We conclude the balance by recognizing and celebrating the change we've made.

The key in Edu-K is that the person experiencing the balance—the client (or "learner")—is the one who's actually in charge. Every step of the process is determined by the learner himself as he senses just what he needs. Brain Gym consultants are trained in supporting the client in noticing those needs and knowing how to facilitate the procedures that are called for, all with the right attitude—not of "fixing" but of *facilitating change*.

I've learned the value of offering the utmost respect to the client in any balance process. An Edu-K balance is not a series of corrections directed by one who decides what's "needed." Instead, it's a means of supporting another person in experiencing his own sense of discovery, the result of which is deep, authentic learning. Processing in this way, he safely recognizes the distance between where he is and where he wants to be. He is naturally drawn to the activities that his mind-body system is ready to benefit from, selecting from a *learning menu* of options. Optimally, the client has enough time to fully experience each step of the balance process, to reap the greatest degree of integration from it.

> A *learning menu* typically includes at least the 26 Brain Gym movements and two repatterning processes developed by Paul and Gail Dennison. (Facilitators who have taken advanced coursework will have additional tools to offer on their learning menu.) A key step in any balance is offering this list to the learner, from which he then chooses his own path to integration by noticing the activities to which he's drawn.

I'll illustrate the balance process by telling the story of one client's session.

Calling on Edu-K balancing

Alexa was a senior in college, majoring in Media Production, with a goal toward working in television or radio. A very right-brained young woman, she'd never done well in certain aspects of academic study, most notably English grammar. She just hated all those punctuation and language rules, and had since childhood. However, Media Production was part of the journalism department, which required an extensive exam in English grammar in order to graduate—and Alexa had already failed it once. Her very thick study guide began feeling bigger and heavier as the days dragged by, and she found more and more reasons not to study. When she did open it, the information just "swam in front of her eyes," and she couldn't focus at all. Her feeling of dread was increasing daily.

Alexa and I began our balance process with PACE, so we were both operating in a state of clarity and integration, prepared for new learning and in tune with each other. I then supported her in creating her goal: "to easily understand and quickly learn English grammar." She was completely engaged, animated, and comfortable as we came up with this language.

I invited Alexa to check her "before" state through various pre-activities, to notice the difference between any parts of her goal that already felt familiar and safe, and where she could see there was room for more learning.

First, I had her cross off the word "to" at the beginning of her goal, and write "I," essentially moving it from hypothetical to *real*. Her written intention, now in first-person present tense, said: "*I* easily understand and quickly learn English grammar." Just looking at this goal now, Alexa stopped breathing. When I had her read the words aloud, they came out flat, in a tone of dread. She said, "I wish it were true, but it feels impossible."

It's not a typical practice in our society to encourage people to observe just how uncomfortable they are. But I've learned that this kind of noticing has a very important role in Edu-K balancing. Fully experiencing how a stress-producing pre-check is affecting our mind-body system is part of what helps us get ready for new learning. And this kind of deep noticing is very helpful later, when we see how different we feel and realize how much the balance has accomplished.

Then I suggested that she act out a scene that represented studying for an English exam. How could she do this here in my office? As it happened, my own high-school English grammar text was in a handy bookcase, and I simply pulled it out and set it down in front of her. She took one look and fell back in her chair, uttering a distressed "Aaagggghhhh!" It was obvious: her mind-body system was not happy about studying English grammar. What a vivid experience of her less-than-integrated state!

When she thought about English grammar, Alexa noticed that:

• She could hardly focus to read a page of text.

• Her eyes resisted tracking across the lines of print.

• Her neck, shoulders, and stomach were unusually tight.

• She was barely breathing.

• When she did her postural checks, she was quite out of balance in all three dimensions.

• Her walking gait was suddenly clumsy and awkward. (A skilled dancer, she's normally very coordinated.)

• She felt anxious, apprehensive, confused, and overwhelmed.

For a refresher on the "postural checks," see the section titled "The Balance of Balance: The Three Dimensions" in Chapter 9, "Theory in Action."

All this was evidence of the switched-off state of Alexa's brain. Of course, she and I were observing these things on the surface, simply noticing how she reacted and how her body moved (or didn't move). I offered Alexa a learning menu of Brain Gym movements and Edu-K processes and invited her to notice which ones drew her attention.

After looking at all the choices, Alexa found that her eyes kept coming to rest on the words "Dennison Laterality Repatterning." She pointed and asked, "What's this? I can't take my eyes off it." I said simply, "I'll show you."

In my experience, this is actually the key point in any Edu-K balance: as "stuck" as a person might feel while immersed in her issue, her awareness is heightened at this point, and the frustration she's feeling has her mind and body primed and ready to make a change. *In this moment, she will find herself drawn to the movements or processes that will most benefit her.* This is what makes Edu-K balancing different from many other modalities: the element of personal choice. *The facilitator doesn't choose—the learner does.*

In fact, Alexa's choice of Dennison Laterality Repaterning (DLR) was not surprising. If a stress reaction were causing her non-leading (left) hemisphere to switch off, it would block her ability to function with details. Going through the steps of DLR would likely help her brain's two hemispheres come into greater communication—"powering up" all of her abilities—and then leave behind a more efficient pattern of brain organization in relation to her issue.

> There are five main steps of Dennison Laterality Repatterning, which involve specific activities in an established sequence. Paul Dennison beautifully explains how he developed and now uses DLR in Chapter 5 of his book, *Brain Gym® and Me: Reclaiming the Pleasure of Learning*. The steps may look simple, but they do require a certain amount of attention to the subtleties of the process to be certain of addressing each learner's unique needs. For this reason, I recommend learning to facilitate balances, especially DLR, through a Brain Gym® 101 course.

I led Alexa through the steps of DLR. As she began each element of this process, she was awkward and uncoordinated, but as she continued, her movements became easy and fluid. I could almost see her mind-body system beginning to access new inner resources as she developed these more natural movement patterns.

When we completed the DLR, Alexa said she felt finished, that there was nothing else she needed. I asked her to think again about studying English grammar. She noticed that:

> For more about this kind of internal noticing, please see the section titled "Honoring the Learner's Noticing" in Chapter 9, "Theory in Action."

- She could focus on a page of text and read easily.

- Her eyes flowed easily across the lines of print.

- Her whole body felt relaxed; tension had vanished.

- Her breath was deep and full.

- All three dimension postural checks were now much more "on."

- Her walking gait was fluid and energetic.

- She felt confident—and surprised!

I asked Alexa to repeat her goal, and she stated: "I easily understand and quickly learn English grammar." Her voice resonated, grounded and calm, and she spoke with authority. She was surprised at the tone of her own voice and said, "Wow—I really mean it this time!"

I suggested she look again at my old English grammar text. She calmly reached for the book and paged through it a bit, saying things like: "Well, I know that part. . . . Oh, I see what that means. . . . Hmm. This is new, but I think I could figure it out." She could actually focus on the text now and pay attention to the material.

She sat back in her chair and said, "I feel really good, like I *can* study English—and understand it. What just happened? This feels huge."

I replied, "Well, I don't have x-ray vision to see into your brain. If I were going to imagine what happened, the story might go like this: You made an intention to change in a specific area, fired up that 'blocked' brain organization pattern by vividly recreating the stress of your issue, and used integrating movements to blend more efficient circuitry into that brain pattern. In essence, you taught your brain a new way to function. Now there's connection where there used to be confusion, which means you can think about English grammar and still be in a whole-brain state." We had fun celebrating with a victorious "high-five."

Six weeks later, Alexa breezed through her exam. She reported, "All of a sudden, it was so easy to study. For the first time, my resistance was gone and things started making sense. And you know what? English grammar is really kind of interesting!"

> "Our movement patterns can change, often in a moment. I see the Edu-K balance process as an opportunity to slow down in our daily lives and 'stop a moment in time' to really observe our circumstances. We can then take a deeper look at the pattern of movement we're using for whatever current goal we've identified, and invite some new ways of moving toward that goal that will draw from a wider array of our resources." [4]
> ~ Paul E. Dennison

So what had happened to create such change? I think of the balance process as a gentle, profound means of educating your mind-body system about the state in which you want it to operate, for any target activity you care to address.

Through balancing, we return to a more whole-brain state and experience all the levels of physical comfort, easy functioning, and positive attitude that accompany it. Taking time to fully notice the difference in how we feel afterward reinforces our awareness of the change we've made. So now when we think about our "issue," it's the clarity of an integrated brain organization pattern that emerges.

This seems like a really different way to make change.

Yes. So many practitioners have "the answer" to our "problem." Go to a doctor and she knows just what medicine will cure our condition. Go to a chiropractor and he knows just what to adjust to relieve our headache. The client is the object of observation and diagnosis and the recipient of the treatment: the "diagnose and fix" model.

> "In Edu-K, our drawing-out process is very much like engaging in a lively dialogue: two people (the facilitator and the learner) are involved in a process of inquiry." [5]
> ~ Gail E. Dennison

Edu-K balancing is very different from this: it's one of "drawing out" from the learner and allowing her mind-body system to adjust and heal itself, rather than making something happen. It acknowledges the learner as an active participant—indeed the primary participant—in the process. When I go through an Edu-K balance to address an area where I'm blocked, I appreciate how involved I am in every step—from identifying the issue and setting a goal to knowing which movements I'm drawn to and noticing the changes I've made. It's very empowering.

> Janet had an extreme fear of driving, which she managed (with great stress) only in the immediate area of her home: to the bank, grocery store, and dry cleaner. She'd learned to drive in her early thirties and had a terrifying accident not long after; she'd spent the next twenty years relying on her husband to take her places or having friends pick her up. Janet is a business acquaintance of mine, and she let me talk her into coming for a balance session "for fun," just to see what the outcome might be. She said, "It will be a waste of your time." I replied with a smile, "Well, it's my time. If you don't mind, I don't mind."
>
> She managed to drive herself to my office for her session. Together, we created the goal, "I drive comfortably anytime, anywhere." In her pre-check, she imagined driving and found herself reliving her typical white-knuckle grip on the steering wheel. For her learning menu, she was drawn to doing some of the simplest Brain Gym movements, and they didn't take long to accomplish. At this point, she found herself glancing out the window at her car. She said, "You know what? I can drive. I know I can drive. Why couldn't I drive before? I feel like I could drive to San Francisco if I wanted to."
>
> After Janet left my office, and for the first time ever, she decided to drive to a store in an unfamiliar part of town that we'd just happened to chat about after our session. She called me that night and said, "It was amazing! And on the way home, I thought, doesn't that freeway go toward my house? So I took the freeway home. All that traffic, and I thought nothing of it!"
>
> She called me a few days later to let me know how well she was doing. She said, "I'd never have believed it if I hadn't experienced it myself. My husband is an M.D., and he's stunned. He just can't understand how I could change like this. I drove us out to dinner last night!"
>
> A few months after our session, I happened to meet Janet and her husband at the shopping mall. She introduced me to her husband saying, "Honey, this is Kathy, who helped me get over my fear of driving." Her husband looked at me, and in the most heartfelt way possible said, *"Thank you!"*

So just what is changing?

As consistently and profoundly as we may experience these kinds of shifts from Edu-K balancing, knowledge of exactly what is changing inside may elude us. What's most important is simply to notice our experience and value the process.

Working with one client, the CEO of a big organization, was a challenge. He was used to understanding everything with his truly detail-oriented mind. Sometimes we could hardly get through his session because he kept asking questions about how and why things worked the way they did: "What just happened in my head?" or "How could I just feel better like that?"

He arrived for his fourth session with a huge grin on his face. He said, "I get it! *I don't have to know!* I don't know how my phone works, either, and I use that all the time. I keep experiencing that Brain Gym works. I can read later about why. Right now, let's just use it." So we did.

Here is another example of the power of the balance process, again using repatterning.

Sandra came for an Edu-K balance session to address a severe obstacle to her business success. A highly regarded interior designer, she could not do math calculation while immersed in her creative work. If a client asked about the cost for a certain window treatment, for example, she'd say, "I'll call you tomorrow with that quote." Then she had to go to bed with the intention of doing math first thing in the morning, before she became involved in other activities. It was a time-consuming struggle to do the computation, and she had to work at it with no distractions.

I asked, "Did you crawl as a child?" I was not at all surprised when she answered, "I'm sure I didn't crawl much. My mother had three children in four years, and I know we all spent great amounts of time in play-pens. Once I *could* run and play, I wasn't allowed to—that was for the boys in the family. I had to sit and read or draw, like a 'lady.'"

We moved forward to address her goal of "fluidly doing math in the midst of creative work." Her balance session included Dennison Laterality Repatterning.

The day after her session, Sandra called to tell me that while in the midst of consulting with a client on design options, he asked a question about costs. She said, "I whipped out my calculator and gave him the answer before I realized what I'd done. I couldn't believe it!"

After years of experience as a Brain Gym consultant, I've come to take stories like Sandra's as an everyday occurrence. Because I observe and experience this kind of shift consistently with Edu-K balances, I sometimes have to remind myself how remarkable these results really are. But one balance session that I facilitated truly surprised me:

Henry had had challenges his whole life. He'd had surgery to correct severe cross-eyes and had worn a patch since age four to strengthen his weaker eye. Clearly intelligent and highly verbal, he still was not able to read at all, despite two years of special-education services in school, plus reading tutors and clinics. His mother said, "He just doesn't get it. We even took him to a vision therapist who has helped him so much—but he still can't read. Not a good start for a second grader."

Henry's mother had attended a meeting where I presented information on Brain Gym. When she heard me mention the importance of crawling and how Brain Gym movements and processes could support children's reading, she immediately recognized Henry in my description because he had completely skipped the crawling stage.

Indeed, when Henry and I went through the PACE warm-up, he had a tremendous challenge with the Cross Crawl. Even with modeling and help, he continually reverted to bringing his elbow down to the same-side knee.

As Henry and I chatted, he expressed how very much he wished he could read. "It would make everything so much easier," he said. I wrote out in large print, "Today is a hot day. It is a hot summer day"—typical first-grade words. I said, "Henry, would you look at these sentences and tell me if there are any words you know?" He struggled across the two lines, mis-calling every word except "a"—and I believe he was guessing at that one.

Henry's Edu-K balance called for Dennison Laterality Repatterning and a few other Brain Gym movements and processes, with lots of fun and chatting in between. This took a total of perhaps forty-five minutes. By the time we finished our movement activities, he was now Cross Crawl-ing easily and fluidly.

At this point, I asked Henry to look at the page again. He instantly spotted the words that appeared in both sentences and said, "Look at this! This says *day*, and this says *day*. . . . This says *hot*, and this says *hot*. . . . *a—a*. . . . *is—is*. . . . " and he used his thumb and index fin-ger to link the word pairs, reading them correctly and without hesita-tion. His mother, astonished, asked, "Henry, can you read that?" I said, "Let's see." The only support I offered was putting my finger under each word; he read both sentences on his own. I glanced over at his mother, who had tears running down her cheeks.

Over the next two weeks, I received the following emails, notes, and phone calls from Henry's mother:

- "What an experience that was today. Henry just seemed the normal Henry except when it came to reading to me tonight. There was no struggle. He read *One Fish Two Fish Red Fish Blue Fish* [a Dr. Seuss book] like an ol' pro. It was amazing."

- "Henry is still improving! I have him going to the reading clinic just to learn all the consonant and vowel sounds he missed last year. And he's tearing up the turf."

- "I'm still seeing improvement. Henry tied his shoes yesterday with no problems. He just acted like it was no big deal—never mind that it has been."

- "Henry loves rhyming books now. He used to hate them, as he couldn't hear the rhyme and thought they were just nonsense. Now he can hear the rhyme, and he loves it!"

- "Henry's occupational therapist says he's writing like a real second grader now instead of a kindergartner. He's like a different child."

- "Henry seems to be hearing all the sounds of his words now. Henry's school speech therapist didn't believe me when I told her about his progress. She said that it just wasn't possible and insisted on testing him. When she saw the improvement for herself, she asked, *'What have you been doing with Henry?'*"

The answer, of course, is Brain Gym. Yet, this balance did not teach Henry to read. Evidently, he had already learned the individual "bits" involved in reading, but he'd had no way to make a cohesive whole out of his knowledge. This, I believe, is what his balance achieved.

For information on how *physical movement* affects the many elements that combine to become the reading process, see Chapter 11, "Ready for Reading."

I was amazed at the learning that Henry accomplished that day, in a single session. Vital pieces for this major shift all seemed to come in the package of this one balance, although he will certainly benefit further from more sessions over time. Children sometimes need several sessions to see the kind of change that Henry made in one day, and we may work and work with a child and see much smaller gains. But sometimes, that one shift is just what the child has been waiting for.

Does balancing make a permanent change?

As we've discussed previously, I find that challenges seem to arise from two main sources:

- lack of initial patterning (due to issues such as retained infant reflexes or insufficient time spent crawling, for example)

- learned reaction patterns that are developed through trauma or stress

When a block exists because the person never got the movement he needed in infancy or childhood, the changes that result from balancing are, in my experience, lasting. It's been six years since Henry's balance, and he hasn't slipped back into *not* being able to read.

When a block exists because of emotional trauma or stress, for which we learned a survival-based compensation, my experience is that a balance helps us return to a more integrated, whole-brain state and creates the strong awareness of the change we've made. In many cases, especially when we are really ready to change, this is enough to completely resolve the old situation. However, we still have the choice of whether to use the new pattern or the old one.

Do you need to keep balancing for the same goal?

The answer often is, "That depends." I like to say that some clients arrive with an "issue" and others arrive with a "project." Phobias, fears, and the emotional charge around certain specific situations or people in a person's life typically fall into the "issue" category. They are usually resolved very well in a session or two, and the change is often quite remarkable. Over time, the person may recognize that addressing the issue again (perhaps from a different angle) would be helpful, but in the meantime, the change achieved is enough to be a tremendous relief. Alexa's resistance to studying English grammar was an "issue."

"Projects," on the other hand, are situations that are grounded in a deeper overall challenge. Progress of some kind may still be seen by the end of the first session, but additional sessions are often necessary for the kind of change the client (or her parent) is seeking. Depending on the nature of the individual, it may take several balances, or a series over a number of months or even years, to do the re-learning necessary to resolve her key challenges.

Of course, it's impossible to know ahead of time if a client is dealing with an issue or a project. I would never have believed that Henry would go from not reading at all to reading fluently in a single session (although by now I have seen that kind of shift again and again). As a Brain Gym consultant, I can make my best guess, but I've learned never to think I know something for sure; I continue to be surprised.

Changes over time

Here's the story of a "project" that continued over about two years, with a learner who had many challenges to overcome.

I started working with Brandon when he was about to enter second grade. Born prematurely, he'd been late in achieving key developmental milestones and still had significant coordination and learning issues.

Our first sessions were a slow introduction to a variety of Brain Gym movements, one or two at a time, interspersed with playing with the various balls, streamers, and hoops in my office. His mother and I always participated along with him.

Initially, our sessions were simply an immersion in these activities. I'd share a new movement, like Lazy 8s, which he would draw over and over on my whiteboard. Then he'd make a beeline for his mother's lap and curl up for several minutes, evidently taking time out to integrate and incorporate this new learning. Then he'd get up and want to do it again. Often he'd continue to do his new movements at home.

Informal goals would arise out of our play experiences. For example, one day Brandon asked for a ball-tossing activity, but he was consistently missing his catches, so I asked, "Which Brain Gym movement do you think will help you today?" He pointed to his choice on my learning menu chart, and his mother and I joined him in rubbing Brain Buttons and then doing a bit of Cross Crawl and Double Doodle. Sure enough, his next attempt showed more coordination, his hands closing more successfully around the ball. Before long, he was catching much more reliably.

Soon he was arriving at my door with his own goals: "I want to be able to run fast!" He'd dash across my office, all elbows and knees and feet stepping unevenly. But after a playful Dennison Laterality Repatterning, his arms were more in sync with his legs, and his stride was more even as he ran.

A bit at a time, I could see that Brandon was building a stronger foundation for coordinated movement. His success was evident in the look on his face as he ran and hopped, skipped and rolled during our sessions. His teacher began reporting that Brandon was participating more fully in physical activities at school, as well, and that his focus was more easily sustained in class.

At this point, Brandon's mother took the Brain Gym® 101 course, where she learned how to support him at home with these simple movements and use a modified balance process to address his goals between our sessions together. She also provided Brandon's teacher with a copy of *Brain Gym® Teacher's Edition*, and soon his whole class was benefiting from the movements as well.

After about six months of sessions, Brandon gained interest in reading. He'd had special help in school and coaching at home since first grade, and he knew the basics of sounding out words, but he'd resisted reading on his own. Now, rather than insist that his mother read to him, he began taking up books himself, spending time immersed in stories.

As we continued our work together, our sessions became focused on his desire to improve in reading, writing, and math. Our bi-weekly sessions had drifted farther apart, to every four weeks or so.

By the end of third grade, Brandon declared, "I think I'm done." Indeed, he'd come a long way. He was now reading at just about grade level and was taking joy and pride in his ability to write and do math. He was also more coordinated as a runner and enjoyed sports activities, at which he was rapidly becoming skilled.

Brandon's mother still brings him back for occasional sessions, but the bulk of our "project" feels complete. She said, "It seems like he's caught up with where he is supposed to be. I'm so happy to see the way he's learning and how pleased he is with his own accomplishments."

Do you need expertise in every client's area of concern?

While some background knowledge of certain conditions may be useful, I take comfort in the fact that I don't need to be an expert in a specific field to facilitate a balance for a person with that challenge. My job is not to resolve someone's medical label, but to support him in making changes in how his body moves when he's immersed in moving toward his goal. By following the steps of the balance process, the learner focuses his intention and then *moves his body* in a way that results in a more integrated brain organization pattern, thereby bringing about his own change. If I'm facilitating correctly, the learner's own mind-body system is in charge of everything we do, and his own innate intelligence makes the right choices. The details may change, but the foundation of the process is the same, regardless of who is balancing and for what goal.

For example, a few years ago I worked with Robert, who was recovering from surgery to remove a brain tumor. I could have declined, since I'd never worked with anyone with brain injury before. I had confidence in the balance process, however, so I proceeded with our first session. I'm very glad; my work with Robert was some of the most rewarding of my entire career.

> "Why does the Edu-K balance process work? The answer to this question has less to do with technique than we think, and more to do with the fact that we are highly skilled at listening to the language of movement; thus we are better able to be there for the person in heart, in pace, and in the new moment. 'Where are you in the center of all this chaos, this nonverbal language?' Perhaps for the first time, the client is really heard at the body level. Someone is there for him; there is confidentiality and honoring of his unique process. There is nothing to do, no place to go, nothing to change." [6]
> ~ Paul E. Dennision

A very intelligent and capable business manager before his tumor appeared, Robert now had significant challenges with simple tasks. He said, "Sometimes I need to lock the door. I can see the key in my hand, but it takes real effort to get the key lined up with the lock. And something as simple as getting my coat on a hanger takes a lot of figuring out." When I introduced the PACE warm-up, Robert could barely accomplish the Cross Crawl, even sitting down.

I asked Robert which goal was the most important to address today, and he selected his "coat" issue. I had him act out the situation, as a pre-check. Standing by the closet, he held his coat in one hand and the hanger in the other and looked at them. He easily put the hanger into one shoulder of the coat, but it took some processing to figure out how to get the other shoulder onto the hanger. Then he pointed to the hanger rod and said, "Now, this is where I really have to think. See how the hanger tops are all lined up one way over the rod? I have to look at this hanger and be sure the top is curved the same direction as the others, so

I can get it onto the rod." I could only imagine how exhausting it would be to live each day this way.

I've learned that in situations like Robert's, it's sometimes helpful to offer a suggestion for a goal, especially one that simplifies the issue down to its essence. I offered this goal: "I understand left and right." His eyes lit up with excitement and anticipation, and he said, "That will help!"

I was not surprised that Robert was drawn to Dennison Laterality Repatterning as his learning menu. At the end of this process, although he was still doing the Cross Crawl sitting down, it was much more fluid: his hand moved without hesitation to the opposite knee. When we returned to the closet, I handed Robert his coat and a hanger. He slipped the coat onto the hanger and hung the hanger on the rod in the blink of an eye! You can imagine the surprised look on his face, and that of his wife!

The next time we worked together, Robert arrived beaming with pleasure, and then he showed me: he could Cross Crawl standing up. He said, "Look what I can do! I was practicing, and it just kind of happened!" We celebrated with an enthusiastic "high-five."

This time, Robert wanted to address his "key in the lock" challenge. In acting out this goal, he took his keys and went to the door, saying, "I always have to look at the key and be sure I'm really lined up with the middle of the lock, and that the key is pointing straight in." I suggested another simplified goal that followed from the previous one: "I know where the middle is."

Robert's learning menu now called for an element from the Edu-K In-Depth Course material, an unstructured movement/dance experience. We imagined gentle music playing, and his wife and I joined him in freely flowing around the room, moving in any way we would like. Then Robert chose some simple Brain Gym movements. Following this, he approached the door again and slipped his key into the lock smoothly and easily. He said, "I didn't have to think about it at all—I just did it."

In my years as a Brain Gym consultant, I've dealt with many "firsts" with clients: all kinds of cognitive or academic issues, test or performance anxiety, fears and phobias, job or relationship challenges, and physical coordination issues (from tying shoes to piano or golf/skateboard/soccer performance). Every "first" shows me that, indeed, the balance process is a tool for everyone. The common denominator is that we all can create an intention for specific change and call on the intelligence of our mind-body system to choose a path to integration.

That said, many Brain Gym consultants who specialize in a certain area (resolving infant reflexes or sensory integration issues, working with senior citizens, business and sales effectiveness, trauma recovery, reading tutoring, sports psychology, etc.) combine Brain Gym tools with their expert work and see huge changes. Indeed, this is where many of the specialized courses in Edu-K come from: skilled consultants develop a means of using the balance process to address specific challenges. It's a world of rich possibilities!

How much change typically occurs in a balance?

In my experience, every balance accomplishes something. Sometimes a single balance completely resolves our issue, and sometimes it can be the first step of the bigger transformation we ultimately want to make. It all depends on the goal we're addressing and how big a shift is appropriate for us to make on that particular day.

It's also important to note that each Edu-K balance simply sets the integration process into motion. While immediate (and sometimes dramatic) change is usually seen after a single session, it may take two to six weeks for the full effect to become integrated and evident in one's life.

Is there anything we can't balance for?

One thing we can't balance for is to change someone else! Occasionally a client says, "I want my (husband, wife, mother, father, child, friend, sibling, teacher, boss, neighbor. . . .) to stop doing _____ (fill in the blank)." I typically say, "Wouldn't it be amazing if we could balance for that person to change—but we can't. We can only balance to change ourselves. So, think of how you react when that person does whatever he does that bothers you. If you could make one shift in *your own reaction pattern* that would make this 'not an issue' anymore, what would that change be?" Clients often say something like, "If I could feel more distant from his words" or "If I could see the humor in the situation." So we balance for that. Very often, our reaction to someone else's behavior is part of the dynamic tension that keeps him or her acting that way. When we change our own behavior, attitude, or perception (shifting our side of the dynamic tension in the relationship), it's amazing how things around us tend to transform.

Also, it's most productive to balance for process, not outcome. A client may want to balance to earn an A on his history exam (outcome). Instead, we look at the process piece that's missing and create a more specific, targeted goal: "I easily study history," "I remember the facts when I need to," or "I calmly take tests."

What if a client wants to balance for a medical outcome?

The Edu-K program offers a means of enhancing access to our innate capacities for growth and change. Rather than focusing on "curing" the symptoms of a condition (for which I'm not trained or licensed), my role as a facilitator is to address the mental/emotional state that might accompany or support any health changes a client would like to make.

For example, one woman wanted to lower her blood pressure. Instead of directly addressing her physical symptom, I asked, "What would your inner state be if your blood pressure were lower?" She said, "I'd be calm, content, and at ease in my life." So we balanced for that.

Along those same lines, when a client arrives wanting to resolve something regarding a medical label, I always ask her more about it, to identify the behaviors or feelings she wants to shift.

Vicky came for a Brain Gym session and said, "I'm here because I'm ADHD." She told me her doctor had diagnosed her as ADHD, and she said she *knew* she was.

Through my years of experience in Edu-K, I've learned not to be a big believer in labels. I know that a diagnosis like ADD (Attention Deficit Disorder: inability to selectively attend) or ADHD (ADD with hyperactivity) is most often arrived at by simply observing a checklist of behaviors. There are myriad reasons for inattentive or hyperactive behavior, from food allergies or mercury poisoning to emotional trauma or retained infant reflexes, none of which is appropriate (in my opinion) to be addressed with ADD/ADHD medications. Vicky felt that her doctor had jumped too quickly to recommend medication without exploring any of the other possible reasons for her behavior. She wanted to find out what Edu-K could offer first and then do other medical testing if necessary for things such as food allergies.

For information on the relationship between retained infant reflexes and hyperactivity, see Chapter 8, "Wired for Ability."

I asked my standard question for this situation, which is, "Why do you think you're ADHD?" Vicky said, "I'm distracted by every little sound and movement around me. I teach high school, and if a student so much as drops a book, I fall apart. I've been this way all my life, and I just hate it. It was very hard getting through high school and college. One little sound in the library while I was studying would really upset me, and I'd lose my focus." Together, we created Vicky's goal: "I easily stay focused around surprising sounds."

At one point, her balance called for an Edu-K process that includes a bit of time to reflect on the issue while sitting in Hook-ups. Out of the blue, Vicky said, "I grew up with an alcoholic father." She continued sitting, obviously thinking or remembering, and then continued: "When he came home from work, I had to have all my toys put completely away. If anything were still out of place, he'd pick it up and throw it at me in a rage. Then he'd throw more things. I was terrified. I always listened hard for the sound of his car so I could get everything picked up in time." She paused and then said, *"Oh my goodness—I've been listening my whole life for the sound of his car."*

With this revelation, Vicky relaxed back into her seat, her shoulders released, and her breathing deepened. She sat that way for quite some time while the impact of this realization sank in, and then we completed the balance. I heard from her weeks later and she said, "Guess what—I'm not 'ADHD' anymore. I hear the sounds, and they just don't bother me now."

Automatic, seemingly "unreasonable" reactions in our lives are like bright little flags waving in the breeze, doing their best to get our attention. They're saying, "Look at me! There's an issue here!" If Vicky had taken medication for her "ADHD," she might never have resolved that old wound. There are many authentic, responsible reasons for taking certain medications, and it's very important to work with your doctor about dosage and duration, but in my opinion, it's also important to be sure you're not medicating something that can be easily addressed another way.

How much practice does it take to become skilled in leading balances?

On one level, the balance process consists of very simple and straightforward steps. On a deeper level, each of these steps has its own elements of variation and subtlety. Experience, astute observation, compassion, and dedication to *support* rather than to *direct* or *fix* all allow a skilled facilitator to make the most of them. Yet, even in the hands of a novice, I've seen the balance process yield remarkable results.

Two women taking their first Brain Gym® 101 course reluctantly paired up for a practice portion of the class. The assignment was for one partner to take the other entirely through a balance from beginning to end, to support him or her in overcoming some chosen issue; then they would switch roles. Neither woman had much faith in her ability to do this. They both felt awkward and unsure; in fact, they said they *knew* they'd mess it up. I encouraged them to simply follow the process they'd learned and reminded them that I would be standing by for support if they got stuck.

The first partner began, gripping her course manual and reading line by line as she led her partner through the steps. Together they crafted the right wording for her goal: "I easily absorb the details in the required reading for my nursing studies." Step by step, she supported her partner in getting the most out of the rest of the balance process, just as she had learned to do earlier in class. Before she knew it, this woman had experienced a huge shift regarding her goal. Now as she looked at her technical reading, the text no longer swam in front of her eyes, and key words popped off the page as she read.

They celebrated this success and switched roles. Soon they were laughing their way through the process, which went more smoothly and just as effectively. This balance recipient felt a huge shift in her goal as well, which was about effectively managing (rather than "mothering") her sales team.

When the group reassembled to share experiences and ask questions, these two women were delighted to share their success. They said, "We didn't believe we could do it, but we did—and it worked!"

The basics of the Edu-K program are actually quite simple to learn. You have a good start just by reading this chapter. But as I've said before, to truly learn Edu-K balancing, I highly recommend that you study with a licensed consultant. A Brain Gym® 101 course taught by such a person will be steeped in the Edu-K philosophy of respect for the learner, which you'll begin to apply in many important ways that make balancing more effective and joyful.

By the end of the course, you'll have learned the basics of the Brain Gym program, and you'll have all the tools you need to balance friends, family, colleagues, or students in your classroom. You'll also be able to balance yourself by simply going through the steps, facilitating your own change.

I do Brain Gym balances for myself frequently. On a typical day, I may notice that I'm reluctant to get started with some task, so I set a goal for efficiently checking emails, returning phone calls, doing a certain errand or project—whatever I seem to be avoiding. Or I may simply wish to enhance the quality of my life and choose a goal, for example, to fully perceive and enjoy the beauty of nature on my morning walk. I'll continue my self-balance by noticing where I feel stuck, looking at the learning menu and doing the processes I'm drawn to, and then noticing the shifts. This can be accomplished very quickly, and I reap immediate rewards.

I love imagining the day when more and more people know about Brain Gym movements and Edu-K balancing and use them in their daily lives. A parent would automatically offer Hook-ups along with the bandage for a scraped knee, to support healing from the inside out. If you were upset, frustrated, or stuck, a friend would say, "Would you like to balance about that?" Every day, teachers would include integrating movement to refresh their students' access to ability. What if these techniques were simply common knowledge? What if your use of Brain Gym was like a pebble in the pond, with ripples expanding throughout your corner of the world?

Chapter 13

A Selection of Brain Gym Movements

Throughout the pages of this book, I have mentioned twelve of the twenty-six Brain Gym® activities. This chapter brings these twelve together, grouping them by category—Midline Movements, Energy Exercises, Lengthening Activities, and Deepening Attitudes—so you can learn more about what they have in common.

In my experience, we get the most out of Brain Gym movements when we do them comfortably, with a gentle but alert presence, noticing how our body moves and how we feel. Brain Gym activities can be adapted for any ability level or physical challenge, by sitting or lying down instead of standing, or doing the movement to a lesser degree. You may wish to explore these movements one or two at a time, calling on them at various points throughout your day, to see just what each one has to offer you.

The Midline Movements

Theory: These movements are thought to support coordination of the left and right sides of the body for physical action, and the left and right hemispheres of the brain for cognitive processing.

> If a person is not able to move or coordinate parts of his or her own body as needed, it's fine for a friend to assist; this is called "motoring" the person through the movement. When assisting someone in this way, it is very important to be gentle and perceptive. Allow the person to initiate each movement as fully as he or she can, and assist only as needed, and with permission. "Less" will very likely be "more" under these circumstances.

Frequent Outcomes:

- Improved eye-teaming while reading, eye-hand coordination for writing, and two-handed coordination for manual tasks, such as tying shoes

- More fluid motor coordination (for walking, running, sports activities)

- Improved accuracy in tasks that require midline awareness and lateral symmetry (such as perceiving the difference between "d" and "b" while reading and writing)

- Easily managing details while holding the "big picture" of a task (spelling and punctuating while writing, recalling math facts while doing long division)

- Ability to coordinate attributes of both brain hemispheres for cognitive tasks

The Cross Crawl

Standing, slowly raise one knee and bring the opposite elbow or hand over to it. Lower that leg and arm and then connect the opposite knee and elbow. Alternate back and forth in this way, allowing your "non-connecting" arm to simply relax at your side.

The Dennisons describe the Cross Crawl as "an ideal large-motor warm-up for all fine-motor skills, such as reading and writing, that require crossing the body's vertical midline." This movement may enhance such skills as eye-teaming, spatial awareness, listening, and left-right coordination.[1]

Lazy 8s

Trace an infinity sign directly in front of you, aligning the center with your own midline. Starting at the center, follow the Lazy 8 up and around to the left, then up the middle and around to the right—over and over again. Repeat with the other hand, then both hands together. Without moving your head, allow just your eyes to gently follow the movement of your hand(s). You can trace Lazy 8s in the air in front of you or on a surface like a whiteboard or paper on a desktop, using a marker, crayon, pencil, or just your fingers.

In drawing Lazy 8s, the eyes and hand practice moving fluidly together (eye-hand coordination), especially across the midline. This may also encourage both eyes to work together for enhanced visual skills such as eye-teaming and depth perception. Practicing Lazy 8s has been known to reduce or eliminate reversals and transpositions in reading and writing.[2]

The Cross Crawl

Lazy 8s

The Double Doodle

Put both hands out in front of you and move them in mirror image patterns and shapes. You can begin as if "conducting an orchestra," and then flow into freeform squiggles and zig-zags. Eventually, you may choose to create specific shapes, such as circles and squares, or people, animals, trees, or flowers. You may enjoy drawing your Double Doodles on paper or a whiteboard, holding a colored marker or pen in either hand.

The Double Doodle

As with Lazy 8s, above, the Double Doodle helps develop kinesthetic and visual left-right discrimination. These movements foster an awareness of the lateral midline as the center point for movement in either direction, a foundation for spatial orientation and correct letter formation. The Double Doodle may also help learners move through any confusion about which hand to use when writing, as only one hand can lead—the other must relax and follow.[3]

Double Doodle play

The Energy Exercises

Theory: These movements are thought to help resolve stress-related disturbances that affect physical balance and emotional equilibrium.

Frequent Outcomes:

- Improved physical and emotional stability and grounding

- Increased ability to recognize one's own feelings and relate positively to others

- Enhanced organization of thoughts and belongings

- Greater ability to feel one's weight and center of gravity

- Improved awareness of one's vertical midline as a reference point for directionality

Brain Buttons

Find the spots just below the collarbones on either side of the breastbone. Give these spots a rub with the thumb and fingers of one hand while resting the other hand over your navel. Switch hands after twenty seconds or so. Throughout, allow your eyes to gently track from side to side, left to right.

Brain Buttons

Massaging these spots may support a state of visual ease, eye-teaming, and the ability to cross the visual midline for reading; eye-hand coordination for writing; and whole-body coordination, as for the Cross Crawl. This may also enhance the sense of postural center and directionality for improved left-to-right scanning and reading.[4]

Sipping Water

Sipping Water

Sip some water, holding it in your mouth for a moment before swallowing. Does this action quench your thirst? Continue consuming water throughout the day and notice any changes in how alert you feel, or how well you work.

Sufficient hydration helps the neural system maintain membrane potential, so nerve cells can transmit messages efficiently. Consuming sufficient water may enhance academic and cognitive skills, concentration, mental clarity, and memory storage and retrieval.[5]

The Thinking Cap

Using your fingers and thumbs, gently "straighten out" the rolled edge of your ear. Start at the top of your ear and work your way around, finishing at the earlobe. You can "unroll" both ears simultaneously; repeat three or more times.

The Thinking Cap

This activity relieves tension in the neck and shoulders (observed by the Dennisons as associated with auditory inattention) and may enhance auditory processing, short-term memory, listening comprehension, and thinking skills.[6]

Balance Buttons

Place the fingertips of one hand right behind your earlobe, on the indentation near the edge of your skull. (If you're not sure just where this spot is, join two or three fingers and cover the entire area behind your earlobe.) Rest your other hand over your navel. After about 30 seconds, reverse hands to cover behind the other ear.

This activity brings attention to the vestibular system (the body-balance mechanism in the inner ear) and the body's center of gravity. The outcome is often a greater awareness of the three elements of directionality—left/right, up/down, and front/back—and may help restore the alignment of the head in relation to the rest of the body. This movement has been known to alleviate symptoms of motion sickness and improve eye-teaming.[7]

Balance Buttons

The Lengthening Activities

Theory: These movements are thought to release the "freeze response" of tendon-guard reflex (the involuntary, stress-induced tightening of muscles on the back of the body) that affects posture and physical balance.

Frequent Outcomes:

• Release of physical tension

• Improved listening and language expression

- More relaxed pencil grip and easier flow of writing

- Enhanced focus and comprehension

- Greater spirit of participation

The Owl

With your right hand, grasp the muscle that runs between your left shoulder and the base of your neck and apply moderate pressure with your fingers and thumb. Inhale a relaxed breath, turn your head to one side and exhale (children—or playful adults—enjoy "hooting" like an owl while they do this). Inhale again, turn your head to the other side and exhale. Cycle back and forth this way, three or more times. When you are finished, drop your chin to your chest as you exhale and relax in this position. Then repeat the process, gripping your right shoulder with your left hand.

The Owl

This movement is a release of the upper trapezius muscle (top of the shoulder), which tenses from the stress of excessive reading or other near-point activities. Using the Owl may diminish squinting or staring habits and promote a more balanced posture. Releasing this tension often re-establishes the ability to listen, think, and access memory.[8]

The Calf Pump

Athletes and dancers will recognize this lengthening movement: it's frequently done to release tension in the back of the legs before physical exercise. Stand and stabilize your position by holding onto a wall, chair, or table and take a long step forward with one foot. With both feet pointing forward, bend your front knee until you feel the muscles just begin to lengthen in your back leg, causing your back heel to rise up a bit. (If your front knee extends past your toes, take a longer stride to keep your knee safely over your ankle.) Now you are in position to begin. Gently allow the heel of your back foot to move toward the floor, creating a lengthening of the calf muscle. Hold for a moment, then rise back onto the toes of your back foot; repeat several times. Remember to breathe as you move. When this release feels complete, switch foot positions and lengthen the muscles in the other leg.

The Calf Pump

The Calf Pump releases tension in the muscles of the feet and lower legs, which tighten when we're under stress (from a "freeze-response" called tendon guard reflex). Releasing tension may help to discharge this fear reflex, allowing a return to normal muscle tone in our legs and supporting a more natural stride.[9] *People of all ages love the Calf Pump, especially after periods of extended desk- or car-sitting; they often find it helps them regain focus, comprehension, and readiness for language expression.*

Arm Activation

This movement is an isometric release of the shoulder, achieved through activating the arm in four directions. Position your right arm straight up overhead

Arm Activation

(or at any comfortable angle in front of you). Place your left hand on the "front" of your right arm, near the elbow. Hold steady with your left hand as you press gently against it with your straightened right arm. Use a gentle action: only 20 percent of your "push power." Continue holding for about eight seconds, or until you feel a release of shoulder tension, and then relax. Now move your left hand to the "back" of your raised arm and exert pressure against it. Repeat in the remaining two directions, repositioning your left hand so you can press "in" toward your ear, and then "away" from your ear. Lower both arms and notice the difference in how they feel. Then—activate the other arm!

This movement releases tension in the muscles of the upper chest and shoulders, where control for both large-motor and fine-motor activities originates. If these muscles are shortened due to stress, we may have challenges with activities like handwriting.[10]

Deepening Attitudes

The next two movements have been given a special category of their own. They relate to the Energy Exercises, however, and are often grouped with them.

Theory: These movements are thought to diminish the fight-or-flight response.

Frequent Outcomes:

Hook-ups Part I

• Release of stress, anxiety, and muscle tension

• Deeper breathing

• State of calm self-awareness

• Access to higher-order thinking skills

Hook-ups

Part I: Cross your ankles. Hold your hands out in front of you, thumbs down. Cross your wrists so you could pat your hands together. Gently interlace your fingers. Bend your elbows and rotate your hands down and in toward your body, bringing them up to rest against your chest. If you like, you can lightly touch your tongue to the roof of your mouth just behind your teeth when you inhale and let your tongue relax when you exhale. Sit like this for a minute or two as you breathe deeply.

Variation for Part I, called Cook's Hook-ups: Sitting comfortably, cross your right ankle over your left knee. Grasp your right ankle with the left hand and cross your right hand over to wrap your fingers around the ball of the right foot. (This may be done in the opposite way, reversing left and right for these directions.)[11]

Cook's Hook-ups
A variation for Part I

Part II: Uncross your ankles and wrists and touch the fingertips of your right and left hands together. Continue to touch your tongue to the roof of your mouth (relaxing it on the exhalation) as you breathe deeply for another minute or so.

When under stress, the body routes blood away from the core and to the extremities, to prepare for "fight or flight." The Dennisons hypothesize that crossing arms and legs over the midline brings attention back to the core and releases that hyper-arousal response. After Hook-ups, people frequently report deeper breathing, a greater feeling of calmness and grounding, and enhanced access to higher-order thinking skills such as choice-making. Doing Hook-ups while standing provides additional benefit by activating the vestibular system and balance-related muscles, which may help to restore equilibrium following physical, emotional, or environmental stress.[12]

Hook-ups Part II

> The Dennisons describe the late Wayne Cook as "a pioneering researcher of bioenergetic force fields" and state that he developed Cook's Hook-ups "as a way to counterbalance the negative effects of electromagnetic fields."

The Positive Points

Gently place your fingertips on your forehead about half-way between eyebrows and hairline, directly above either eye. These points are on the "frontal eminence" or "brow ridge" of the skull. (In some people, this ridge is more pronounced; in others, it's quite subtle.) You can use both hands or cover both points with one hand. Allow your fingers to simply rest on these spots with an ultra-light touch for a minute or so (or longer).

The Positive Points

After holding these points, people often notice greater access to "executive functions," such as planning, choosing, and initiating positive social behavior, as well as diminished fight-or-flight hyper-arousal response, which suggests that this movement may stimulate the prefrontal cortex.[13]

Learning more about the Brain Gym movements

As I've mentioned before, there are twenty-six Brain Gym activities in all. If you use just those found throughout these chapters (and described above), you'll have a very good assortment of Brain Gym tools to call upon. And—you may wish to explore all the others as well to see what they have to offer you!

A variety of books describe the Brain Gym movements and their many benefits. Some provide extensive background information as well. Here are three good choices to begin with:

- *The Brain Gym® Teacher's Edition*

- *Brain Gym® for Business: Instant Brain Boosters for On-the-Job Success*

- *Hands On: How to Use Brain Gym® in the Classroom*

You may also choose to learn directly from a Licensed Brain Gym® Instructor/Consultant. In a workshop or private session, he or she will model each movement and show you how to get the most out of it. And if you take the Brain Gym® 101 course, you will learn all of the movements in the context of the dynamic Edu-K five-step balance process.

Please see the Appendix A for a more extensive list of book titles and how to find a course or contact a Licensed Brain Gym® Instructor/Consultant in your area.

Now that you have experienced several Brain Gym movements and learned some foundational concepts of the Brain Gym/Edu-K program, let's explore how all these come together in practical application, starting with the workplace.

Brain Gym
in Action

The Brain Gym®/Edu-K program
brings vitality, focus, and ease
to all aspects of daily living

. . . . from the workplace and home life,
to sports, education, and personal growth.

Chapter 14
Brain Gym in the Workplace

By this point in your Brain Gym® exploration, you've read the theory and experienced the activities; perhaps you've gained some perspective on why challenges may arise and how movements that have an integrating effect on the mind-body system can help to dispel them. This section of the book is all about putting this information to practical use in your life. Since Brain Gym is a tool for all ages, let's begin in a world common to many adults: the workplace.

I believe that everyone comes to his or her work situation with good intentions. Business teams and office employees are carefully chosen for their training and expertise. Systems are developed to support the optimal functioning and goals of the firm. Everything ought to be in place for success.

However, even the best of us can feel challenged by our work environments. Over time, tensions can build, communication can go off-track, and entire teams can lose their effectiveness. And keep in mind that adults are essentially grown-up kids! Chances are excellent that any learning or processing challenges they had as students have followed them right into the workplace.

And a day at work can be demanding. We've already learned how key portions of our brain "switch off" when we're experiencing stress, resulting in slower reading and poorer comprehension, limited hearing, and diminished processing overall. How productive can we be in that state? All of these are reasons why Brain Gym® movements and Edu-K balancing are so valuable in the business world: Using these tools can actually improve not just employee morale but the company's bottom line. Let's explore a bit about why this may be so.

Brain Gym as a productivity booster

I sometimes give business seminars and presentations where I explain our bodies' stress responses and how each element of the PACE warm-up contributes to ease and effectiveness. Once participants get over their reluctance and actually begin moving their bodies in a room full of colleagues (humor helps here), they frequently share how different they feel after doing each Brain Gym movement.

By the end of the seminar, all of the attendees have typically found at least one activity that they say worked noticeably well for them and that they are looking forward to incorporating into their business day. Many want to know more.

One participant wrote to say:

> That seminar was a pleasure. It is hard to believe that in just one short workshop you taught us techniques that are fast, easy to use, and practical. My cold calls are a lot less stressful and calls to existing clients are more relaxed. I continue to recommend Brain Gym to people who mention that they want to manage their stress better.

An excellent support for workplace effectiveness is the book *Brain Gym® for Business: Instant Brain Boosters for On-the-Job Success*, co-authored by Paul and Gail Dennison and Jerry Teplitz. Along with brief descriptions of all twenty-six Brain Gym movements, it offers illustrations of adults in business attire doing each activity. An extensive index lists which movements are recommended to enhance performance in specific job tasks—from organizing, communicating, and finishing projects on time to dealing with data and keyboarding.

Movement at work

It's simple to blend a Brain Gym movement or two into your day, perhaps during a quick break or trip to the water cooler. Many activities, like Brain Buttons, can be done almost invisibly. Some people find a place to do the PACE activities without others watching, while others declare themselves the office "Brain Gym-ite" and humorously lead colleagues in a few of the movements in the break room.

One such "Brain Gym-ite" reports that, at first, his co-workers were reluctant to join him in doing PACE, and he ended up cajoling them into action. After a while, on days when he'd get busy or forget, people started coming by his desk asking, "Isn't it time?" Then he found colleagues leafing through *Brain Gym® for Business* and taking themselves through some of the movements!

Sometimes doing what's best for us means stepping out and risking the questioning looks of our work associates. When we allow ourselves to move, we support our mental health and physical well-being. And others benefit as well when we model such helpful practices.

Different people take to different Brain Gym movements. An executive secretary I know says, "I just love the Cross Crawl. When I get overwhelmed, I step away from my desk and Cross Crawl for a bit. Then I'm fine. I can't believe what a difference it makes." Other people have dedicated themselves to drinking more water, releasing shoulder tension through the Owl, or sitting regularly in Hook-ups. Whatever works and supports you, do it! Even a little bit of Brain Gym can go a long way.

What business issues respond to Edu-K balancing?

Regardless of a person's work title or level of responsibility, Edu-K balancing is an excellent means of resolving blocks that get in the way of productivity. Here are some goals that clients have addressed to deal with work situations:

I relax and do my best.

I focus on one project at a time.

I comfortably allow messages to wait while I complete other tasks.

I fluidly balance work and home.

I quickly spot important content as I scan the page.

I consistently keep my files organized.

I finish my reports on time.

I confidently join my new work team.

I easily ignore the sounds in cubicles around me.

I prioritize tasks and accomplish the right things each day.

Several of my clients are busy professionals who regularly schedule balance sessions to resolve issues that sap time and energy from their day and distract them from achieving their goals.

One business manager said that he was always exhausted. When I asked him why, he described a day of doing his own work plus closely supervising the work of all the people who reported to him. I asked, "Don't they do good work on their own?" to which he replied, "Well, yes—they're excellent professionals. I actually never even find anything wrong—I'm just a compulsive checker. I'm always so worried that something will slip through the cracks." So we balanced for the goal: "I easily relax and trust that others are doing their work." Following that session, his behaviors quickly changed. He and his team created a system for reporting progress on projects with regular updates and only occasional direct supervision. He found that he really could trust others to do their best, and the feeling of overbearing responsibility lifted. My client found that he was much more comfortable, and the entire team became more productive.

Edu-K balancing can create deep, spontaneous change. As one business owner stated after two balance sessions, "I don't even have to think about it; I'm simply operating differently now."

One woman's employer paid for two Brain Gym balance sessions and her tuition in a three-day Brain Gym® 101 course. The employer told me, "The benefits I've seen this employee gain through balancing and workshops far exceed the kinds of change I see her co-workers come back with from 'believe-in-yourself' seminars. This is real change, and the best use for my training dollar."

Managing stress with Brain Gym

The high-pressure world of commerce can require astute judgment and quick action at all hours of the day. If our schedules are long and relentless, we can get so bound up in managing events that our health ends up at risk.

Sipping Water

Mike is the president of a small computer software company. Two years prior to seeing me, he'd had to sell a thriving business because he had made himself ill with stress. It had taken him the past two years to regain his health, and with the pressures of his new position, his previous physical and emotional symptoms were re-emerging: he couldn't sleep, even bland food upset his stomach, and he had chronic headaches. Sometimes his heart would just start racing. The doctor reported that Mike had no identifiable illness and suggested medication for stress, which gave him uncomfortable side effects. He knew he had to do something different. After a friend told him about Edu-K balancing, he made a commitment to give it a try.

Following our first balance session, focused on "dealing calmly with work events," and a week of using PACE four times a day, Mike reported feeling considerably better. He was working more effectively than before and no longer hit what he had described as his 1:00 p.m. "productivity wall." He found that he could easily slip the PACE movements into his day, and many could be done discreetly. For instance, even during a business meeting, he could slip his hand up to one Brain Button at a time, and give it a bit of a rub. He also put a large pitcher of water on his desk each morning and made sure he'd consumed it all by the end of the day.

"The Brain Gym movements serve as the kind of easy and effective self-help tools that we need to optimize our performance and on-the-job satisfaction in the business environment and it is possible to achieve this optimal performance and satisfaction by doing the movements for just a few minutes each day." [1]
~ Paul E. Dennison

In subsequent sessions, Mike balanced for "calmly evaluating the options," "easily keeping the overall goal in mind," and "comfortably responding to the personalities of the board of directors." In addition to PACE, Mike had created a program that included doing about half the Brain Gym movements throughout each day. He said, "This is my health break."

Two months later, after his fourth session, Mike described himself as feeling stronger, more relaxed, content, focused, effective—and relieved. Now that he was no longer at the mercy of his stress, his symptoms had all but disappeared. Although this had been a most hectic and demanding two-month period, he'd been able to weather it with what he described as "grace under fire." Instead of internalizing criticism and feeling overwhelmed by the responsibilities of his position, he's now acting from a place of clarity, confidence, and effectiveness. His new ability to respond, rather than react, has improved relationships with his colleagues and board of directors, and he's even more able to relax and enjoy time with his wife and family.

Brain Gym in the air

Of all the corporate worlds where stress is an issue, the airline industry is likely toward the top. Dealing with unpredictable weather, travel delays, and missing luggage could daunt the most cheerful sales agent. Here's a story of how one Brain Gym instructor is making headway in supporting her entire corporate structure, using elements of the Brain Gym program.

Pam August, a Brain Gym® instructor in Calgary, Alberta, is an Organization Development Specialist for Canadian carrier WestJet Airlines. She has brought Brain Gym into many elements of her training programs, including instructor and leader development and flight crew fatigue management. She also uses the Brain Gym five-step balance process as the framework for one-on-one and team coaching, to help individuals and teams move toward their goals with more ease.

Pam first encountered Brain Gym as a faculty developer at the Southern Institute of Technology in Calgary. After experiencing the benefits of Brain Gym in a faculty in-service, she immediately knew she wanted to learn more about how to integrate intention, noticing, and movement into her teaching practice. She became a Licensed Brain Gym® Instructor/Consultant in 2005, at the same time she joined WestJet.

Known for its positive corporate culture, WestJet employees readily embraced Brain Gym as a tool that supports their development and brings out their best every day. Pam introduced PACE to a group of leaders as an energizer, at a leadership conference in 2005 where they also experienced Lazy 8s and the Thinking Cap. Leaders continue to ask for "those brain exercises" at learning sessions Pam facilitates.

One of Pam's first success stories involved a Customer Service Agent trainee who was experiencing extreme anxiety during performance testing for her role. Pam facilitated a balance for her, and the agent continued to do PACE throughout her training, which she successfully completed. One year later, as Pam was visiting a base across the country, she was flagged down by the agent who told her she still used Hook-ups when things got stressful, as they often do in the airline industry! Pam continues to offer Brain Gym balancing as part of the internal coaching support she provides, and the majority of her clients experience break-throughs through the balance process. "Calm, invigoration, a whole new perspective, the ability to flow through change" are all outcomes that have resulted through Brain Gym.

While most WestJetters have been very receptive to Brain Gym, Pam has experienced a bit of reluctance from those who spend more time living "from the neck up." In order to help make connections that make sense, Pam provides simple explanation about how the mind and body work together and what happens to us under stress—something we can all relate to. This was the case in introducing Brain Gym to flight crews as a fatigue management counter-measure.

Fatigue is a significant challenge that all flight crews face, and the Brain Gym movements offer simple "wake up your brain" strategies that can be done anywhere, anytime. Pam developed a core team of pilot train-ers to facilitate sessions, to further lend credibility and support to the program. This core team reports great success with the Brain Gym sec-tion of each training—it's always the highest rated part of the day—and report that pilots and flight attendants are continuing to the do Brain Gym movements "on the line." One of the trainers, once a bit skeptical, now does Brain Gym as part of his flying routine because, as he states, "It makes a big difference!" In 2011, all of WestJet's 1,100 pilots and 2,400 flight attendants experienced all the elements of PACE, plus several other key Brain Gym movements, through the "fatigue management" section of their annual training program. Recently, one of Pam's colleagues was facilitating a training session and two differ-ent participants asked to do "those brain exercises" to perk themselves up. Pam says, "It's funny—people may forget what it's called, yet they don't forget the movements!"

Perhaps one day soon, you will see WestJet guests watching a Brain Gym demo to add to their flying experience!

Research on business applications

When applied consistently and with skill, the Brain Gym system can improve diverse aspects of business. Here's an example:

Jerry Teplitz, co-author of *Brain Gym® for Business*, has adapted the Brain Gym work to address productivity in the business world, includ-ing courses such as Switched-On Selling (SOS). The South Carolina Farm Bureau, an insurance company, conducted its own study on the effectiveness of this program by having one-third of its sales force attend the one-day SOS seminar, with the remaining two-thirds acting as the control group by not attending.

Course participants learned to balance for such goals as "I handle rejection well," "It is easy for me to make cold calls in person," and "It is easy for me to ask my clients for referrals." The company tracked both groups for four months after the seminar, comparing everyone's sales figures from the previous year against those from the current year. Salespeople who attended the SOS seminar increased sales 39 percent and premium levels 71 percent over those who did not attend the seminar.[2]

Edu-K balancing and group goals

While the balance process is used most often with individuals, remarkable shifts may also occur when those individuals come together to address a common goal. Following a balance, office staff or management teams may find themselves communicating more effectively, feeling more aligned as a group, and cooperatively solving challenges that arise.

I was invited to work with a business that was having serious cooperation issues. It was a small, recently merged office. The two owners (now partners) brought with them distinctly different personality styles and sets of office systems, and employees steeped in those disparate systems. As one of the owners stated, "The challenges for our newly-merged support staff are considerable and lead to conflicts that drain our time and energy."

The Total Team Effectiveness™ program I've developed uses the Edu-K model to specifically address challenges within groups. It consists of a workshop covering the basics of the Brain Gym process, followed by individual balances with each team member, and then at least one more session with the entire group, focused on a collective goal.

In the case of this company, each participant chose to use his or her private session to address a specific personal issue, with the overall understanding that balanced team members create a more balanced team. When they got together a few days later for their group session, they chose to focus on improving their ability to communicate and generate harmonious solutions.

The owners later wrote to say that their office was now more productive and focused on accomplishing their business goals. One of the office staff members commented, "It isn't that conflict went away. We just seem to find solutions so cooperatively and easily now."

Not all businesses have a need—or the time—for such in-depth work. Sometimes just a quick balance-boost can resolve a specific situation.

I facilitated a short workshop for the executive committee of a small private college at the beginning of a day dedicated to creating a three-year strategic plan. This school was facing a real challenge: each department's program was growing, and the building wasn't. There had been some very heated "discussions" among department directors about the usage of classrooms and whose program "deserved" what space. All the directors attended this meeting.

In the workshop, I briefly explained the basics of Edu-K balancing and introduced the PACE warm-up. Then we discussed what they wanted to accomplish together. The participants all knew they needed to improve their teamwork and blend the interests of the various departments of the school. To develop a group goal, I asked them to list the qualities that would help their team be more effective, which I scribed on the board. They mentioned such things as respect, flexibility, open communication, and willingness to hold a team view. Once all these words were contributed, I had everyone look at them and notice their reaction. Their comments ranged from "I can't even look at the word *cooperation*" to "Making this change seems totally impossible."

I suggested they each put a hand over any place where they noticed discomfort in their body, and soon they were covering stomachs, heads, necks, jaws, and lower backs. One man said, "I need more hands!" Then I pointed to a poster of all the Brain Gym movements (our learning menu), and invited members of the group to simply notice which movements they were drawn to. One person said, "I can't take my eyes off the words 'The Calf Pump.' What is it?" I replied, "I'll show you," and then led the group in that movement. After a few movements done this way, I noticed everyone sitting back in their chairs, seeming quite content. When they looked again at the words on the board describing their goal, they had various comments: "My stomach feels fine and my headache is gone." "I can do that now." "I can look at our goal and breathe now—and even smile." "I'm ready—let's get to work."

The director of public relations for this school later wrote to describe what happened during the meeting that followed their Brain Gym workshop:

We found that we were able to complete our tasks in record time with great camaraderie. Starting with concerns of "turf wars" between members of the team, we found we spent the day enjoying and respecting one another more than we could have anticipated. In fact, we accomplished the outline of our Three-Year Strategic Plan by 5:00 p.m. that same day!

Even though several weeks have passed since our retreat, members of the Executive Committee are openly using the techniques in front of our employees and discussing the benefits of the processes with their staff. Many of our employees have sought out the *Brain Gym® for Business* books that we brought back with us so that they, too, can benefit from the exercises.

We hope to include you in a future all-school meeting. In the meantime, we are all ambassadors for "Brain Gym" techniques!

Whether it's a quick productivity boost or in-depth balancing, Brain Gym and Edu-K can help to transform the atmosphere of your work setting. It's amazing what can happen when individuals really prepare themselves for success, and teams balance to hold a shared vision.

Chapter 15
Brain Gym and Physical Activity

One of the most compelling aspects of the mind-body connection is how quickly changes in our state of internal balance are reflected in our actual *physical* balance. Whole-brain integration often results in a more stable, comfortable posture and the skilled motor control involved in many daily activities—from walking, to driving, to simply guiding a pencil. And, of course, this kind of mind-body coordination is absolutely essential in the world of sports.

This chapter offers an abundance of stories that illustrate both the many ways that physical coordination "glitches" can get in our way and the power of Edu-K balancing to resolve them.

A balanced brain, a balanced body

You may recall reading in Chapter 9, "Theory in Action," about the Three Dimensions of Edu-K: Laterality, Centering, and Focus. I described a set of *postural checks* you could use to experience just how integrated any of these three dimensions might be. This is more than idle curiosity; noticing what's "off" gives us a gauge by which we can experience our movement back toward balance, so we can perform at our best.

This is very helpful in many areas of physical endeavor; here's one client's story of using Brain Gym® in the high-stakes world of professional golf.

Marie had played golf at the highest amateur levels. She had won several statewide tournaments and qualified not only for two national championships but also the prestigious LPGA Futures Golf Tour, where amateur golfers prepare for pro competition. When we met, she was determined to fully qualify as a professional and wanted to refine her skills.

For more on the "postural checks," see the section titled "The Balance of Balance: The Three Dimensions" in Chapter 9, "Theory in Action."

Among the obstacles she was addressing was her lack of consistency in stance as she prepared to hit the ball. One day, she'd notice a tendency to lean a bit forward, for example, so she'd put more weight on her heels. That worked fine until she found herself putting a bit more weight on her heels all the time—even when she didn't need it—and she'd end up leaning too far back. The adjustments she was making were minute, but at the level at which she was playing, being off even a tiny amount was too much; it drained energy from her focus on other aspects of the game.

Then she learned how to use Brain Gym movements to adjust her stance. She'd notice how stable she felt in each of the three dimensions: leaning a little to the right or left (Laterality Dimension), not feeling grounded (Centering Dimension), or tipping to the front or back (Focus Dimension). She said, "It's so simple. If I feel 'off' in any direction, I just do a few Brain Gym movements while I'm walking down the fairway or standing off to the side, waiting for someone else to make his or her shot. Then I'm right back in balance, with no more need to compensate through my posture!" It's doing wonders for her game.

From golf to skiing and gymnastics, from soccer to horseback riding and ballet dancing—if an activity involves physical coordination, Brain Gym movements and Edu-K balancing can work wonders.

Anne scheduled a session to resolve what she described as "not just a block—a huge boulder" that was keeping her from accomplishing her lifelong goal: learning to fly a helicopter. She could take off, maneuver, and land just fine—it was hovering that she simply couldn't do. Lesson after very expensive lesson, she'd come home in tears of frustration, feeling that she'd never be able to hover.

Flying a helicopter places great demands on one's ability to function in all three dimensions simultaneously. Greatly simplified, the pilot must control two functions with each hand (moving the controls left to right and front to back) and one with each foot (moving the pedals up and down). Hovering requires making subtle adjustments, sometimes in three directions simultaneously. When Anne had to work at this level of coordination, she felt completely overwhelmed.

As Anne balanced for her goal of "effortlessly hovering a helicopter," she was drawn to Three Dimension Repatterning (3DR). This process is slightly different from Dennison Laterality Repatterning, and the outcome is expanded: while DLR creates integration between the two hemispheres of the brain (Laterality Dimension), 3DR simultaneously creates integration in three dimensions (Laterality plus Centering and Focus Dimensions) of the mind-body system.

After going through the 3DR process in relation to her goal, Anne was much more prepared for the coordination tasks of hovering a helicopter. At her next flying lesson, she managed quite well, and in the lesson after that, she hovered perfectly.

A balanced body, a balanced brain

Interestingly enough, doing Brain Gym movements and Edu-K balances to achieve athletic goals has an automatic spillover into academics and other forms of mental processing. Many skills acquired through sports also apply in the classroom: focus, concentration, eye-teaming and tracking, as well as performing under pressure. After balancing for skill in sports, many students just naturally improve academically as well.

A student may not care so much about improving in reading, but definitely wants to easily pass and receive the ball in soccer, or score from the free-throw line in basketball. We always use the goal that's most important to the person doing the balance.

Simon, age sixteen, arrived very reluctantly for his Brain Gym session. His mother wanted him to improve in academics; Simon wanted to improve in soccer. He said that keeping track of the ball was usually easy. "But if it's traveling straight at me," he said, "my stomach sinks and I just freeze up." As a pre-check, I tossed a small pillow straight to him. His eyes got wide and he actually fumbled catching it. Then I asked him to walk up and down the length of my office. He noticed that his feet were dragging and catching on the carpet. He said, "That's just what happens—my body freezes up. My feet don't want to move, and I feel awful!" I asked Simon if he ever felt that same way in school, and he said, "Yeah, when the teacher calls on me. I hate answering questions in class."

I knew that Simon's mother was bringing him to me specifically to address reading, so I used his comment to create a bridge from sports to academics. I said, "I'm collecting stories on the relationship between soccer skill and reading. Would you be willing to give me a sample of your reading before we do the soccer balance?" He agreed, and I pulled out an age-appropriate book. He read slowly and without expression.

Simon's balance included several Brain Gym movements as well as Dennison Laterality Repatterning. In his post-check, he easily caught the pillow I tossed to him and said, "I could actually see it coming toward me!" This time, when Simon walked the length of my office, there was a spring in his step and a smile on his face. When we re-checked reading, his voice was more confident and he read with expression—and a big grin.

Simon's soccer game definitely improved. He could now fluidly manage the ball when it came toward him. And, almost immediately, he became more comfortable with being called on in class. This was the beginning of a big shift for him academically; within four weeks, his grades went from Ds to Bs.

What had been the source of Simon's blocks in academics and soccer? We may never know. The previous chapters of this book describe the many ways in which lack of neural patterning, infant reflex issues, and learned compensations may contribute to performance blocks. One thing I love about the balance process is that we don't have to identify just where the block comes from. Often, if we just add integrating movement to our day, or use Edu-K balancing to move toward our goals, the mind-body system does all the rest.

What kind of physical coordination goals can people balance for?

From whole-body movement to fine-motor control, Brain Gym helps improve coordination and skill, through goals such as these:

I kick the ball where I want it to go.

I always know where my teammates are on the playing field.

I keep my eye on the ball.

I *enjoy* my sports participation.

I easily balance on my skateboard.

I quickly learn new dance steps.

I coordinate both hands as I play piano.

My fingers type accurately while I look at the text I'm copying.

I write clearly and on the line.

I shift gears fluidly while I drive.

I safely chop vegetables as I cook.

Once the goal is identified, we can move forward with the rest of the balance and make dynamic change!

The psychology of sports

The world of professional athletic coaching is beginning to adopt Brain Gym tools and techniques. It helps athletes hone their skills, as well as the mental game that can be a bigger challenge than the physical one!

Rachael Grant Dixon is a sports psychology consultant, as well as head coach for boys' volleyball at a high school in San Diego, California. She uses Brain Gym tools extensively with her clients and students, many of whom are working at the highest levels of amateur (school, regional, Olympic) competition in a variety of sports.

She says, "I graduated with a master's degree in kinesiology, with an emphasis on sports psychology, and yet I still felt there was something missing. For example, I could see athletes' pre-competition anxiety (mind) and understood just what was happening to their coordination and performance (body), but I didn't have the right techniques to deal with it. I was frustrated, since I wasn't as effective as I instinctively knew I could be. When I came across Brain Gym, it brought both worlds together for me."

Now Rachael brings Brain Gym movements and Edu-K balancing into her work with athletes at every level, teaching them to be self-sufficient in their use of these activities. She says, "When athletes ask, 'Can you help me?' I reply, 'I can give you tools to help yourself.' The power is in them, not me. They have the tools to overcome adversity or blocks; they have the power to do it."

She leads her high-school volleyball team through Brain Gym movements and sees the difference they make, and so do the athletes themselves. Rachael says, "At competitions, without me saying anything at all, my boys will be on the sidelines standing in Hook-ups. They know others may think they don't look 'cool,' but they realize that it helps them stay calm, and then they play better. They don't care why; they just care that it works."

Rachael regularly leads her athletes through mental imagery exercises, which she finds are even more effective if they sit in Hook-ups and then hold their Positive Points throughout. One day, she and her volleyball team were finishing the last practice before departing for a very important semi-final match against a top-ranked team. She was walking toward the door when one of her players said, "Coach, don't go yet! We haven't done our brain stuff!" She was surprised, since this particular boy's body language had never shown that he appreciated Brain Gym. Of course, she returned and didn't leave until they all felt mentally prepared. It should be noted—they won that semi-final match.

Rachael says, "With my team, I don't often have time for formal balances, so I'll simply have each player contribute a word to a group goal on the whiteboard in our training room; they'll add such things as *focus*, *control*, or *communication*. Sometimes we don't even have time to write out goals, so I tell everyone to simply think of something they want to do better personally, or I provide an image for the team as a whole, such as working in a unified way. Then we do a quick Dennison Laterality Repatterning and go out and play—better and better.

"One of the things I love about Brain Gym is that athletes can use it 'on the fly' when they're out in the field. These athletes are performing at an elite level, and they don't have time to come to my office and chat about every issue. Brain Gym is something they can do quickly and independently. And they do. One day I got a text message from Robbie, who was away participating in the boys' volleyball Junior Olympics. He wrote, 'Coach, I'm so glad you taught me the brain stuff—it works!' That, to me, was awesome, since I could tell he'd been using these tools all on his own."

Balancing for performance

In Rachael's consulting work with individual athletes, she can take the time to support them in going deeper, to overcome specific blocks to performance.

Gianna was new to Brain Gym, but she was concerned about a specific coordination issue and allowed her mother to talk her into attending one of Rachael's workshops on mental skills and then a private session. As a middle blocker in volleyball, Gianna's job was to continually move left and right along the net to block the opponents' incoming ball, but she was confounded by her lack of coordination in managing this lateral movement. In her balance pre-check, Rachael observed in Gianna what she called a "delayed reaction time" that kept her from being able to get where she needed to be with split-second accuracy. Gianna's learning menu called for Dennison Laterally Repatterning, plus a few other Brain Gym movements.

Rachael said, "When I started leading Gianna in the steps of DLR, she looked at me like I was just nuts. I told her, 'You need to just trust me and then we'll do the pre-activity again.'" After this process was complete, Gianna again executed her typical middle-blocker moves and was astonished: "Wow! What a difference!" And Rachael could see it too: Gianna now had total freedom to move laterally, and the difference was immediately evident in her game.

Another client, Sarah, one of the top 100 college-recruited athletes in California, suddenly was struggling to execute her volleyball serves during games. It was bad enough when she lost confidence in herself; when her teammates and coach lost faith in her, she was devastated—and embarrassed. "Rachael," she said, "why am I not serving well?" She really wanted to know. Together they created a goal for Sarah to "get out of her thinking mind and be confident."

In Edu-K, movements may be done on one's own in the days after a session to reinforce the integration process and are called "homeplay" (as opposed to home*work*).

When Sarah did a sample serve as a pre-check, her eyes were down, her whole body language reflecting lack of motivation. Her learning menu called for a modified Total Core Repatterning, after which her body language was still somewhat the same, but her panic about this challenge had grown into true resolve to overcoming it; she agreed to do Brain Gym movements on her own in the following days.

Almost immediately, Sarah was competing at her best again. She said, "Yeah, I went back and knew I could serve—I knew I could do it." And she did.

Tools for self-management

Rachael tells the story of another athlete who made an amazing shift from constantly blaming others to taking ownership of his own growth and change:

"Mark came for a Brain Gym session to address the aggressive, emotional outbursts he'd been having on the basketball court. He was constantly blaming other people for his own lack of coordination and poor shooting. Full of excuses for his on-court behavior, he showed little regard for how his actions affected others, and his coach had no option but to remove him from games. Now, Mark wanted me to fix his attitude so he could keep his emotions under control.

"He spent the better part of thirty minutes going on and on about basketball, his team, his coach, and all his problems on the court. Throughout it all, I began to suspect that his emotional outbursts had nothing to do with basketball, but I wasn't quite prepared for what happened next. I asked him, 'Mark, what do you really want? If you want to improve your behavior, what would your goal be?' I gave him a few minutes to think about it silently and then I handed him a marker and asked him to write his goal on the whiteboard. I was completely taken aback: He'd written 'To easily receive love and feel happy.'

"It all came down to the basic human feelings he was ready to have come into his life. We balanced for his goal, and he felt wonderful when we were finished. He left my office with a smile on his face, ready to come back for another session. I didn't 'fix' his problem; I showed him he had the power to fix it himself."

More on the mental game

What had been the source of Mark's challenges? Again, we may never know—and it really doesn't matter. What matters is that he was able to change his behavior. However, sometimes during the balance process, we may gain insight into a past incident or circumstance that's subtly playing itself out in our current sports performance. Here's one such story:

Lloyd enjoys fencing for both exercise and recreation, and he had advanced to where he had achieved national standing in his classification. Yet, despite his skill, he could never seem to win against his toughest opponents. He came for a balance session to address this significant obstacle. He said, "I'll do great in competition, until I'm on the verge of actually winning my final matches. Then something pulls me back, and my opponent scores the last points."

We talked a bit about this issue, and then Lloyd mused, "I think it all boils down to this: When I was young, the people who were considered 'winners' in my world were very unpleasant—actually, one in particular was quite merciless. I think I have a feeling deep inside that if I become a winner, I'll end up that way as well." Together we created a goal: "I retain my sense of integrity and still win."

Lloyd's pre-check for this balance was quite revealing. He chose to role-play the last moments of a fencing competition against a skilled competitor, pausing and strategically lunging forward again and again as if holding a fencing saber in his hand. He said, "I'm moving, but my brain is whispering in the background, 'Don't be too good!' I can feel myself losing energy and focus."

We continued with Lloyd's balance, which included Dennison Laterality Repatterning and a few other Brain Gym activities. When these were complete, Lloyd felt much more at ease. After again role-playing the last moments of a competition, he said, "Wow—that was really different. There was no sabotaging voice in my head, and I could literally see myself making point after point on my competitor."

When I saw Lloyd a few weeks later, I asked how his fencing was going. He said, "I'm noticing a significant difference in focus and determination. I still haven't won all my tournaments, but it's not because of that little sabotaging voice in my head—that's completely gone. I just need to hone my skill."

The idea of whole-brain integration has also made it into the world of professional race car driving.

The book *Inner Speed Secrets*, by Ross Bentley and Ronn Langford, grew out of the seminars and workshops they teach to high-performance race car drivers. These seminars focus on the principles of preparing the mind-body system for winning on the racetrack. They say that most race car drivers "spend serious dollars on developing the car, but they seldom spend anything on developing the driver."[1] Among the mind- and intention-building practices they recommend is "Inner Speed Secret #12: Integrate to get in the flow." What's included in this "secret"? The importance of switching on and integrating the two sides of your brain for improved coordination and perception, through activities like the Cross Crawl, Lazy 8s, and Hook-ups.

When groups do Brain Gym movements together, or participate in a balance toward a common goal, they become more integrated, both as individual players and as a team.

Kevin McCormack was head coach for the South Australia Senior Women's State Soccer Team. He states, "Our team sessions. . . . provided the extra boost we needed to reach the grand finals in the National Championship for the first time in twenty years. Players who regularly used the program were more confident and reliable in a crisis on the field. They were able to execute on the field with greater efficiency, and as an added bonus, experienced less injury. In addition, I found the team spirit that this team developed to be quite remarkable. I highly recommend [Brain Gym] as part of your program to aid coaches and players reach their highest potential."[2]

Fine-motor changes

Physical coordination also plays itself out on a smaller scale as we use our eyes and hands together for such activities as writing.

Regina came for a balance session because she had severe dysgraphia: she struggled to put her thoughts down on paper. She said, "I can go through six or seven drafts, just writing a simple note to my daughter's teacher." I could only imagine what it had taken for Regina to accomplish what she had in her professional career. Together we created the goal: "My thoughts flow onto the paper." I watched Regina struggle with a writing sample as a pre-check. She made two false starts and wrote hesitatingly, with poor handwriting.

On inspiration, I asked, "Do you ever feel coordinated with your hands?" She said, "I'm at my best when I'm decorating cakes. I have total control—very different from handwriting," and she pantomimed using both hands on the frosting bag, slowly squeezing out the words and decorations. I was struck with a thought, and said it aloud: "Are you sure you're right-handed? What if it's really your left hand that's skilled at frosting cakes?"

Regina had no memory of being forced to change from being left-handed to right-handed as a child, but she was willing to experiment. Shifting the pencil into her left hand, she wrote a bit that way. Her handwriting was shaky, but the thoughts and words emerged more rapidly; she was astonished at this difference.

The learning menu for Regina's balance called for Dennison Laterality Repatterning and then some writing, alternating back and forth between her right and left hand. When she was finished, she picked up the pencil in her right hand and wrote—a lovely, fluid sentence. "That was different!" she exclaimed, "I could actually think and write at the same time! I feel like my brain is finally talking directly to my right hand."

Regina was not actually interested in becoming a left-handed writer but certainly appreciated her newfound access to right-handed language expression.

And on an even smaller scale, coordination affects the world of those who work with minute physical movements, such as surgeons:

My ophthalmologist, Dr. Dennis Cooper, is one of the foremost eye surgeons in Scottsdale, Arizona. One day, he shared with me that while he was very comfortable and confident in the operating room, on occasion he experienced a specific challenge. He described how eye surgery involves using very tiny instruments in a confined and fragile space, with the patient's nose often getting in the way. This sometimes required that he reposition himself to address the eye from a different angle. It would be so much easier, he said, if he could simply switch his instrument to the other hand. I suggested that Edu-K balancing might help him make that kind of coordination change, and he agreed to visit my office and give it a try.

After his session, Dr. Cooper reported a significant shift: "I am amazed to see that I am now equally coordinated with either hand—the nurses even comment on it. And I always do the PACE warm-up before performing surgery just to have these skills even more available."

What's your game in life? Whether it's on the athletic field, in the classroom, or in the workplace, Brain Gym movements and balance sessions allow you to play with freedom, skill, and confidence.

Chapter 16

Brain Gym in the Classroom

As you may have noticed, the Brain Gym® program refers consistently to "the learner." While we may think of learning mostly in the context of a school environment, this term actually applies to everyone—we are all learners. Daily life involves acquiring new skills, such as mastering equipment or technology, or developing ways to handle situations. Brain Gym is beneficial for anyone to use as a means to move through new circumstances with ease.

In this chapter, however, we will focus specifically on the classroom, where we'll explore the process of introducing Brain Gym to students of all ages and share tips for using these tools to enhance learning at all levels.

Let's begin with the teacher, and see how Brain Gym can be of benefit to the leader of a busy learning community.

Brain Gym as teacher self-care

Oh, how I wish I'd known about the Brain Gym program when I was a classroom teacher—and not just for my students! I would have done various movements throughout the day, right alongside my class, to release stress and keep myself at my best. I enjoyed my years of teaching, but I certainly remember "those days" when pressures built up and my students always seemed to misbehave. Then I began to notice that when I came to school feeling happy and light, their behavior was invariably so much better. How much of

> Truly speaking, everything about Brain Gym has to do with *learning*; therefore, many of the concepts already covered in this book naturally pertain to the world of education. This chapter will revisit some of these topics and introduce new ones as well, focused now on *practical classroom application*.
>
> As you read, keep in mind that Brain Gym does not replace good teaching. Nothing replaces good teaching! Brain Gym movements and processes simply help each child take the greatest advantage of the learning opportunities all around him.

the classroom atmosphere was a direct result of the state I was in when I walked through the door?

Until I came across Brain Gym, I had no idea that such simple tools for achieving and maintaining inner balance even existed. I had lived most of my life bouncing back and forth between feeling effective and feeling stuck, not knowing there was another way to operate. Now if I feel stuck or resistant, I can do a few Brain Gym movements and get right back on track.

I recommend doing PACE, the Brain Gym warm-up, every day. When we do these movements, we're reminding ourselves that we choose inner balance, and we can act to bring that about. It's great to observe before-and-after shifts: breathing, body tension, racing thoughts—whatever presents itself to be noticed. And prepare to be surprised. I've been refining my noticing skills for years, and yet, as I finish PACE, I'll find myself breathing more deeply and think, "I really wasn't aware of that tension before, but it must have been there because I feel so much more relaxed now!" Sharing awareness like this with your students supports their growing ability to notice their own inner process.

Balanced life, balanced teacher

Teachers often discover Brain Gym as a means of helping their students, but they become even more enthusiastic about it because of how it supports them personally. They are under incredible pressure to assure adequate learning in all students (as measured by standardized test scores), not to mention all the other academic and administrative tasks they're expected to manage. A teacher's day requires focus, diplomacy, creativity, patience, perspective—all of which can vanish under stress.

And while simple use of the movements alone is very helpful for teachers, the Edu-K balance process can support them in making even deeper change. Recent clients have balanced for classroom goals such as these:

I see the best in all my students.

I stay aware of my whole class while dealing with individuals.

I efficiently handle all paperwork.

I calmly respond to "challenging" children.

I focus on one task at a time.

I flow with interruptions.

I cooperatively plan with my team.

I comfortably balance time at work and home.

If you are a teacher and begin smoothing out issues like these, you may find your days taking on a whole new dimension of ease and productivity. You can learn the process for balancing in a Brain Gym® 101 course, and if you attend with a friend or colleague, you'll have a partner with whom to practice, share, and grow as you both balance for goals that support you in your personal and professional lives.

Preparing for a good beginning

Teachers are frequently introduced to the Brain Gym program through a workshop at their school, where they experience a few key movements and learn some of the foundational concepts. Following such a workshop, many teachers are excited about bringing these tools to their students and want to begin right away. It's fine to just jump in! Share what you know, with a sense of enthusiasm and discovery, and have a good time.

If you're less certain about how to move forward, you may want to prepare a bit first. I recommend becoming familiar with the movements yourself. Make friends with them one or two at a time; see what kind of difference they make in your life. This way, you'll have your own experience to fall back on as you explain and demonstrate.

> While it's optimal to learn each movement from an instructor who can explain it fully and guide you in getting the most out of it, it's possible to extend your exploration of the twenty-six Brain Gym movements through books I've mentioned previously, such as *The Brain Gym® Teacher's Edition*, or *Hands On: How to Use Brain Gym® in the Classroom*.

And you don't need to be an expert on every movement you introduce. Make your copy of *Brain Gym® Teacher's Edition* available to your students, see what interests them—and remember: keep it fun!

Teachers who model using these movements for themselves create an environment of shared exploration and trust, rather than that of "using Brain Gym to fix kids who need help." When teachers lead by example, students are more likely to approach Brain Gym with interest and curiosity, and discover for themselves how it supports them.

You can say such things as, "I'm feeling really distracted (or upset, frustrated, lacking focus, or whatever) right now, and I can tell my body needs some movement. Let's see. . . . which one do I want?" And then simply do a movement or two, or three—whichever ones you're drawn to—until you feel back on track.

A tool for all learners

Brain Gym may appear first in special-education classrooms because they have what's sometimes described as the "greatest need and deepest pocket." And Brain Gym is indeed very effective for children who have a history of learning difficulties.

However, many high achievers (in school and in life) also benefit from Brain Gym, since they may incur a high personal cost to perform at that level. Year after year, as a classroom educator, I watched high-strung, overachieving children who were hard on themselves and often hard on others. Brain Gym gives these students the tools they need to reduce this sense of pressure and make learning more authentic and enjoyable.

And Brain Gym is valuable for all the children in between: the ones who struggle along, never quite qualifying for special help but not doing really

well, either, and the middle-of-the-road children who mostly do
just fine, and yet may find themselves stuck as they move into
new material.

It's important for us all—students, teachers, parents, adminis-
trators—to have tools that can help release stress. Then, we can
return again and again to a state that allows for full expression
of who we are—at our best.

Accepting each stage of participation

By its very nature, new learning—even of very good things—is accompanied by the stress of uncertainty. Some learners are so capable that this stress
is minor or fleeting. But if someone is in a survival state, new experiences
may seem overwhelming or even threatening; the tendency then is either to
withdraw or act out. Moving from survival to safety often requires a period
of permission to begin slowly, perhaps simply observing on the sidelines or
participating to a lesser degree.

Managing these situations calls on the teacher's ability to recognize such behaviors and provide appropriate direction. Some "survival state" children will
actually get a lot out of simply watching others do the Brain Gym movements. You could say, "It's fine to sit and watch, and imagine that you're
doing this movement, too. Can you pretend that your body is doing the Cross
Crawl (for example), even though it isn't moving?" You can plant the seeds of
inner noticing by asking, "Is today a watching day or a doing day?" Children
can also participate on the sidelines by drawing a picture of classmates doing
a particular Brain Gym movement, or simply tracing Lazy 8s as the others
complete their own activities.

Although the examples above pertain to our youngest learners, this process is
true for anyone, of any age. It's important to offer alternative activities that
are age-appropriate.

Drawing out each learner's best

For a more complete explanation of the "drawing out"
model, please see Chapter
12, "Make Lasting Change
through Brain Gym Balancing."

The word *educate* comes from the Latin *educere*, which means "to
draw out," and the most significant role of any educator is to draw
out potential from within the student: to interact in such a way that
the student takes the lead in his own learning. This is a very different process from many traditional educational practices that focus
primarily on "stamping in" the knowledge through rote learning
and drill with little positive emotional connection to the content.

By allowing the innate knowledge within each one of us to drive
the learning process, we absorb information easily, deeply, and
enjoyably. And a teacher who takes care of his or her own needs
is more capable of teaching in this way.

Part of this drawing-out model includes offering children the
opportunity to notice ways in which they may feel hesitant or

stuck, which movements they are drawn to, and how they feel after doing them. Once children are introduced to these concepts, they love using Brain Gym tools to solve their own problems, feeling creative and empowered in the process.

"Noticing" in the classroom

The most wonderful things happen when we nurture inner noticing in learners of any age: they develop self-awareness, which is the foundation for self-control and personal responsibility. Time spent cultivating this skill is rewarded as students become more thoughtful and engaged learners.

When introducing the concept of noticing to young children, it's best to begin simply, perhaps by playing observation games about things that are external and tangible. You could invite students to identify items around them that are blue, fuzzy, sharp, or heavy. Over time, you can choose a more subtle quality to search for: objects that seem comforting, delightful, complicated, or rigid.

Then this process can be brought to external body noticing. While doing Hook-ups, for example, you might say, "Which way do your ankles feel like crossing today, right over left or left over right? … Good noticing! They might be happy like that today and want to cross differently tomorrow. Won't it be interesting to see?"

As you shift to inviting noticing on the inner level, it's helpful to start by modeling it yourself, sharing with your students that you notice tension in your shoulders, you're feeling refreshed after a break, or that a story makes you feel excited, sad, or quiet inside.

> "New learning cannot occur without noticing. As toddlers learning to walk, as first graders learning to print, or as a couple learning to communicate, we will keep doing the same thing over and over until we are able to reflect on what we are doing and the effect it is having." [3]
> ~ Gail E. Dennison

To draw out this kind of internal noticing from young children, you could say: "Sometimes if we pay attention to our middle, our tummy, it will help us know how we feel inside. Do you know what it's like to have a happy tummy, or an upset, angry one? Pay attention to how your tummy feels right now… and see what happens as we go into Hook-ups." *Now pause—really pause—to allow time for inner noticing.* "Is there a difference in how your tummy feels? Does any other part of you feel different?" *Accept all answers.*

Many children are conditioned to think it's best to answer quickly, and will be hasty in their response. Over time, especially as you reinforce the concept that all answers about inner noticing are "right," children will become more introspective—and accurate.

Realize that most children (and adults as well) are not very experienced in noticing what's really going on internally. This could be because many of us have a childhood history of grown-ups telling us what we think or feel. In this way, we may have come to distrust our feelings or shut off access to them altogether. In fact, some people may not notice an inner difference after doing Brain Gym movements until they've done them over several days, in an environment where it's safe to relax and participate. Once students are more adept at noticing, you can help them recognize internal signals from their mind-body system for movement that will help them learn easily again.

> "There is no more important skill to be gained from the Brain Gym experience than noticing. Noticing, with the self-awareness and self-directed decision making that it requires, represents the optimal development of the prefrontal cortex, working in concert with the brain stem and sensory system, and is the key to high-level cognitive functioning." [4]
> ~ Paul E. Dennison

For example, when stumped on a math problem, a child might feel frustrated. Resist the temptation to say, "But that's easy," or "You know how to do that." Instead, you can invite him to put his hand on the place where he feels that frustration and ask, "Which movement is that spot asking for right now?" By supporting his inner noticing, you validate his experience of frustration and his own ability to do something about it. Over time, he will discover that he can meet his own needs without having to come to you.

You can even have children share stories about a time when they felt frustrated (or angry, confused, irritated, etc.) and used Brain Gym activities to help themselves release the feeling and return to their best learning or playing. In the beginning, some children may fabricate stories about this. This is fine; they're rehearsing how to do it in the future. Eventually, you'll see more and more children using "movement in the moment" to bring out their best—especially if they see you doing it, too!

Introducing Brain Gym to young students

What a joy it is, sharing Brain Gym with youngsters! Most often they embrace it immediately and participate enthusiastically. You may want to start slowly, introducing one activity at a time, and take two or three days for the children to become familiar with it before moving on to another.

> Paul Dennison offers his method of introducing Brain Gym movements into the classroom starting on page 188 of his book *Brain Gym® & Me: Reclaiming the Pleasure of Learning.*

Once children have learned all the steps of the PACE warm-up, you may look for various ways to bring it into your daily routine. Some teachers select a specific piece of music as the "PACE song" for the class. When the children hear it begin, they know it's time for water. As they sip the water, they rub their Brain Buttons and then move into the Cross Crawl. As the final verse of the song begins, they know to be sitting, or standing behind their chair, in Hook-ups. Children love showing that they can participate responsibly in this activity.

Variety keeps it fun!

When doing Brain Gym with children, it's important to keep things fun and lively and, as much as possible, allow elements of variety and choice.

Double Doodle Drawings

Depending on the age or nature of the class, this can be achieved by varying such things as who gets to lead the activity, what music is playing during Brain Gym time, which movements are done above and beyond PACE, and whether the students do Brain Gym as a group or independently.

Children also love expressing their natural curiosity, enthusiasm, and understanding about Brain Gym movements through the creation of skits, dances, art projects, class presentations, and more:

- What movement does this music remind you of? Let's do that movement while we listen. Does the music change? What movement should we do now?

- Can you create a Brain Gym skit, song, poem, or rap to present to your class, or to a younger class?

- Can you do Double Doodle play? Holding a marker in either hand, draw both sides of a tree (or some other object) at the same time, in mirror image to each other. Or draw identical, mirror-image forms side by side.

- Can you turn your Lazy 8s into something imaginative?

- Can you find a way to do a Brain Gym movement with a partner?

- Who can do two Brain Gym movements at one time?

- Can you stand in Hook-ups? Can you stand in Hook-ups with your eyes closed?

- Who would like to draw from this basket of Brain Gym cards and lead us in that movement?

Lazy 8s Fun

Gail Dennison has developed a one-day course titled "Double Doodle Play: A Window to Whole-Brain Vision." This course combines the Double Doodle and other movements from Brain Gym and Vision Gym® to explore and enhance visual perception and artistic expression—and to have fun!

Variety keeps children's interest alive. "When it becomes routine, it becomes boring." This is the motto of Isabel Cohen and Marcelle Goldsmith Shaman, authors of *Hands On—How to Use Brain Gym® in the Classroom*, which offers myriad ways of adapting and extending the Brain Gym movements through games, songs, raps—and more. After *Brain Gym® Teacher's Edition*, this book is a "must" for every classroom teacher or home-schooling parent who would like to add even more interest, fun, and creativity to his use of Brain Gym over time.

Movement at work in the classroom

Students need to move so they can then sit still, listen, and learn. You may soon begin to recognize wiggles and distracted behaviors as cries for activity to wake up the brain—and naturally create focus. Then you can say, "It's been a while since we've done some Brain Gym. Is your body asking for the Cross Crawl or maybe Lazy 8s?" Depending on the class or the moment, you can lead everyone in a specific movement or two, or build inner noticing and independence by saying, "You decide which one is best for you right now." Eventually, children can learn to interpret their own behaviors and help themselves with the appropriate Brain Gym activities.

When we allow students to move, especially in ways that are integrating to the brain and body, they're more prepared to take in information and make use of what they know. They're simply more capable.

Introducing Brain Gym to older students

Teens and pre-teens may approach Brain Gym differently from younger children. They appreciate understanding how the mind-body system works, how stress gets in the way of being an effective learner, and how the movements can help.

Sometimes I'll invite students to do a "Brain Gym experiment" in three steps: Notice, then Brain Gym, then Notice again. I ask them to read a bit to themselves from one of their textbooks and observe such things as whether their eyes were easily tracking left to right, what their level of focus was, and how much they understood and remembered what they read. Then I take them through the PACE warm-up, explaining a bit about how each element may be helping them learn more easily, and then have them read again. At least one student is sure to speak up and say, "Wow! I can read easier! Why is that?" This builds curiosity and interest in learning more.

To expand the lesson, I might ask about times when they've felt stuck in studying or writing a report and what the outcome was: "How long did it take? Did your test results or report turn out the way you wanted it to?" There are plenty of replies about how challenging that can be.

> A good resource for use with teens is the book *Brain Gym® for Business*. It's written for a more mature reading audience, and older students will appreciate the simple, straightforward approach to knowing which Brain Gym movements will help them with specific work tasks, as that's the main focus of this particular book.

Then I ask, "Why?" Often, at least one student replies with a quick, "Because I'm stupid." I immediately counter with, "No—you're not stupid. Your mind and body are most likely just feeling the effects of stress. It happens to everybody in one way or another, and it's not your fault." (Students have told me later—usually privately—that they were incredibly relieved when they learned this!)

And then I'll say, "What if you could just shift into easy reading, clearer writing, or remembering what you're studying? What if you could instantly improve in your favorite sport or video game? Would you be interested?" They generally are. Sometimes I share a story or two of students or athletes using Brain Gym movements and pull out my copy of *Inner Speed Secrets* by Ross Bentley and Ronn Langford, the book that shows how even race car drivers are learning integrating movements (like the Cross Crawl, Hookups, and Lazy 8s) in seminars to boost their performance on the racetrack.

Sports as the opening

If you do athletics with students of any age, you have a natural opportunity to introduce Brain Gym from the "outside in." In any sport, participants do better if they have good balance, eye-teaming skills (ball tracking), eye-hand coordination (catching, throwing, batting), and whole-body movement (running, kicking, dodging other players). In this way, we see how the fundamentals of academic agility also show up in a very physical way on the playing field. Even doing the postural checks for the three dimensions takes on a whole new meaning when the student is about to engage in a demanding physical activity and wants to be at her best.

> You can learn more about the "postural checks" in Chapter 9, "Theory in Action."

I recently did a series of classroom visits to introduce Brain Gym at a local public school. One group of special-education students, ages eleven to thirteen, started out politely disinterested. Then I began asking questions about their favorite sports (soccer, football, basketball), and we discussed how much physical stability was required for each one. I offered to show them how they could make sure they were ready for the demands of their sport and taught them the postural checks for the three dimensions: side to side, up and down, front to back. They were amazed to see the different ways they were tippy or otherwise out of balance. Then I took them through the PACE movements, and we did a recheck: Every student found he was now more stable. Then came the comments: "Wow, I feel so much more solid and in control! I can just do these funny movements and be better at soccer? Cool!"

At this point, I shared how, when we're in *physical balance*, things we do with our *mind* are easier. And another student said, "You mean—I can do this before MATH?" I joined the whole class in laughter.

The teacher of this class now has a group of enthusiastic Brain Gym users. She can come into the room and say, "You have five minutes to check your three dimensions, notice what's 'switched off,' and bring everything back on." The students all stand and do their postural checks with much concentration and noticing and then do the activities they can tell will be helpful. They call it their "secret weapon" in both sports and school.

Making it their own

Especially in the upper grades, it's important for students to see Brain Gym as a tool that they can choose to use for themselves. Once they are familiar with the movements, they can learn to observe ways in which they feel momentarily "switched off" and use Brain Gym to shift back into gear—for reasons they really care about.

Stepping into an eighth-grade classroom to deliver something to the teacher, I observed a student get up from her desk while everyone was reading silently. She walked to the back of the room and did a few Brain Gym movements. Passing by me on her way back to her seat, she caught my eye and softly said with a smile, "I couldn't read! But I bet that helped." She slipped back into her seat and went right back to reading. I loved that this teacher had offered Brain Gym tools to her students, and they were *using* them. This approach may take a shift in teaching style and classroom management, but more often than not, students show that they can handle this kind of responsibility.

Inviting participation

As a teacher, I have seen that while most young people are interested in and curious about Brain Gym, some are a bit self-conscious or reluctant initially to participate. My philosophy is that it's always a choice; however, it may be appropriate to encourage such students to at least experience what these movements have to offer.

It's fine to modify Brain Gym activities for learners of any age. Sometimes I teach "stealth" variations that they can do without drawing attention to themselves:

- Hook-ups can be done without bringing the arms up to the chest, leaving crossed wrists on the lap. Or arms can cross over the chest, hands under armpits.

- Fingers can casually rub one Brain Button at a time.

- The Cross Crawl can be done while seated, alternating hand to opposite (slightly raised) knee.

- An almost invisible Cross Crawl can be done by moving one index finger and the opposite foot or toe!

- Lazy 8s can be traced on a student's leg or doodled on notepaper; the student can follow tiny Lazy 8s with his nose, or envision and track a large Lazy 8 with his eyes.

- Fingers can be on the Positive Points while a student leans his head on his hand, in a resting position, elbow on the table.

- A quick massage of the shoulder, moving the head a bit, has many of the benefits of The Owl.

- A simple seated Calf Pump can be achieved by stretching one leg out straight and flexing and releasing the foot.

Once students know more Brain Gym movements, they may invent their own Brain Gym adaptations.

> "The Brain Gym work is based on the premise that, when teaching fully engages the sensory system rather than compromising it, conscious, aware noticing becomes available and we can take charge of our own learning. I see learning as that magical thing that takes place in a split second and changes us forever." [5]
> ~ Paul Dennison

You may also solicit their feedback by asking directly: "How would you suggest we teach Brain Gym to teenagers so they feel okay doing it?" The trick is to know your students and what's likely to be accepted.

And be aware that it could look like some students aren't paying attention at all, but they're really reaping great benefits from what you're explaining. Here's an email from a high school resource teacher:

I had a very "hyper" tenth-grade girl in my room the other day. I showed her how to do PACE, but I thought she wasn't paying attention because she was so angry about something going on with her friend in the next classroom. I looked over a few moments later and there she was, practicing the PACE movements on her own. She said, "Hey, Mrs. Curtis. This funny stuff totally calmed me down!" She was right.

A bit later, I noticed that another student was really stressing about a history exam. I asked him if he would like to try something that would help him study and remember things for the test. He was reluctant until that same girl explained the PACE movements to him and taught him how to do them. Now they both use PACE every day!

An effective classroom management tool

Brain Gym movements are a wonderful way to support young people in gaining self-control. Many teachers tell me that even the most active children in their room have learned to recognize when they need Hook-ups and take a moment to do this. When students aren't successfully managing their own behavior, a creative teacher can bring a bit of Brain Gym into the situation.

Many classrooms adopt the "two-minute guideline." Children who have been in a scuffle or disagreement drink water and then sit in Hook-ups for two minutes; then they are able to discuss the situation rationally with their teacher, and with each other.

> When children (or adults) are in the stress of the moment, they are incapable of seeing another person's point of view. After they've "gotten out of their brain stem," they have more access to reason, and so are more able to discuss the situation responsibly.

Some teachers find that when they stand quietly in Hook-ups, everyone ends up following along. The whisper goes around the room: "Mr. Baker is in Hook-ups!" Soon all the children are in Hook-ups as well, and the teacher has gotten everyone's attention without raising his voice—or even saying a word.

Brain Gym consultant Jeanette Franck gave a Career Day presentation to six groups of students in grades seven through twelve. She shares:

Hook-ups Part I

> My first five groups of students were polite, and we had an enjoyable interchange of demonstrations, questions, and answers. Then, the seventh graders entered the room! I stood there wide-eyed, observing how the group jumped around, chattered loudly, and noisily found seats. With the upper grades, I had quietly waited for them to settle down. I soon realized, however, that this technique was not going to work with the seventh graders. As I began to speak, I noticed that some students were tilting their desks, while others were moving their arms and bodies all around. Questions flew from every direction, but no one paused for an answer to be given.
>
> I suddenly realized what I needed to do first. I asked them if they would like to do some exercises for their brains, called Brain Gym. They were excited about doing anything that gave them freedom to move! As I introduced them to PACE, I explained the benefits of each element—but I purposely omitted the fact that the activities might calm them down.
>
> When we finished, I scanned the room. All the students were sitting quietly and attentively. Then I deliberately glanced at the teacher. His mouth was literally hanging open as he, too, scanned the room. He turned toward

me with a pleasantly puzzled expression on his face and asked, "What did you do?" I simply responded, "Isn't Brain Gym wonderful?"

I shifted my attention back to the seventh graders and resumed my presentation, problem-free. Before the class got up to leave, one young student politely raised his hand and said, "Excuse me, Mrs. Franck. Before we go, could you show us a technique to get our wild energy back?" I just laughed and replied, "Not today."

Out the door they filed, a lot calmer than when they came in. Brain Gym had turned a potentially frustrating session into an experience that was the most enjoyable one of the day for me![6]

Positive attitudes emerge

"Classroom teachers tell us that, when the Brain Gym system is put into practice, children and teachers . . . enter a play space in which all feel themselves to be on the same team as they enjoy the game of learning." [7]
~ Gail E. Dennison

Shifts in attitude naturally come along with shifts in ability. When a child can actually do what the teacher's been asking her to do, she is likely to be much more willing to do it. Teachers often report significant improvements in student behavior when they begin using Brain Gym movements regularly. Here's an example of a shift not only in learning and behavior, but the entire atmosphere of the classroom:

I teach a self-contained seventh- and eighth-grade special-education class in a middle school. These students are so far behind in academics and have such poor focus that they cannot be in a regular classroom; most have a variety of emotional problems as well, which used to cause regular flare-ups during the day. This year, after taking the Brain Gym course, I taught my students all the Brain Gym movements, a few at a time, and explained how and when to use them to get "unstuck" in their studies. They started spontaneously choosing to use these movements at various times of the day to help themselves when they wanted to do better. Their homework and test scores started improving in all areas: math, reading, science, and history.

But I was amazed to realize the other difference that occurred this year. My students (many of whom I knew well, as they had been in this special class last year also) were suddenly shifting their attitude and getting along so well together. They cooperated in ways I'd never seen before, and the typical nagging and teasing almost vanished. They really became a learning team and seemed to enjoy the victories and gains of their classmates as much as they enjoyed their own.

Beyond the movements, and into the balance process

Simply adding a bit of Brain Gym to the school day will be the perfect mind-body boost for learning, achievement, and attitude. I have seen children's skills and behavior improve tremendously through consistent use of Brain Gym movements in this way. However, some students have more significant challenges and will benefit more deeply from the Edu-K five-step balance process. These sessions can be done individually, in small groups, or with an entire class.

Through Brain Gym, learners can address the many diverse challenges they may experience at any age. Here are some academic goals my young clients have addressed:

I read easily.

I easily scan for the important details.

I remember which way to make "b" and "d."

I keep my things organized.

I hear what the teacher says.

I relax and feel fine when it's test time.

I quickly learn my math facts.

I take notes and still hear the lecture.

I get along with my teacher.

And students may also choose to balance for behavior goals:

I stop and think.

I say things at the right time.

I share nicely with others.

I wait my turn at games.

I remember to use Hook-ups when I'm angry or sad.

I notice my feelings and talk about them at the right time.

Group balances in a school setting

It's possible to do a whole-group process in just a few minutes, to prepare for any specific activity, such as math, writing, spelling, or testing.

I visited a fifth-grade special-education classroom just as the students were returning from the library. These children all had considerable reading challenges, so I asked the teacher if she'd like me to lead everyone through a quick balance for reading.

Working in the short time I had available, I simply asked, "Who would like to be able to read their book really easily and remember what you read?" Every hand shot up. This essentially set our goal for our session.

I asked everyone to open his book and read a bit to himself. Most of the children nervously flipped from page to page; eyes darted about all over the reading material; chairs scraped the floor as feet fidgeted under desks.

Then I led the class through several Brain Gym activities, starting with the PACE warm-up, plus Calf Pump and Lazy 8s. It was the first time they'd ever done Brain Gym, so I explained a bit as we went along. We didn't have long, so those few activities had to be enough for the moment.

To conclude, I had them read again. They sat so still, and all we heard was the sound of pages slowly turning for a good five minutes! The teacher had never seen these children read so enthusiastically.

Balancing one-on-one in school

With creative planning, it's possible for even a classroom teacher with a room full of students to find a way to accomplish quick sessions with individual children.

A teacher who had taken the Brain Gym® 101 course decided to schedule five minutes each day for balance work with one child at a time. Her goal was eventually to lead all of her students through Dennison Laterality Repatterning (DLR). Luis was a fourth grader who knew some of his addition facts but consistently failed the timed tests that were part of the weekly curriculum. He never got more than a few correct out of thirty, no matter how often this teacher worked with him or how much he practiced.

One day, the teacher noticed that Luis had correctly answered seventeen out of thirty on his most recent test! Amazed, she looked back in her records and found that she had done a DLR with Luis just six days before, as he focused on his goal of "easily understanding math." On his next timed test, Luis correctly answered twenty-nine out of thirty, and after that, he never scored less than thirty out of thirty. He began asking when he could take another timed test! Luis also began enjoying addition games, even finding ways to add to their complexity, making them more challenging for himself.

What a remarkable shift for Luis. And all because his teacher set aside a few minutes of her classroom time to take him through this powerful, integrating balance process.

The possibilities

What would change in children's school performance if teachers brought Brain Gym movements and processes into student activities on a daily basis? What if a trained professional on each campus could facilitate balances with children to help them not just manage or cope, but overcome blocks, and blossom?

Think about the stories you've read in this book, about students who experienced such remarkable changes using Brain Gym. Once they were operating in an integrated state, and their abilities were more available, their grades improved *and so did their behavior*. They were finally able to do what they'd been trying to do all along: Read. Comprehend. Feel good about themselves. We're all capable of this, and we all deserve this.

A bit of Brain Gym is so easy to use and incorporate into a classroom day. I invite you to start simply, and see where inspiration—and integration—takes you.

Chapter 17
Brain Gym as "Un-Therapy"

Sometimes people ask, "Are you a therapist? And is Brain Gym® therapy?" Brain Gym and Edu-K can have a huge impact on how we experience many aspects of our lives, but are not therapy in the typical sense of the word. In fact, I sometimes call Edu-K balances "un-therapy."

Un-therapy? What do you mean?

Traditional therapy is extremely helpful for many people. A skilled therapist can help us identify core issues, clarify where we want to take action, suggest means toward new behaviors, and support us as we go through the process of making change.

I've explored a number of different kinds of therapies throughout my life and have benefited from most of them. However, what I realize now is this: Edu-K balancing offers a means to faster, more focused, and recognizable change than any other process I've ever experienced.

In an Edu-K balance session, the point is not to analyze the block a person is experiencing. It's not necessary to know what kind of trauma (childhood or otherwise) created a given pattern of behavior. In fact, the client and I discuss his target issue only for the purposes of clarifying it, so he can develop the language he'd like to use in his goal. Choosing movements from a learning menu becomes his own personal journey from "stuck" to "ready" as he creates new patterns that are active and available for him to call on when the need arises.

Some people choose to combine Edu-K sessions with traditional therapy. On-going dialog with a skilled therapist may lead to clarity on core life issues, which can then be targeted in the balance process, increasing the benefits of both approaches.

What kinds of personal changes can people make?

I have seen people make shifts in areas they never thought possible. Attitudes, reactions, fears—these all can be related in some way to compensation patterns we've taken on through stress or trauma. And these are areas for which Edu-K balancing is extremely effective. Here are some personal goals for which my clients have balanced:

I flow easily with life's events.

I see the best in myself.

I take time to hear what my children are saying.

I comfortably experience heights/tight spaces/airplane travel.

I deal positively with _____'s temper.

I move confidently into my new job.

I relax and do my best.

I take time each day to nurture myself.

I am immune to negativity.

I stand up for myself diplomatically.

As we make changes such as these, we smooth out the wrinkles in the fabric of our lives, allowing us to move forward more comfortably and competently in relationships, self-care, and sense of personal direction.

A client named Bradley said that he wanted to get over a feeling of frustration and limitation that seemed to permeate his life. He never found success in any of his career choices, and he enumerated the many areas where he felt dysfunctional. Rather than engage in prolonged conversation about all these issues, I gently asked, "If you could make one shift that would change this pattern, what would you want it to be?" He paused for a moment—actually, a long moment—and then said, "I want to believe in myself." So there it was, the perfect goal for his balance: "I believe in myself."

Bradley's learning menu included a variety of Brain Gym activities. At one point, while he was doing some Cross Crawl, he remembered an event from his teenage years. One of his best friends, a very adventurous and outgoing boy whom everyone liked, had died in a climbing accident. At age fifteen, Bradley had been one of the pallbearers at his funeral.

"Wow," he said, sitting down. "I haven't thought about that in the longest time. What do you think it means?" I didn't reply. Bradley thought for quite a while, moving into his next chosen movement, Hook-ups. Finally he said, "He was so alive, and all of a sudden he was gone. After the funeral, I just quit functioning. . . . You know, I think I decided right then that life is risky, and I shouldn't plan on much." We discussed the impact that a lesson like that could have had on his life. Bradley said he could see how that may have prevented him from committing to a job or a sense of future.

When our conversation ended, Bradley looked quite different. He was breathing much more easily. His walk had a quicker, springy step full of energy and intention. His face was softer and more relaxed. Now when he stated his goal—"I believe in myself"—it had the ring of truth and personal conviction.

It took some time for the entirety of Bradley's shift to fall into place, but he eventually enrolled at a local university. With a new sense of purpose and dedication, he earned a degree in landscape architecture and is now building a career he enjoys.

Did I know about Bradley's childhood trauma and construct a session to re-solve it? Not at all. The trauma around that memory was simply there, ready to be released when the door was opened through focused intention, sup-ported by a powerful vehicle for change: the intelligence of Bradley's own mind-body system at work.

It wasn't even necessary for Bradley to remember this event. People frequently go through the steps of a balance without any particular memory or strong emotion arising. This process simply supports them in creating new response patterns and retiring the ones that no longer serve them, regardless of wheth-er the old memories surface.

This moment, right now

My belief is that one of the most powerful aspects of the Edu-K balance pro-cess is simply this: it keeps us in the present moment. If we're analyzing or regretting, we're in the past. If we're fearful or anxious, we're in the future. Yet, the only point where we can make internal change is this moment, right now.

That's not to say that analyzing and planning aren't good, in their place. But when they involve elements of self-criticism and defeatist attitudes, we may become immobilized, unable to see the possibilities of life. Doing integrating activities can move us out of a frozen, fear-based state and return us to the present moment, where we can make new choices.

The language of movement

Movement dissolves fear and the trigger of negative emotions—then we can be rational. The emotional component of any block we're experiencing is a product of our limbic system, and the survival component is a product of the brain stem.

It's important to realize that the limbic system and the brain stem *do not understand language*: not English, not Chinese, not French—none of them. However, they do speak the language of movement. Movement gets us out of our brain stem or limbic system, where we are confined to reacting, and into our neocortex, where we can respond and have access to conscious choices.

Hook-ups and
Positive Points

While physical touch of this type may be very therapeutic, it is important to adhere to any guidelines that apply in schools, agencies, etc. I could have invited Brooke to hold her own Positive Points after concluding her Hook-ups.

One day I worked with Brooke, a fifth grader. Very needy and emotionally immature, she had attached herself to the school nurse and found reasons to appear at her door several times a day. The day I worked with Brooke, she'd found out that the nurse would be at another school next year. She was distraught and couldn't stop sobbing—in fact, she'd been in tears for hours—and the drama all tumbled out as we began our time together.

Rather than engage her in conversation, I said, "I see you're upset. Let's do some things that will help." I invited her to sip some water and then sit in Hook-ups. I received her permission to place my fingertips on her forehead and gently held her Positive Points while she talked about how sad she was that the nurse was going away. Her tears slowed down, and she began talking about how scared she was about next year. "Who will I talk to? Who will help me?" At this point, I said, "You can think about that while we do our next movement. What shall it be?" She reluctantly stood and began a slow Cross Crawl. We did a few other Brain Gym activities, each with its own powerfully integrating effect.

Before long, Brooke noticed a book on the table and mentioned that she'd read it and how good it was. We began talking about books and then movies. Soon we were laughing about a TV show we'd both seen. Fifteen minutes after arriving in tears, this girl was talking calmly and easily. Finally, I asked, "What will you do next year when the nurse is at another school?" She was quiet for a moment. "Well," she said, "nobody stays anywhere forever. We might move this summer, too. I guess I'll find a friend wherever I am."

I didn't know Brooke or her history, or what other issues she was dealing with. However, I know what I observed in my few moments with her: a shift from uncontrollable tears to calm and reasonable. I didn't tell her to stop crying. I didn't tell her she was wrong to feel sad. I didn't try to "fix" her.

Indeed, it's not anyone's responsibility to "fix" anyone else, *nor can they*. Integrating movement, touch, and laughter kept returning Brooke to the present moment. And it's in the present moment that we truly heal ourselves.

Chapter 18
Brain Gym and Relief from Stress, Distress, and Trauma

Stressful situations arise in everyone's life: from traffic jams and difficult colleagues to financial challenges, separation or divorce, and illness. Stress arises in children's lives as well, through failure in school, peer issues, family disruptions, or other conflicts. When such stresses are ongoing, they may evolve into *distress*, which could be defined as suffering caused by grief, anxiety, or unhappiness. Distress over time, or with sudden impact, may result in *trauma*: severe emotional shock, often with long-lasting psychological effects.

As a Brain Gym® consultant, I have worked with many clients who have described traumas of one kind or another, often a vivid event or period of time that significantly changed how they lived their lives. In this chapter, we'll look at the subject of trauma more specifically, exploring how it registers in the body and how Brain Gym movements and processes help provide relief from it.

The effects of trauma

Our reaction to an event is determined solely by the meaning it holds for us. The death of a grandparent, for example, may have little impact on one child but be devastating to her sibling. Events that look inconsequential to an outside observer can have deep and damaging effects on the person involved. For example, a sarcastic comment to a sensitive child, meant to be humorous, could profoundly affect him for years to come.

Some distressing experiences (perhaps those that are minor in nature) may truly be healed by time. Some we think are resolved,

Please note: While many people experience relief from stress, distress, and trauma as a result of the goals they balance for, the Brain Gym®/Edu-K program is educational in nature and not therapy; it is not a substitute for appropriate medical treatment. Anyone experiencing extreme symptoms should seek help from a professional who offers specialized trauma-recovery services.

but they're only hiding as we create and refine techniques for burying or ignoring them. Putting our emotional reactions on hold is actually a very important short-term coping strategy: it allows us to do what must be done in the moment. But the temptation is strong never to return to finish our healing process.

"Forgotten" or simply unrecognized trauma can be at the root of many of our conditioned responses. For example, I became surprisingly emotional when doing life insurance and estate planning with my husband; then I realized that this topic was touching strongly on a childhood memory from more than forty years prior: the shock of my father's sudden death when I was eleven years old, and the challenges my family experienced afterward. It's important to recognize trauma in our life for what it is, or was, and address it consciously, at the right time.

Calling on Brain Gym

September 11, 2001, was a day of devastating terrorist strikes in the United States. I was in Germany, enjoying the last afternoon of a course that followed the 2001 Brain Gym® International Conference, at the moment we heard the news.

We were shocked, confused, upset—and had only the sketchiest details. In class, we instinctively began using Hook-ups, the Positive Points, and other Brain Gym processes as we supported each other. Brain Gym tools may seem so simple, but as we shared them, a spirit of calm began to fill the room. The confusion and grief were still there, but the tremendous sense of anxiety and shock slowly began to diminish.

When class ended, I returned to my hotel room. My husband had arrived just the day before, to join me for a post-conference travel holiday, and together we saw it all on television: the awful destruction. Thousands dead. My heart ached as the impact of the day's events sank in.

I was grateful that I had Brain Gym movements and Edu-K balancing to fall back on. Every time I felt overwhelmed by what was happening, I'd go through the PACE process, often concluding by sitting in Hook-ups for perhaps fifteen minutes or more. I'd feel tension slowly release and a more relaxed state begin to return; I'd feel my thoughts calm down and emotional numbness abate as my breathing deepened and the awareness of my own heart increased. Sometimes I'd lead myself through an entire Brain Gym balance with the goal of being in the present moment: "I am here, now, and I am safe."

The travel that my husband and I managed to do seemed quite surreal: driving through vineyards and touring castles, knowing that the wreckage of the World Trade Center was still smoldering back home. The fantasy of visiting exotic places, juxtaposed with the reality of world events, became an emotional roller coaster.

Finally, the airlines were operating again, and we were on a flight from Germany to New York. Distress and pain were all around, in the faces of airline employees and fellow travelers. It was a palpable force in the very air of that flight.

I kept calling on my Brain Gym tools to relieve the stress of the moment and return to as balanced a state as was possible: doing PACE as I waited in the airport, Hook-ups and Positive Points in my seat on the airplane, and other movements as I stood to stretch during the flight. I did them *all*.

I was relieved to finally be home, but then was faced with the incessant media coverage of ongoing events. Everywhere I turned, news reports refreshed the trauma in my mind-body system. I turned again and again to my Brain Gym tools. It's not that Brain Gym made my days easy or comfortable; as for everyone, it was truly a time of shock and mourning. But I was grateful for the way it allowed me to deal with the emotions that came up and remain as clear as possible.

Moving out of trauma

As we have discussed throughout this book, we are most at ease when our main brain structures are able to share information with one another. But under stress, our mind-body system automatically prepares for self-preservation: less vital resources are switched off and energy is routed to the brain stem. Access to formal reasoning vanishes and we become hyper-alert, our nerves on edge.

The strong emotional component provided by the limbic system bonds to the memory of where we are and what we are doing at the time of a traumatic event. The entire picture of this moment becomes vividly established in our body's memory, ready to emerge when we're reminded of the situation. This process is intended to protect us, so we can avoid repeating the injury. The challenge comes when the pattern outlives its usefulness, and we are left with an automatic stress response that no longer serves us.

When we are faced with a stress reaction and call on Brain Gym movements or Edu-K balancing, we help our mind-body system return to a state of greater ease. Taking time to deeply notice these changes reinforces our awareness that a new, integrated pattern has been established. If the emotion resurfaces, we can address it again with Brain Gym movements or balancing. Eventually, our impulse to return to the old, un-integrated pattern begins to fade.

Sharing tools that help

About six weeks after September 11, I was at a conference where many of the participants were from New York City. Over lunch on the first day, a few of us began talking about where we had been at the time of the terrorist attack. One Manhattan resident spoke of her apartment being enveloped by the billowing, choking dust; another described hearing the awful sounds of disaster: screams, sirens, and more. One had lost a dear friend in the buildings' collapse. Many talked of the emotional toll from watching the nonstop news coverage.

One person now couldn't sleep; another kept feeling a continual knot in his stomach. Our conversation brought up the pain that I was still carrying about this event. A familiar grief crept back into my heart and my muscles tightened: I had vividly "called up" the trauma pattern that became established that awful day.

Hook-ups Part I

Hook-ups Part II

At the height of our conversation, I found myself leading everyone into Hook-ups and then Positive Points. We all became quite still. Before long, I heard the sounds of deeper breathing in those around me and noticed that I was breathing more deeply, as well. Shoulders gently dropped as everyone began to release long-held tension. Furrows on foreheads began to soften as faces relaxed, and I noticed that my own thoughts had slowed down. I could now feel my heart beating, and it felt soft, yet strong and available. Looking around, it was clear to me that a significant shift had occurred.

The Positive Points

At this point, I suggested that everyone think again about the events of September 11. It took some time for people to speak. One woman finally shared, "I can remember what happened that day, but it's more distant. It's like it was much longer ago." Another person said, "I can think about it and still breathe. This is different." A third said, "I keep looking around inside for that sharp pain, and it's just not there. I don't get it."

Severe post-traumatic stress should be treated appropriately. Depending on the individual and the circumstance, this could include a combination of psychotherapy and Brain Gym sessions or other interventions as well. But you may find that Brain Gym techniques alone are very helpful in profoundly reducing the immediate effects of trauma.

The next day the "sleepless" woman shared that she had actually slept through the night. "I lay down and just drifted right off to sleep. I feel rested for the first time in weeks." Another person reported he wasn't "carrying such a heavy burden anymore." Everyone shared that they were experiencing a positive change. One man had actually called his wife and described Hook-ups over the phone so she could use it herself and share it with their children. Several people reported how much it helped to use Brain Gym when the old feelings came up again (as they will do).

Clearly, the events of September 11 were extraordinary, and nothing is a "magic fix." We talked about how trauma affects us on many levels and that we may need to address it over time, through whatever modalities work best for each of us.

If my telling of this story about September 11 has brought up unpleasant memories for you, you might like to experience these same Brain Gym movements now.

> ▶ Notice first how you feel when you recall the events of that day. Then, gently move into Hook-ups. Become aware of anything shifting or releasing: your level of muscle tension, depth of breathing, whatever presents itself to be noticed. At some point, you may feel ready to move to Part Two of Hook-ups. After a while, bring your fingertips to your forehead and gently hold your Positive Points. What do you notice now when you recall the events of that day? You can repeat this process as often as you like.

Sometimes, just these few movements can make a significant difference.

An organic intervention

> A teacher I know quite well is trained in Brain Gym. On the morning of September 11, just after the news of the attacks had been announced in her school, she went to as many classrooms as she could and spoke about what had occurred. Many children talked about how upset and fearful they were. Then this teacher led the children in Hook-ups and Positive Points. In every class she visited, the children said they felt a lot better after doing this. One boy said, "I was really scared. But my tummy settled right down." The teacher encouraged the students to use these Brain Gym movements any time they wanted to, and to teach their family members what they'd learned.

I believe there would be less residual stress stored in our bodies if we used techniques like these as soon as possible after any traumatic event. Doing something helpful doesn't take much; this teacher spent perhaps fifteen minutes in each classroom. I can only imagine what the benefit would have been if every teacher in that school (in our city? in our country?) had known about these simple techniques and used them right away with his or her class, and from time to time after that, when discussing this horrifying day. We can't foresee all the challenging experiences that life may hold for us, but by addressing trauma promptly with effective tools, we can diminish the impact on our mind-body system.

Tools for everyday use

Most of us will (fortunately) never directly experience the kinds of devastating events described above. However, stress, distress, and trauma come in all shapes and sizes, from being sorely embarrassed, to failing in math again and again, to being injured in a fall. How reassuring to have something so simple and effective to use in times of need!

Hook-ups and
The Positive Points

I walked into the locker room at my gym and found an elderly woman holding icepacks on her cheekbone and knee. She'd slipped on a puddle as she returned from her water-exercise class. Falling holds real terror for elderly people, considering how fragile their bones may be. This woman's eyes were wide open and she was trembling, despite her claims of "I'm fine. . . . " I introduced myself and told her I might be able to help her feel better soon with a couple of quick techniques, to which she agreed. While she sat in Hook-ups, I held her Positive Points.

After just a few moments, I felt her almost melt under my hands as the tension drained out of her; her rigid body relaxed and she slumped against the back of her chair. She looked up and said, "I really do feel a lot better! How did you do that?" I showed her again how to sit in Hook-ups and where her Positive Points were so she could do these movements at home, and I went on my way.

We resolve trauma a bit at a time. And, I believe, when we address it immediately, the simplest of actions can bring powerful resolution. Hook-ups and the Positive Points: I invite all of you to use these tools and share them with others, whether dealing with trauma or just the stresses of daily life.

Chapter 19
Brain Gym at Home

Of all the places where Brain Gym® may be used, I believe the most important could very well be the home. After all, this is where we spend most of our time! Ideally, it's a place of healing, comfort, and regeneration, where we enjoy the company of family and friends.

When Brain Gym becomes part of the shared language and experience of our household, we have a vocabulary for communicating about what we're feeling. We also have tools for supporting each other in moving beyond any challenges that may arise.

In this chapter, I'll share stories about using simple Brain Gym processes to maintain a happy home environment. I'll also offer suggestions for sharing Brain Gym with family and friends and for taking care of yourself, which is the foundation of your ability to care for others.

Starting with yourself

Life inspires us to devote time and attention to the needs of so many people: the child with learning challenges or a busy sports schedule, the spouse with a stressful job, the parent with cognitive decline, or the friend going through a divorce. If we are to truly have anything to offer in situations like these, if we are to share from a place of plenty rather than exhausting responsibility, our first job is to care for our own well-being. Then we can be at our best while tending to the details of our busy lives.

Often, it doesn't take much. Clara noticed positive changes when she simply added the PACE warm-up to her daily routine:

All I did was PACE, first thing in the morning. After a few days, my husband commented that I was humming as I made breakfast and that I seemed cheerier as I got ready to go to work. Then I noticed that traffic on my commute didn't seem to bother me as much, and I was arriving at the office in a much better mood. Even my co-workers noticed a difference. How could something so quick and easy smooth out life in this way?

Simply bringing integrating movement into your life can have a positive impact. Adults who regularly use the PACE warm-up often find that they are more resourceful in meeting the demands of a busy day; clients report that they're more patient with their children (or students, co-workers, etc.) and that the right words to deal with a situation are much more likely to manifest. See what might change in how you operate after a full week of this one quick addition to your schedule.

Home life in balance

And, of course, adults may choose to use the balance process to address home-related issues, such as these:

I effectively prioritize and accomplish daily tasks.

I consistently maintain healthy boundaries for my children's behavior.

I easily handle the maintenance and upkeep on my house.

I take time to enjoy the holiday season.

I patiently manage my mother's care schedule.

I efficiently organize my bills and pay them promptly.

I calmly listen to my roommate when she expresses work frustration.

I comfortably allow my children appropriate opportunities for independence.

I diplomatically talk with my neighbor about his barking dog.

Here is an example of one woman's balance about her role as a working mom:

Elizabeth was frustrated with what she experienced as the daily turmoil in her life and chose this intention for her balance: "I enjoy my children after work and relax in their company." When she stated her goal aloud, she said, "That is totally untrue! I can't see myself relaxing at all!" When I suggested she envision her typical arrival home from work, all she could see were the dishes in the sink, piles of laundry, and dinner not yet made. As much as she loved her children, their presence felt like an intrusion when she was faced with these tasks. When she focused on her body, she noticed that her neck and shoulders felt particularly tight, and her breathing was shallow.

Elizabeth's first choice from the learning menu was the Cross Crawl. At first, she felt awkward doing this activity, but as she continued, her movement became more fluid and balanced.

She then selected the Owl, which left her with more relaxed shoulders and a greater ability to turn her head from side to side. Her third choice was Balance Buttons. This time, she noticed how much more present she felt and described her thoughts as having shifted from "racing" to "calm."

Finally, she paused, rather bemused, and said, "I feel quite good—I think I'm done." Now, when she envisioned her arrival home from work, she saw herself simply chatting with her children and hearing about their days. All her household tasks were still there, but they'd faded into the background. Elizabeth knew she would accomplish the laundry and cooking but could also see herself taking time for her life's biggest priority: her children.

A week later, Elizabeth shared that her evenings at home were "transformed." She said, "I still have a lot to do, and the kids are still there, but I enjoy their company now. It's easier to experience them in a loving way—and that's changing how they behave, as well. Now when I'm making dinner, they're less 'needy' and seem happy just to be playing nearby."

A natural introduction

At some point, you may decide you'd like to share a bit of Brain Gym with your friends or family. Where do you start? My suggestion is to begin wherever they express interest or curiosity. And—my clients and students report that this occurs most often when they're using Brain Gym movements for themselves, and others can see the changes and benefits in them! Ava's story is a case in point:

When I took my first Brain Gym workshop, I was excited and couldn't wait to use every thing I'd learned with my daughter, Delaney. She was twelve years old and had struggled for years with schoolwork. What a mistake it was to jump in like that! I realize now that I had not only overwhelmed her with something she'd never seen before, but my attitude of "fixing" her was definitely less than helpful.

I had to step back and regroup. I could see that, though I'd done everything with the best of intentions, I'd gone about it backwards. So I decided to use the movements daily, *for myself*, to see what I could get out of them. Sometimes Delaney would ask why I was doing a particular

A mother and daughter sharing Hook-ups and The Positive Points

Sitting in Hook-ups while another person holds your Positive Points often feels quite nurturing and relaxing. When I experience this, I feel ultimately supported and cared for.

activity, and I'd reply (for example), "Well, I was reading, and found I couldn't really focus on the words. This Calf Pump always seems to help." It took a while, but she actually began doing a bit of Brain Gym with me from time to time, especially once she discovered how much she enjoyed it. She loved Lazy 8s and the Double Doodle, and she began choosing to do the Calf Pump or Cross Crawl before reading.

Sometimes I'd ask Delaney for some help, saying, "I'm feeling really stressed right now (or tired, upset, etc.). Would you hold my Positive Points while I sit in Hook-ups?" I'm sure she could see how my tension would just melt away. Before long, she wanted to try it herself, and she loved it! Now we share this activity regularly.

Once Delaney knew a few Brain Gym movements, opportunities to use them sometimes came up when I was helping her with homework. If she was stuck on a math problem, I might ask, "Which movements do you think would be best right now?" Most often, just one or two got her back on track, and soon she was choosing movements on her own. She could see the results in her schoolwork, and her grades began improving.

This "ease-in-slowly" process was definitely the way to go. And, I must say, I'm not sure who benefited more, Delaney or me!

Fun with Brain Gym

There are lots of ways to make room for Brain Gym activities in the home. Parents can provide the space and materials for their children to do creative variations on Lazy 8s or the Double Doodle. In addition to using typical art materials, it's fun to do these activities in sand, in shaving foam on the table, or "painting" with water on the driveway, using big brushes. And these two movements really come alive when the children are holding streamers in their hands, especially with enjoyable music playing.

The Double Doodle

One mother I know took digital snapshots of her young children doing various movements and posted them in their playroom, on what became a "Brain Gym wall." They would giggle and point to the various photos as they chose their favorites to do each day. Over time, they added their Double Doodle and Lazy 8s art creations.

Double Doodle Drawings

Another mother tells of her teenage daughter, who decided to learn all the Brain Gym activities so she could use them when babysitting. This girl found that her young charges often behaved better and shared toys more nicely with each other after they had done their Brain Gym play!

Lazy 8s Play

When children "own" Brain Gym themselves

One of the things I most love is when children tell me that they're using Brain Gym on their own. When I do repeat visits to schools, I'm often met in the hallway by clusters of students delighted to tell me how they've used movement to help themselves achieve something they care about at home, on the playing field, or in the classroom.

Children frequently tell me about the various circumstances in which they've used Hook-ups on their own: calming down after waking from a bad dream or feeling more comfortable before a test, game, or recital. Recently, one nine-year-old boy told me that he uses Hook-ups while his father and uncle are watching scary movies; in their very small apartment, he couldn't get away from the sounds and images, and then he'd have trouble falling asleep. I was sorry to know that his home environment was so stressful but glad he had such helpful tools available and that he was using them.

Lazy 8s with a streamer

I love knowing that when children are solving their own problems this way, it means they have noticed what's not working and have taken initiative in making a positive change, a true sign of developing maturity.

Brain Gym as part of the home culture

A good friend of mine has two pre-teen children who definitely see the difference in their day when they start it off with the PACE warm-up. They make a practice of including these movements in their morning routine, even if they quickly do them while their mother is making their lunches and they're about to dash for the school bus.

On days when they have more time, the mother—or father, or both—will join the children in doing PACE and say, "What kind of day do you want to have today? Is there something you'd like to go particularly well? Let's keep that in mind while we PACE." And, of course, the parents will also share what they want to go smoothly in their day.

During shared Brain Gym activities such as these, it's important for every family member to address what he finds important. In this way, each individual's interests are validated as worthwhile. Over time, this adds to the cohesion of the family and the sense of trust in each other.

Introduced in this way, your children will realize that they can do PACE to prepare for anything: sports, play practice, orchestra rehearsal, etc. Then, it's likely that the children themselves will realize that it might be helpful to do Brain Gym before standardized school exams and other high-stress events.

Once children make friends with Brain Gym, it can truly become part of how they live their lives. I love this story:

A dear friend and colleague, Colleen Gardner, has been a Brain Gym instructor for more than twenty years. She balanced all through her two pregnancies for such goals as moving and sitting comfortably, feeling safe during delivery, and receiving these infants with joy. Needless to say, her children grew up with Brain Gym—it was woven into their family's daily life. Over the years, she shared balances with her children, their friends, and even their entire soccer teams.

A few years ago, Colleen was here in Phoenix to teach a course when her son, Michael, then age fourteen, was due to participate in his statewide competitive speech finals. As she talked to him on the phone, I heard her start to say, "Remember to do your. . . . " and then she stopped and smiled. When she ended the call, she laughed and told me his comment: "It's okay, Mom—I've been doing Brain Gym since I was in your womb. I'll remember!" He did remember, and he actually won first place.

Brain Gym and senior citizens

An ever-increasing part of home life is dealing with the health and well-being of aging parents and grandparents, including the issues of mobility, independence, and cognitive decline. Some Brain Gym consultants have created a specialty of working with this population, offering group programs in community centers or balancing for goals in one-on-one sessions. When I think of the topic of aging populations, two more of my colleagues come quickly to mind.

Claire Hocking, a licensed Brain Gym instructor in Australia, spent years using Brain Gym with her father, who had been diagnosed with Parkinson's disease. Claire shares:

"Dad had typical Parkinson's symptoms and was finding it difficult to even hold a cup of coffee, as his hands shook so badly. I would balance him every few weeks or so, including lots of balances for the Fear Paralysis and Moro Reflexes, which greatly lessened his symptoms. The last time he was admitted to hospital (with the flu), he saw a neurologist whom he had not seen before. The neurologist was surprised to see Parkinson's medication listed on his chart, as he could not see that my dad had any symptoms of this disease.

"At one point, Dad had a brain scan, which showed that large parts of his brain were 'missing.' The doctors thought the scanning machine must have malfunctioned, as he had no other signs of deterioration. (The doctor told me 'He is functioning just like you and me—we cannot understand it.') They redid the scan with the same results. The doctors were baffled and labeled him as a 'medical mystery.'"

Claire now offers "Brain Gym with the Aged" workshops and reports that many Australian aged-care institutions use Brain Gym as part of their residents' daily routine, with outstanding results.

Karen "Freesia" Peterson is a licensed Brain Gym instructor in Hawaii. She has developed the award-winning Giving Back® Fall-Prevention Program to address a major cause of injury and death for those of advanced age. Karen recruits active senior citizens and trains them in Brain Gym techniques, which they then share as they mentor frail, at-risk elders. The result has been significant improvement in their standing, posture while walking, attention span, and mental acuity. All of these enhance the seniors' quality of life, but more importantly, they lower their risk of falling. Karen says, "This program is about honoring our elders, keeping them healthy and fit so they can *give back* their gifts to the community."

The Giving Back website is full of testimonials on the many ways their lives have improved, beginning with enhanced ability to think and solve problems, sense of directionality and coordination, language expression, emotional well-being, and motivation to return to enjoyable activities they'd given up. Of course, all of this is in addition to greater physical balance, and confidence and safety in sitting, standing, and walking. Jean, one of the participants, shares, "I have limitations, but I see the possibilities. The world is opening up. . . . I shout your praises to all."

For more information on the Giving Back® Mentoring Program, visit www.giving backmentoring.org.

In recent years, I have begun working with a very special senior citizen—right in my own family.

My 93-year-old mother was recovering from a leg fracture, which required three months in a skilled nursing/rehabilitation center. Once she got home, her physical therapist (PT) was helping her continue to improve her movement and stability. Her typical hunched-over posture meant that she took short, shuffling steps, not the true stride the PT was looking for, leaving her at higher risk for falls.

As Mom practiced with the PT's guidance, my attention was drawn to her shoulders. I know how much stress I tend to hold in my own shoulders and how that can affect my whole body, so I wondered: could the key to her short stride be the fact that her shoulders seemed so raised and frozen? Later, I asked Mom if she'd like to experience one simple Brain Gym movement that might help, and she agreed. While she was sitting, I supported her in doing Arm Activation by having her raise her arm and "push just a bit" against my own hand in all four directions: forward, backward, toward her ear, away from her ear. Then I gently held her wrist as she lengthened that arm overhead, releasing all the way from waist to fingertips. She loved the feeling of relaxation in that shoulder and arm, and we repeated with the other.

Then I had her stand up, and she said, "Kathy, I'm looking right at you!" She was experiencing the fact that, for the first time in many long months, she wasn't hunched over. Her shoulders had spontaneously come into improved alignment, leaving her chest more open and her head up. She said she even felt taller.

Then I had her walk, and she took lovely steps, much longer than before. She was so pleased with herself! Later that afternoon, Mom and I demonstrated Arm Activation for some other family members, and this time she stood even straighter, her chin held high. Her gait was even more fluid and confident—a true stride.

Along with her physical recovery, Brain Gym helped Mom to make an easier emotional recovery, too. On occasion, she would talk about how stressful the whole incident had been—her fall, the emergency room, and her time in the hospital. I would invite her to notice how that memory made her feel (tight stomach, not breathing), and then I'd hold her Positive Points while she sat in Hook-ups. I'd watch her relax, her breathing becoming deeper and more even. Then she'd reflect on the difference: "It's like it was longer ago. I can remember without feeling bad."

I would also take her through simple balances for such goals as "I trust my leg to hold me," or "I walk with confidence." We often used the most basic of learning menus—just Hook-ups and Positive Points, or Lazy 8s. Even so, every balance we did made a positive difference in her outlook and helped her return to more comfortable daily living.

Brain Gym as a relationship tool

Many aspects of life at home revolve around maintaining harmony with family, extended family, roommates, and friends. When challenging situations arise, it's possible to use the balance process with others to address shared goals such as these:

We safely discuss our feelings.

We cooperatively share household tasks.

We make room for each other's belongings and projects.

We co-create parenting tactics that work for both of us.

Even without engaging in a formal balance, Brain Gym activities can help smooth out the bumps in the road that come up as we live, work, and play together. People often find that, as they do Brain Gym movements with each other, they feel more cohesive as a group or as partners.

Carla Hannaford, author of *Smart Moves*, often tells of the years when her daughter Breeze was a teenager. Before discussing a "charged" issue, they would set the stage with "Heart 8s," Carla's loving adaptation of the Lazy 8s movement. Standing face to face, they would trace the Lazy 8 with their joined right hands, following along with their eyes; then they'd join left hands and do the same. Finally, they would connect both hands, and gaze into each other's eyes as they traced the lateral 8 between them at heart level. After just a few minutes, Carla and Breeze felt much more in tune with each other. Stress would diminish or even melt away, and they were ready to talk with each other calmly and from the heart.

This is such a lovely activity! It's actually great to share anytime, with family or friends, just for the enjoyment of it.

Brain Gym at every age

Brain Gym movements and the Edu-K balance process can be used at every stage in life: from developing foundational skills to managing our learning process or daily life tasks; from regaining lost or diminished capacities, to enhancing our ability to communicate openly and with integrity. We can use these techniques for ourselves and with each other. When offered with respect and love, these "elegantly simple" tools have the potential to deepen the sense of connection and community in every home.

Two sisters sharing the final step in Heart 8s, Carla Hannaford's variation of Lazy 8s

As a physiologist, Carla describes her understanding of why this activity has such a beneficial outcome (beyond the nature of the Lazy 8s itself). Because of all the sensory input from the hands, which take up so much territory in the sensorimotor cortex, we're activating large territories of one side of the brain, then the other, then both sides together when we join both hands—a very integrating activity.

The Possibilities

Chapter 20
Moving Forward

You're nearing the end of this book, and you've covered a lot of material! Now that you're familiar with the PACE process and other movements, elements of background information, and various ways in which the Brain Gym® program can be implemented, you may be wondering, "Where do I go from here?"

As always, my first answer to this question is, "Begin simply, with what you know." You could start with what you've learned in this book, incorporating new movements into your life a few at a time. Then you may choose to read other Brain Gym books or take a workshop, course, or private session.

However, a further answer goes deeper into my real intention for writing this book: a vision of life made easier and more joyful, and a return to our innate nature as spontaneous learners. In fact, we can achieve this through movement.

To that end, my wish is that you. . . .

Move forward, conscious of the need for each child to crawl, walk, and run; skip and play; climb and tumble, using his whole body in purposeful activity to build a foundation for skilled physical movement and, therefore, the ability to focus, think, and learn.

Move forward with the awareness of how vital it is to wait until children are developmentally ready to benefit from formal academic instruction, and until that time, to provide opportunities to build and refine key cognitive skills through art, music, language play, and exploration of the intriguing world around them.

Move forward, mindful that many learning issues have nothing to do with how much a person cares or how hard he tries; they often spring from a lack of appropriate internal "wiring" and the resulting layers of stress, frustration, and sense of defeat.

Move forward knowing that, at any age, it's possible to develop—or regain— the integrated processing patterns through which we can experience the joy of natural, spontaneous learning.

Move forward with new understanding when learners of any age express resistance to lessons or tasks that are challenging for them, remembering to suggest *movement* as a tool for regaining access to their innate abilities.

Move forward with the intention to use integrating physical activities yourself and experience what may change in your perspective on life.

And move forward, open to opportunities to share what you've learned with others, always aware of the right timing and how much to offer.

I'd like to close with this story:

> Donna teaches a class of severely and multiply-challenged children. After taking the Brain Gym course, she started incorporating Brain Gym movements—in particular, the PACE warm-up—into their day. She and her classroom aides adapted the movements for these special-needs children, "motoring" some of them through things like the Cross Crawl and Brain Buttons. She found that their attention for circle time, when they practice things like colors, letters, people's names, and social skills, was so much better when they'd done their Brain Gym first, and that the children were making unusual progress that year.
>
> One day, Donna was reading a story to conclude the group's circle time. Brandon, a boy of twelve who has Down Syndrome, simply would not focus on the story, no matter how many times he was reminded. Finally, Angela, age ten and also with Down Syndrome, went over to Brandon and gently helped him into Hook-ups, at which point he became completely focused and attentive.

What a beautiful and spontaneous way Angela found to support Brandon. How wonderful it would be if we could all share Brain Gym movements and processes, noticing how we feel, being in tune with those around us, and supporting each other in such a loving way. This is my goal and my heartfelt wish.

Appendix A

Educational Kinesiology/ Brain Gym Resources

Finding a Brain Gym® consultant near you:
The names of Licensed Brain Gym® Instructor/Consultants who are professional members of Brain Gym® International are listed on the Brain Gym website by country, then by state or province and city. Some countries outside the United States maintain their own listings. Please inquire at Brain Gym® International, info@braingym.org.

Finding a Brain Gym® 101 course near you:
Brain Gym and Edu-K courses around the world are posted on the Brain Gym website, www.braingym.org. (Again, some countries outside the United States maintain their own listings. Please inquire at info@braingym.org.)

Many Brain Gym instructors are happy to offer a workshop or Brain Gym course (or shorter workshop) specifically for your school, group, or agency, tailored to your needs.

Becoming licensed as a Brain Gym® Instructor/Consultant
The process of becoming a Licensed Brain Gym® Instructor/Consultant is one of ongoing exploration, practice, and personal growth. Each course in the Edu-K core curriculum is a rich opportunity to learn more about oneself and to balance regarding issues in one's life using the new tools being taught in each successive course. In this way, one learns the process from the inside out and will have experienced all the techniques he or she will be facilitating with others in the future.

Specific details of the licensure process vary in different regions of the world. In the United States, licensure currently includes a series of core Edu-K curriculum courses and electives supported by ongoing Brain Gym balance sessions with a licensed consultant and culminating with a four-day teacher practicum. Entering this program requires no specific prior training or degree. While professionals in many disciplines are drawn to Edu-K, so are people with no post-secondary training at all. Current licensing requirements are available on the Brain Gym website, www.braingym.org, where you will also find date and location listings for key courses. (For information on licensure in countries outside North America, please contact Brain Gym® International.)

Once you are a Licensed Brain Gym® Instructor/Consultant, you are entitled to charge a fee for Brain Gym services, state in your promotional materials that you are licensed in Brain Gym, and teach the Brain Gym® 101 course and shorter workshops. (In some countries, becoming a Brain Gym® 101 teacher requires additional training.) Until you are licensed, it is fine to use what you learn informally with friends and family as well as to blend a bit of Brain Gym into any work you are already doing with individuals or groups: in your role as teacher, counselor, physical therapist, etc. The first step in becoming licensed as a Brain Gym® Instructor/Consultant is taking the Brain Gym® 101 course.

Additional Educational Kinesiology Curriculum

Educational Kinesiology offers an extensive curriculum of courses through which you can expand your skills and knowledge base. Some are part of the licensure curriculum; others go far beyond it, to areas such as sensory integration, infant reflexes, developmental delay, and even sports performance. Please see www.braingym.org for current course listings and topics.

Research on Brain Gym

The Brain Gym website offers a volume of collected research studies, as well as back issues of its publications, many of which hold articles on studies.

Contact Information

Brain Gym® International
1575 Spinnaker Drive, Suite 204 B
Ventura, CA 93001
805-658-7942
800-356-2109 (toll-free in the United States and Canada)
info@braingym.org
www.braingym.org

Edu-Kinesthetics, Inc. (U.S. Publisher of Brain Gym® books in English)
P.O. Box 3395
Ventura, CA 93006-3395

805-650-3303
888-388-9898 (toll-free in North America)
edukbooks@aol.com
www.braingym.com

Please see Appendix B for additional books, programs, and learning materials that may be of interest. And visit www.EducateYourBrain.com for an updated listing of books, courses, and programs.

Books and Materials about the Brain Gym® program

There are many books and materials relating to the Brain Gym/Edu-K program, and they can all be found at www.braingym.com. These are good resources to begin with:

The Brain Gym® Teacher's Edition: The Companion Guide to Brain Gym®: Simple Activities for Whole-Brain Learning. Paul E. Dennison and Gail E. Dennison. Ventura: Hearts at Play, 2010.

Brain Gym® and Me: Reclaiming the Pleasure of Learning. Paul E. Dennison. Ventura: Edu-Kinesthetics, 2006.

Brain Gym® for Business: Instant Brain Boosters for On-the-Job Success Dennison. Gail E. Dennison, Paul E. Dennison, and Jerry V. Teplitz. Ventura: Edu-Kinesthetics, 1987.

Brain Gym®: Simple Activities for Whole Brain Learning. Paul E. Dennison and Gail E. Dennison. Ventura: Edu-Kinesthetics, 2000.

Edu-K for Kids. Paul E. Dennison and Gail E. Dennison. Ventura: Edu-Kinesthetics, 1987.

The Dominance Factor: How Knowing Your Dominant Eye, Ear, Brain, Hand & Foot Can Improve Your Learning. Carla Hannaford. Salt Lake City: Great River Books, 1997.

Hands On: How to Use Brain Gym® in the Classroom. Isabel Cohen and Marcelle Goldsmith. Ventura: Edu-Kinesthetics, 2000.

The Learning Gym: Fun-to-Do Activities for Success at School. Erich Ballinger. Ventura: Edu-Kinesthetics, 2004.

I Am the Child: Using Brain Gym® with Children Who Have Special Needs. Cecilia (Freeman) Koester with Gail E. Dennison. Reno: Movement Based Learning, 2010.

Smart Moves: Why Learning Is Not All in Your Head. Carla Hannaford. Salt Lake City: Great River Books, 2005.

CD/Book: *Movement & Learning: The Children's Song Book and Music CD.* Brendan O'Hara. Victoria, Australia: The F# Music Company, 1991.

CD/Book: *Movement & Learning: The Wombat and His Mates Song Book and Music CD.* Brendan O'Hara. Victoria, Australia: The F# Music Company, 1991.

DVD: *A New Paradigm in Reading Instruction: Keynote presentation on DVD.* Paul E. Dennison, Ph.D., Educational Kinesiology International Gathering 2000, Kapaa, Kauai. Ventura: Edu-Kinesthetics, 2000.

Posters: The four PACE activities (child and teen/adult).

Posters: The 26 Brain Gym activities (child and teen/adult).

Activity Cards: The 26 Brain Gym activities

Brain Gym®/Edu-K Courses

Brain Gym® International lists the entire curriculum of Educational Kinesiology courses, from the entry-level Brain Gym® 101 to upper-level, specialized courses. For current course titles and locations, please see the website: www.braingym.org.

Several courses in the Edu-K curriculum directly address infant reflexes or sensory development, or pertain to children with special needs. At this writing, they include the following:

170 – Brain Gym® for Special-Education Providers (SN)

213 – Integration of Early Childhood Reflexes and Reactions (IECR)

214 – In Synch I—Integrating the Senses through Movement (INS)

221 – Movement Exploration I (MEI)

222 – Backing Up to Move Forward (BMF)

311 – Total Core Repatterning (TCR)

321 – Movement Exploration II (MEII)

345 – Integration of Dynamic and Postural Reflexes into the Whole Body Movement System

---

If you're interested in the topic of infant reflexes and child development, please visit www.EducateYourBrain.com, for an updated listing of books, courses, and programs that address infant reflex issues.

Appendix B
Additional Recommended Reading and Resources

For books, learning materials, and courses specifically about the Brain Gym®/Edu-K® program, please see Appendix A or www.braingym.com and www.braingym.org.

Complementary Programs or Courses

Bal-A-Vis-X: Balance/Auditory/Vision/eXercises for brain and brain-body integration. A series of exercises of varying complexity, all of which are deeply rooted in rhythm. Exercises are done with sand-filled beanbags and racquetballs, sometimes while standing on a balance board. Developed by Bill Hubert. www.bal-a-vis-x.com/

Giving Back Mentoring "Fall-Prevention" program. A not-for-profit program for training active senior citizens in the use of Brain Gym movements, and then having them work with frail elders to improve balance and cognition, toward the overall goal of preventing elders from falling. Developed by Karen "Freesia" Peterson, Licensed Brain Gym® Instructor/Consultant in Hawaii. www.givingbackmentoring.org/

Masgutova Neuro-Sensory-Motor and Reflex Integration (MNSRI). A set of programs focused on the restoration and maturation of primary movements, reflexes, coordination systems, and skills for optimal performance of natural mechanisms, developmental processes, brain functioning, and sensory-motor integration. Developed by Svetlana Masgutova, Edu-K International Faculty for Poland. www.masgutovamethod.com/

Rhythmic Movement Training (RMT). Dedicated to bringing integration and balance to children and adults with specific learning challenges (including ADD/ADHD, dyslexia, autism), motor problems, postural imbalances, emotional and behavioral problems, and general life overwhelm. Works at integrating infant reflex patterns through replicating developmental movements, gentle isometric pressure, and self-awareness. Developed by movement specialist Harald Blomberg of Sweden. www.haraldblomberg.com or www.rhythmicmovement.com

Touch for Health. A means of quickly easing the discomfort of common aches, pains, and stresses in daily living through gentle, safe, and effective acupressure/touch techniques. Developed by John Thie, D.C. www.touch4health.com/

Quantum Reflex Integration (QRI). A means of quickly integrating infant reflexes using touch/massage techniques or low-level laser energy on specific points on the body. Developed by Bonnie Brandes, Licensed Brain Gym® Instructor/Consultant and infant reflex specialist. www.reflexintegration.net

Infant/Child Development and Parenting

The Absorbent Mind. Maria Montessori. New York: Henry Holt, 1995.

Awakening the Child Heart: Handbook for Global Parenting. Carla Hannaford. Captain Cook: Jamilla Nur, 2002.

Bright from the Start: The Simple, Science-Backed Way to Nurture Your Child's Developing Mind from Birth to Age 3. Jill Stamm. New York: Gotham, 2007.

Creative Art for the Developing Child: A Guide for Early Childhood Education. Clare Cherry. 3rd edition. Greensboro: Carson-Dellosa, 2001.

Creative Play for the Developing Child: Early Lifehood Education through Play. Clare Cherry. Belmont: Fearon Pitman, 1976.

Dear Parent: Caring for Infants with Respect. Magda Gerber. Los Angeles: Resources for Infant Educarers. 2002.

Einstein Never Used Flash Cards: How Our Children REALLY Learn—and Why They Need to Play More and Memorize Less. Kathy Hirsh-Pasek and Roberta Michnick Golinkoff. Emmaus: Rodale, 2003.

Is the Left Brain Always Right? A Guide to Whole Child Development. Clare Cherry, Douglas Godwin, and Jesse Staples. Belmont: David S. Lake, 1989.

Last Child in the Woods: Saving Our Children from Nature-Deficit Disorder. Richard Louv. Chapel Hill: Algonquin, 2005.

Living Joyfully with Children. Win and Bill Sweet. Lakewood: Acropolis, 1997.

Raising Humane Beings, 2nd edition. Jane Fendelman. Phoenix: Phoenix Rising, 2006.

Save Your Baby—Throw Out Your Equipment. Laura Sobell. Santa Barbara: Whole Family Press, 1994.

The Superconfitelligent Child: Loving to Learn through Movement & Play. Denise C. Hornbeak. Cardiff-by-the-Sea, CA: PEAK Producers, 2007.

What's Going on in There? How the Brain and Mind Develop in the First Five Years of Life. Lise Eliot. New York: Bantam, 1999.

Your Self-Confident Baby: How to Encourage Your Child's Natural Abilities—from the Very Start. Magda Gerber and Allison Johnson. New York: Wiley, 2002.

Infant Reflexes, Sensory Integration, Developmental Delay

Attention, Balance, and Coordination: The A.B.C. of Learning Success. Sally Goddard Blythe. West Sussex, UK: Wiley-Blackwell, 2009.

Does Your Baby Have Autism? Detecting the Earliest Signs of Autism. Osnat Teitelbaum and Philip Teitelbaum. Garden City Park, NY: Square One, 2008.

The Light Barrier: Understanding the Mystery of Irlin Syndrome and Light-Based Reading Difficulties. Rhonda Stone. New York: St. Martin's Griffin, 2003.

Raising a Sensory Smart Child: The Definitive Handbook for Helping Your Child with Sensory Integration Issues. Lindsey Biel and Nancy Peske. New York: Penguin, 2005.

Reflexes, Learning and Behavior: A Window into the Child's Mind. Sally Goddard. Eugene: Fern Ridge Press, 2002.

Sensorcises: Active Enrichment for the Out-of-Step Learner. Laurie Glazener. Thousand Oaks: Corwin, 2004.

Sensory Integration and Learning Disorders. Jean Ayres. Los Angeles: Western Psychological Services, 1972.

Sensory Integration and the Child. Jean Ayres. Los Angeles: Western Psychological Services, 1991.

Sensory Secrets: How to Jump-Start Learning in Children. Catherine Chemin Schneider. Siloam Springs: Concerned Communications, 2001.

Stopping Hyperactivity: A New Solution. Nancy E. O'Dell and Patricia A. Cook. Garden City Park, NY: Avery, 1997.

Too Loud, Too Bright, Too Fast, Too Tight: What to Do If You Are Sensory Defensive in an Overstimulating World. Sharon Heller. New York: HarperCollins, 2002.

Why Motor Skills Matter. Tara Losquadro Liddle. Chicago: McGraw-Hill, 2004.

CD/Book: *Catch a Brain Wave Fitness Fun: Energizing Movements for Brain Development*. RONNO and Liz Jones-Twomey. Long Branch, NJ: Kimbo, 2006. CD/ Book:

CD/Book: *Feelin' Free: Songs & Stories for Sensory Integration*. Eve Kodiak. Temple, NH: Eve Kodiak, 2006. CD/Book. www.evekodiak.com/

CD/Book: *Rappin' on the Reflexes: a Practical Guide to Infant Reflexes: Songs & Movement Games for Children*. Eve Kodiak. Temple, NH: Eve Kodiak, 2004. www.evekodiak.com/

Program/Training: Masgutova Method: Neuro-Sensory-Motor and Reflex Integration. Svetlana Masgutova. www.masgutovamethod.com

Program/Training: Quantum Reflex Integration. Bonnie Brandes. www.reflexintegration.com

Program/Training: Rhythmic Movement Training: Reflex Integration. Dr. Harald Blomberg. www.haraldblomberg.com and www.rhythmicmovement.com

Learning Theory and Practice

Blame My Brain: The Amazing Teenage Brain Revealed. Nicola Morgan. London: Walker, 2008.

The Complete Infinity Walk. Deborah Sunbeck. Rochester: Leonardo, 2002.

Dreamers, Discoverers & Dynamos: How to Help the Child Who Is Bright, Bored, and Having Problems in School. Lucy Jo Palladino. New York: Ballantine, 1999.

Endangered Minds: Why Children Don't Think—and What We Can Do About It. Jane M. Heal. New York: Touchstone, 1990.

Eyegames: Easy and Fun Visual Exercises. Lois Hickman and Rebecca E. Hutchins. Arlington, TX: Sensory World, 2010.

Eyes for Learning: Preventing and Curing Vision-Related Learning Problems. Antonia Orfield. Lanham: Rowman & Littlefield Education, 2007.

The Gift of Dyslexia: Why Some of the Smartest People Can't Read . . . and How They Can Learn. Ronald D. Davis and Eldon M. Braun. New York: Penguin Perigree, 1997.

Kids Learn from the Inside Out: How to Enhance the Human Matrix. Shirley L. Randolph, and Margot C. Heininger. Boise: Legendary, 1998.

The Learning Differences Sourcebook. Nancy S. Boyles and Darlene Contadino. Los Angeles: Lowell, 1998.

Learning with the Body in Mind: The Scientific Basis for Energizers, Movement, Play, Games and Physical Education. Eric Jensen. San Diego: The Brain Store, 2000.

If you're interested in the topic of infant reflexes and child development, please visit www.EducateYour Brain.com, for an updated listing of books, courses, and programs that address infant reflex issues.

Making the Brain-Body Connection: A Playful Guide to Releasing Mental, Physical and Emotional Blocks to Success. Sharon Promislow. West Vancouver, BC: Kinetic, 1999.

The Myth of Laziness. Mel Levine. New York: Simon & Schuster, 2003.

Overcoming Dyslexia: A New and Complete Science-Based Program for Reading Problems at Any Level. Sally Shaywitz. New York: Vintage, 2005.

The Physical Side of Learning: A Parent-Teacher's Guidebook of Physical Activities Kids Need to Be Successful in School. Leela C. Zion. Byron, CA: Front Row Experience, 1994.

Seeing with Magic Glasses: A Teacher's View from the Front Line of the Learning Revolution. Launa Ellison. Arlington, VA: Great Ocean, 1993.

Smart Kids with School Problems: Things to Know and Ways to Help. Priscilla L. Vail. New York: E. P. Dutton, 1987.

Smart But Stuck: Emotional Aspects of Learning Disabilities and Imprisoned Intelligence. Myrna Orenstein. Binghamton, NY: Haworth, 2001.

Switch On Your Brain: A Guide to Better Reading, Concentration, and Co-ordination. Allen Parker and Margaret Stuart. Sydney, NSW: Hale & Iremonger, 1986.

Teaching with the Brain in Mind. Eric Jensen. Alexandria, VA: Association for Supervision and Curriculum Development, 2005

The Well Balanced Child: Movement and Early Learning. Sally Goddard Blythe. Gloustestershire, UK: Hawthorne, 2004.

What Happened to Recess and Why Are Our Children Struggling in Kindergarten? Susan Ohanaian. New York: McGraw-Hill, 2002.

Developing Movement Skills at Any Age
(See also the Brain Gym/Edu-K listing in Appendix A.)

The Body Has a Mind of Its Own: How Body Maps in Your Brain Help You Do (Almost) Everything Better. Sandra Blakeslee and Matthew Blakeslee. New York: Random House, 2007.

Dynamic Alignment through Imagery. Eric Franklin. Champaign: Human Kinetics, 1996.

Inner Speed Secrets: Race Driving Skills, Techniques, and Strategies. Ross Bentley and Ronn Langford. Osceola: MBI, 2000.

Move into Life: The Nine Essentials for Lifelong Vitality. Anat Baniel. New York: Harmony, 2009.

Sensing, Feeling, and Action: The Experiential Anatomy of Body-Mind Centering,® 2nd Edition. Bonnie Bainbridge Cohen. Northampton: Contact, 2008.

Program/Training: *Aligned and Well.* Katy Bowman. www.alignedandwell.com/

Business
Switched-On Selling: Balance Your Brain for Sales Success. Jerry Teplitz and Tony Alessandra. Virginia Beach: Happiness Unlimited, 2010.

Programs/Trainings: *Switched-On Selling, Switched-On Management, Switched-On Network Marketing.* Jerry Teplitz. www.teplitz.com

Stress and Depression
The Boy Who Was Raised as a Dog, and Other Stories from a Child Psychiatrist's Notebook: What Traumatized Children Can Teach Us About Loss, Love and Healing. Bruce D. Perry and Maia Szalavitz. New York: Basic, 2006.

Fighting Invisible Tigers: A Stress Management Guide For Teens. Earl Hipp. Minneapolis, MN: Free Spirit, 1985.

Healing Depression: A Holistic Guide. Catherine Carrigan. New York: Marlowe, 2000.

Managing Your Stress in Demanding Times: Succeeding in Times of Change. Jerry Teplitz. Virginia Beach: Happiness Unlimited, 2010.

Putting Out the Fire of Fear: Extinguishing the Burning Issues in Your Life. Sharon Promislow. West Vancouver, BC: Enhanced Learning & Integration, 2002.

Trauma Recovery: You Are a Winner. Svetlana Masgutova and Pamela Curlee. Fairfield, IA: First World, 2004.

Waking the Tiger: Healing Trauma. Peter A. Levine. Berkeley: North Atlantic, 1997.

What to Do When Your Brain Gets Stuck: A Kid's Guide to Overcoming OCD. Dawn Huebner. Washington, DC: Magination, 2007.

Why Zebras Don't Get Ulcers: The Acclaimed Guide to Stress, Stress-Related Diseases, and Coping. Robert M. Sapolsky. New York: Henry Holt, 2004.

CDs: *Breathing: The Master Key to Self Healing.* Andrew Weil. Louisville, CO: Sounds True, 1999.

CDs/Workbook: *Travel Stress: The Art of Surviving on the Road.* Jerry Teplitz. www.teplitz.com

Aging
Overcoming Senior Moments: Vanishing Thoughts—Causes and Remedies, Advancing Memory Function for All Age Groups. Frances Meiser and Nina Anderson. Sheffield: Safe Goods, 2006.

Brain, Body, Mind, and Neuroscience
The Attention Revolution: Unlocking the Power of the Focused Mind. B. Alan Wallace. Boston: Wisdom, 2006.

Big Brain: The Origins and Future of Human Intelligence. Gary Lynch and Richard Granger. New York: Palgrave MacMillan, 2008.

Brain Matters: Translating Research into Classroom Practice. Patricia Wolfe. Alexandria, VA: Association for Supervision and Curriculum Development, 2001.

Brain Rules: 12 Principles for Surviving and Thriving at Work, Home, and School. John Medina. Seattle: Pear, 2008.

The Brain that Changes Itself: Stories of Personal Triumph from the Frontiers of Brain Science. Norman Doidge. New York: Penguin, 2007.

A Celebration of Neurons: An Educator's Guide to the Human Brain. Robert Sylwester. Alexandria, VA: Association for Supervision and Curriculum Development, 1995.

Evolve Your Brain: The Science of Changing Your Mind. Joe Dispenza. Deerfield Beach: Health Communications, 2007.

The Executive Brain: Frontal Lobes and the Civilized Mind. Elknonon Goldberg. Oxford: Oxford UP, 2001.

The Future of the Brain: The Promise and Perils of Tomorrow's Neuroscience. Steven Rose. New York: Oxford UP, 2005.

Images of Mind. Michael J. Posner and Marcus E. Raichle. New York: Scientific American Library, 1997.

Keep Your Brain Alive: 83 Neurobic Exercises to Help Prevent Memory Loss and Increase Mental Fitness. Lawrence C. Katz and Manning Rubin. New York: Workman, 1999.

Left Brain, Right Brain: Perspectives from Cognitive Neuroscience. Sally P. Springer and Georg Durtsch. New York: W.H. Freeman, 1989.

The Left-Hander Syndrome. Stanley Coren. New York: Vintage, 1993.

Mapping the Mind, revised and updated edition. Rita Carter. Berkeley: U of California P, 2010.

The Mind & the Brain: Neuroplasticity and the Power of Mental Force. Jeffrey M. Schwartz and Sharon Begley. New York: Harper Perennial, 2002.

Playing in the Unified Field: Raising & Becoming Conscious, Creative Human Beings. Carla Hannaford. Salt Lake City: Great River, 2010.

The Scientist in the Crib: What Early Learning Tells Us About the Mind. Alison Gopnik, Andrew N. Meltzoff, and Patricia K. Kuhl. New York: HarperCollins, 1999.

Spark: The Revolutionary New Science of Exercise and the Brain. John J. Ratey. New York: Little, Brown, 2008.

Train Your Mind, Change Your Brain: How a New Science Reveals Our Extraordinary Potential to Transform Ourselves. Sharon Begley. New York: Ballantine, 2007.

A User's Guide to the Brain: Perception, Attention, and the Four Theaters of the Brain. John J. Ratey. New York: Pantheon, 2001.

Water: For Health, For Healing, For Life: You're Not Sick, You're Thirsty! F. Batmanghelidj. New York: Warner, 2003.

The Water Prescription: For Health, Vitality, and Rejuvenation. Christopher Vasey. Rochester, VT: Healing Arts, 2002.

A Whole New Mind: Why Right-Brainers Will Rule the Future. Daniel H. Pink. New York: Riverhead, 2006.

Additional Resources

For information on EEG and Brain Gym®

Sue Maes-Thyret, Achievement & Learning Centre, Strathroy, Ontario, Canada. www.suemaes.com

Appendix C
Basic Structures of the Brain

The brain is made up of many component parts, which have various functions. This Addendum will mention only a few key elements of brain structure.

Cerebrum and its cortex

The cerebrum is the largest portion of our brain. Its surface is the *cerebral cortex*, a gray layer about a quarter of an inch thick, which is formed into many hills and valleys. This is where scientists have "mapped" the many movement and processing areas of our brain.

Under the folds of the cortex lies a white mass of densely packed *neurons* (nerve cells) that are going to and from the different parts of our brain, like the wires in a very busy telephone switchbox. The white color of this area comes from *myelin*, an insulating substance that our body lays down on frequently used neural pathways.

The cerebrum is divided into two *hemispheres*, each of which is comprised of four *lobes*, or sections, that have specific functions. The cerebrum is the location of what we think of as our "intellect"—our ability to reason.

Motor cortex, sensory cortex

Two special areas of the brain's cortex run approximately ear-to-ear over the top of the head. The *motor cortex* issues commands that control various parts of the body (these commands are carried out by the *cerebellum*). The *sensory cortex* receives information (pressure, temperature) from all parts of the body. These two structures are often spoken about together as the *sensorimotor cortex*.

Corpus callosum

Our two hemispheres share information through a special bundle of fibers called the *corpus callosum*. When we use our two hemispheres simultaneously, our body lays down *myelin* on these connecting fibers as well, facilitating efficient inter-brain communication.

> "Cortex" is Latin for "bark" or "rind." If all the convolutions of the cortex were flattened out, it would be about the size of a pillowcase!

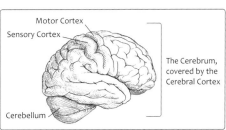

Motor Cortex

Sensory Cortex

The Cerebrum, covered by the Cerebral Cortex

Cerebellum

> We also have myelinated nerve pathways throughout our body, in our spinal cord and peripheral nervous system. Certain diseases, such as multiple sclerosis, are caused by loss of this myelin sheath.

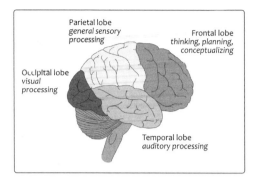

Parietal lobe
general sensory processing

Frontal lobe
thinking, planning, conceptualizing

Occipital lobe
visual processing

Temporal lobe
auditory processing

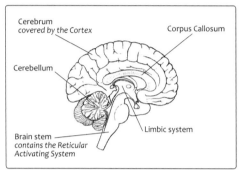

Cerebrum
covered by the Cortex

Corpus Callosum

Cerebellum

Brain stem
contains the Reticular Activating System

Limbic system

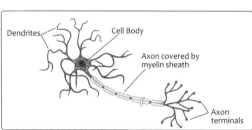

Dendrites

Cell Body

Axon covered by myelin sheath

Axon terminals

Axons can be anywhere from a few millimeters to three feet or more in length. A single axon can reach from your spine all the way down your leg to your toe!

Limbic system

Inside the cerebrum at about the middle of the brain lies the *limbic system*, which is actually a cluster of small structures: the pineal gland, thalamus, hypothalamus, hippocampus, and amygdala. The hippocampus is where we build internal "maps" for sense of organization and spatial orientation; it's also essential for long-term memory. The amygdala is in charge of processing and memory of emotional reactions, especially fear.

Emotions are generated in the limbic system. Because of the strong relationship between the limbic system and the cerebrum, we learn best when we have an emotional tie (preferably positive) to the content we're learning or the situation we're experiencing.

Brain stem

Below and behind the limbic system is the *brain stem*, which is formed from the nerves that emerge from the top of the spinal column. It is the first area to receive neural messages, which it then transmits on to the rest of the brain. It oversees our most basic life-support systems, including breathing, heartbeat, blood pressure, and digestion, and coordinates our survival response.

Reticular activating system

The brain stem houses the *reticular activating system* (RAS), which is in charge of alerting us to incoming signals and filtering out the less necessary ones. It also controls access to our higher cortical reasoning, which it allows only when our midbrain (limbic system) is relaxed.

Cerebellum

Attached to the back of the brain stem is the *cerebellum*, which means "little brain." The cerebellum coordinates voluntary motor control, balance, equilibrium, and muscle tone.

Messenger cells and their networks

Neurons are specialized cells that carry messages through the body. Each one may have a multitude of extensions called *dendrites* that receive impulses from other neurons. Each neuron also has a single extension called an *axon*, which may have many branches. Each branch ends in a *terminal*, which aligns across a tiny *synaptic gap* to a dendrite from another neuron.

When its dendrite receives an impulse, the neuron body generates an electrical charge that ripples down the superhighway of its axon, at up to 200 miles per hour. When the electric charge reaches a terminal, chemicals called *neurotransmitters* are released, which move across the synaptic gap and are received by the next neuron's dendrite. When neurons are fired frequently (as we practice a skill or repeat a movement), their axons develop a coating of myelin, the insulating substance that speeds the transmission of the impulse.

A common saying in the world of brain science is that "neurons that fire together wire together." Repeated physical activities (signing our name) and mental processes (memorizing math facts) call on the same neurons again and again, which then "wire together." The resulting *neural networks* in our brain allow us to do these activities easily and automatically.

Appendix D
The Meridian System

Along with the many body systems we're familiar with (digestive, circulatory, skeletal, muscular, nervous, etc.), there exists another system that is only now becoming known in the western world. *Meridians* are pathways of very subtle energy flow that allow communication between the parts of the human body. The foundation of Oriental medicine for more than 3,000 years, meridians have now been measured and mapped by several different modern technological methods, including electronically and radioactively, and now, through the use of electron microscopy, physically.[1,2,3,4,5] While not anatomically visible, one theory is that meridians may flow through the collagen fibers of the body's connective tissues.[6]

The disciplines of acupuncture and acupressure, which are based on the meridian system, are approved for the treatment of pain by the American Medical Association. Many medical doctors are now cross-training in these practices, so they can provide just such services to their patients.

There are fourteen main meridians in the body. Two of these are on the body's lateral midline, one in front and one in back. The other twelve meridians exist in matched pairs on either side of the body. Though these meridians are named and identified separately, each one begins where the previous one ends, and the result is a continuous flow (actually two matching flows, one on either side).

The state of each meridian is said to relate to the functioning of a certain organ or system of the body, as well as specific emotional states. Stimulation of points along these meridians is what creates changes in physical or emotional symptoms from practices such as acupuncture and acupressure.

One of the body's many paired meridians, the "kidney" meridian, begins on the underside of each foot at the front of the arch, runs around the ankle, up the inside of the leg, and alongside the front midline of the body, and ends at the clavicles, or collarbones. These "K-27" points (the 27th acupuncture points along these kidney meridians) are where your Brain Buttons are located.

In one vivid 1985 study, Pierre de Vernejoul of France injected small amounts of a radioactive isotope at selected spots on the body and, with gamma camera imaging, followed its migration through the tissues. When injected at classic acupuncture points (which are all on meridian lines) the isotope quickly *followed the meridian* (thirty centimeters within four to six minutes), dispersing over "several dozen of minutes." When injected elsewhere (not on an acupuncture point), the isotope quickly dispersed through the venous (vein) route, disappearing in less than a minute. [7]

The "K-27s" are sometimes described as key energy points in the meridian system, a "switchboard" for subtle energy flow in your body. When we are in a state of "dis-ease" or stress, the Applied Kinesiology practitioner uses massage or other touch techniques here to release the resulting "blocks" to this energetic flow; the acupuncturist uses needles for the same purpose.

How can rubbing these points make such changes?

Applied Kinesiology uses the term "reflex point" to describe a spot on the body that, when touched or massaged, prompts a change elsewhere in the body. For example, rubbing *neurolymphatic* reflex points, such as those running down either side of the spine, encourages lymph to flow in areas some distance from the area being worked on.[8] Holding *neurovascular* reflex points, most of which are on the skull, affects vascular circulation in parts of the body far removed from the point being stimulated.[9] While Western medicine does not (yet) offer an explanation for these effects, they are nonetheless documented as occurring.

Appendix E
Exploring Lazy 8s

In a conversation with Paul Dennison, I learned some very important information about Lazy 8s, one of our most frequently used Brain Gym® movements.

First, just what is Lazy 8s?

The Lazy 8s movement is done by tracing a lateral 8, or "infinity" sign, over and over, sweeping across the lateral midline of the body again and again, activating both brain hemispheres and encouraging them to work together. The Lazy 8s movement looks so very simple, yet many people find over time that reading and writing are easier after doing Lazy 8s for just a few minutes, even reducing or eliminating letter-writing reversals.

I invite you to experience Lazy 8s for yourself. Draw a large lateral 8 figure on paper, either flat on a table or vertically on a wall, and place it so that the center of the 8 is directly in line with your midline.

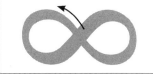

Now, trace the 8 with one hand: begin at the center of the 8 and follow the line, flowing first up the middle and to the left, then up the middle and around to the right, again and again. Holding your head still, allow your eyes to follow your hand. Trace this pattern for a while with one hand, then the other, then with both hands together. Each time you switch hands or begin anew, start in the middle and flow up and to the left. Notice your ability to follow the flow of the Lazy 8; more importantly, notice any areas of resistance, as these will illumine areas where your brain is experiencing "glitches" in how your two brain hemispheres work together, or how your eyes and hand work together. As you continue to use Lazy 8s, it will become much easier, and you will likely find certain aspects of reading and writing easier as well.

New information from Paul Dennison about Lazy 8s

For a long time, we encouraged learners to trace the Lazy 8 pattern only in the "up the middle" pattern. Any learner who was inclined to trace "down the middle" was gently guided in the "up the middle" pattern. For some learners, this was quite a challenge and resulted in more than a bit of frustration.

Paul Dennison now recommends allowing learners to trace Lazy 8s in whichever direction they are most inclined, especially at first. He says that learners inclined to trace Lazy

8s "down the middle" are helping themselves to experience their body more fully, to feel more grounded. Once learners are able to more fully experience their body this way, they will easily make the transition to the "up the middle" pattern.

So—the new Lazy 8s guideline is this: Allow learners to trace Lazy 8s in whichever direction they are inclined, at least at first. Regularly model the "up the middle" pattern; invite learners to notice which direction their body feels like flowing, while encouraging eventual movement to the "up the middle" pattern.

This guideline can also be used with The Elephant, which is essentially a whole-body Lazy 8; however, the original "up the middle" pattern is always used when doing Alphabet 8s, which rely on that flow for correct letter formation. In fact, Paul Dennison states that the Alphabet 8s and letter formation should not be attempted until the learner has integrated Lazy 8s in both directions, up and down.

No matter which form of 8s the learner is doing, it is still optimal to start at the center and move first to the left, so he or she is activating the "ease" aspect of the gestalt hemisphere.

I have been playing with this new information and have had very interesting experiences. When I trace Lazy 8s "down the middle" I'm much more aware of my body—my feet even feel more connected to the floor. Then, when I trace "up the middle," I'm less aware of my body and very aware of my mind—I can almost feel the hemispheres of my brain switching on!

Paul Dennison explained, "Thirty years ago, I worked with delayed learners who basically had a good sense of their body but needed more integrated brain function. Typical Lazy 8s were quite effective, and we didn't realize that they might ever need to be done another way. Now, many of us are working with learners who do not have a good awareness of their body. We need to support these learners in developing body awareness so their experience of brain integration will be more appropriate and complete."

I love this new information, because it helps me understand why learners might be inclined to trace Lazy 8s the way they do! Now my job is simply to notice direction of flow the learner is using, continue modeling the "up the middle" flow, and notice change as it occurs (sharing with the learner, as appropriate) with appreciation for the process.

> For information on how to
> make and use Lazy 8s boards, visit:
> www.EducateYourBrain.com
> and click on "Free Tools."

Endnotes

Origins of the Brain Gym Program
[1]   Dennison, Paul E. *Brain Gym® and Me—Reclaiming the Pleasure of Learning.* Ventura: Edu-Kinesthetics, 2006. 34.

Introduction
[1]   Begley, Sharon. *Train Your Mind, Change Your Brain.* New York: Ballantine, 2007. 156-160.

Chapter 1 ~ A Brain Gym Beginning
[1]   Ratey, John J. *A User's Guide to the Brain.* New York: Pantheon, 2001. 148.

Chapter 2 ~ Water: Charge Up Your Body's Battery
[1]   Robbins, Jim. *A Symphony in the Brain.* New York: Atlantic Monthly Press, 2000. 29.
[2]   Batmanghelidj, F., M.D. *Water for Health, for Healing, for Life: You're Not Sick, You're Thirsty!* New York: Warner Books. 2003. 53.
[3]   Hannaford, Carla. *Smart Moves: Why Learning Is Not All in Your Head.* Salt Lake City: Great River Books, 2005. 178.
[4]   Benton, David and Naomi Burgess. "The effect of the consumption of water on the memory and attention of children." *Appetite* 53 (2009): 143–146.

Chapter 3 ~ Brain Buttons: Clear Out the Cobwebs
[1]   Dennison, Paul E. and Gail E. Dennison. *Brain Gym:® Simple Activities for Whole Brain Learning.* Ventura: Edu-Kinesthetics, 2000. 56-57.
[2]   Walther, David S. *Applied Kinesiology: Synopsis.* 2nd Edition. Pueblo: Systems DC, 2000. 431-432.
[3]   Frost, Robert. *Applied Kinesiology: A Training Manual and Reference Book of Basic Principles and Practices.* Berkeley: North Atlantic Books, 2002. 85-86.

Chapter 4 ~ The Cross Crawl: Power Up Your Hemispheres
[1]   Baniel, Anat. *Move into Life.* New York: Harmony Books, 2009. 19.
[2]   Hannaford, Carla. *Smart Moves.* 24.
[3]   Hannaford, Carla. *Awakening the Child Heart: Handbook for Global Parenting.* Captain Cook: Jamilla Nur, 2002. 26.

Chapter 5 ~ Hook-ups: Shift Out of Your Brain Stem and into the Flow
[1]   Dennison, Paul E. and Gail E. Dennison. *The Brain Gym® Teacher's Edition.* 68-69.

2   Dehaene, Stanislaus. *Reading in the Brain.* New York: Viking, 2009. 69.
3   Maes-Thyret, Sue. *"Biofeedback and Brain Gym.®"* Brain Gym® International Conference at Victoria, British Columbia, 1999. Audio recording.
4   Dennison, Paul E. *Brain Gym® & Me: Reclaiming the Pleasure of Learning.* Ventura: Edu-Kinesthetics, 2006. 119-120.
5   Maes-Thyret, Sue.
6   Hannaford, Carla. *Smart Moves.* 63.
7   Perry, Bruce D. and Maia Szalavitz. *The Boy Who Was Raised as a Dog And Other Stories from a Child Psychiatrist's Notebook.* New York: Basic Books, 2006. 49.
8   Boyles, Nancy S. and Darlene Contadino. *The Learning Differences Sourcebook.* Los Angeles: Lowell House, 1998. 206-207.

Chapter 6 ~ PACE: Bringing it All Together

1   Dennison, Paul E. and Gail E. Dennison. *The Brain Gym® Teacher's Edition*, 27.
2   Honegger, Debra. "Pilot Study: First Grade Students Improve Their Writing Skills." *Brain Gym® Journal* 18.1 (Mar. 2004): 3-5.
3   Hannaford, Carla. *Smart Moves.* 126. Chart used with permission from the author.
4   Morrison, Gillian. "Moving to Learn in Country Schools." *Brain Gym® Journal* 16.3 (Nov. 2002): 6--7, 13.
5   Irving, Jan, "PACE Research Keeps in Pace with First-Year Nursing Students: A Report on a Doctoral Thesis Completed by Jan Irving, Ph.D." *Brain Gym® Journal* 10.1 (Apr. 1996): 3--4.
6   Dennison, Paul E., Whole-Brain Reading Course, Phoenix, AZ, March 8-9, 2002.

Chapter 7 ~ Move into Learning

1   Hannaford, Carla. *Smart Moves: Why Learning Is Not All in Your Head.* Salt Lake City: Great River Books. 2005. 41.
2   Dennison, Paul E. and Gail E. Dennison. *The Brain Gym® Teacher's Edition.* 82-83.
3   Ibid. 66-67.
4   Maes-Thyret, Sue.
5   Jensen, Eric. *Teaching with the Brain in Mind.* Alexandria, Virginia: Association for Supervision and Curriculum Development, 1998. 87.
6   Hannaford, Carla. *Smart Moves.* 40.
7   Dennison, Paul E. "The New Classroom: Embodied Teaching, Embodied Learning." *Brain Gym® Journal* 16.1 (Mar. 2002): 3.
8   Dennison, Paul E. and Gail E. Dennison. *The Brain Gym® Teacher's Edition.* 9.
9   Jensen, Eric. *Teaching with the Brain in Mind.* 84.
10   Dennison, Gail E. and Paul E. Dennison. *The Brain Gym® Teacher's Edition.* 1.
11   Cherry, Clare. *Creative Play for the Developing Child.* Belmont: Fearon Pitman.1976. 59.
12   Ibid. 53.
13   Ohanian, Susan. *What Happened to Recess and Why Are Our Children Struggling in Kindergarten?* New York: McGraw-Hill. 2002.
14   "Recess is 'In Recess' as Schools Cut Child's Play." *Education Reporter* 189 (Oct. 2001). 11 Feb 2005. http://www.eagleforum.org/educate/2001/oct01/recess.shtml
15   Sorci, J., principal, Balsz School District, Phoenix, AZ. Personal communication.
16   Ratey, John J. *A User's Guide to the Brain: Perception, Attention, and the Four Theaters of the Brain.* New York: Pantheon, 2001. 156.

Chapter 8 ~ Wired for Ability

1   Cherry, Clare. *Creative Play for the Developing Child.* 52.
2   Sobell, Laura. Personal communication. 18 Jan. 2008.
3   Hannaford, Carla. *Smart Moves.* 171.

Chapter 9 ~ Theory in Action

1   Carter, Rita. *Mapping the Mind.* Berkeley: U of California P, 1999. 38.
2   Shaywitz, Sally. *Overcoming Dyslexia: A New and Complete Science-Based Program for Reading Problems at Any Level.* New York: Vintage, 2003. 76-77.
3   Hannaford, Carla. *Smart Moves.* 90-91.
4   Dennison, Paul E. *Brain Gym® & Me.* 77.
5   Ibid. 39.
6   Ibid. 107.
7   Dennison, Gail E. "The Noticing Bridge." *Edu-K® Update* 61 (Jun. 2003): 2.
8   Ayres, A. Jean. *Sensory Integration and the Child.* Los Angeles: Western Psychological Services, 1979. 148.
9   Freeman, Cecilia, with Gail E. Dennison. *I Am the Child: Using Brain Gym® with Children Who Have Special Needs.* Reno: Movement Based Learning, 2010. 18-19.

Chapter 10 ~ Cultivating Natural Focus

[1] Dennison, Paul E. "Brain Gym®, Attention, and Brain Science—How Neuroscience is Validating Movement-Based Learning." *IAK-Kongress 2009 mit Edu-K® -Gathering: Bewegung, Lernen und Gehirn.* Kirchzarten bei Freiburg, Germany: IAK Institute für Angewandte Kinesiologie GmbH, 2009. 59.. 69.

[2] De Quetteville, Harry, "Waldkindergärten: the forest nurseries where children learn in Nature's classroom." *The Telegraph* 18 Oct. 2008. Accessed 13 Jun. 2012. http://www.telegraph.co.uk/education/3357232/Waldkindergarten-the-forest-nurseries-where-children-learn-in-Natures-classroom.html

[3] Häfner, Peter, "Natur- und Waldkindergärten in Deutschland—eine Alternative zum Regelkindergarten in der vorschulischen Erziehung." PhD diss. U of Heidelberg, 2002.152-161.

[4] Paul E. Dennison, personal communication, June 18, 2009.

[5] Dennison, Paul E. "Brain Gym®, Attention, and Brain Science. 69-73.

[6] Ibid. 69-70.

[7] Dennison, Paul E. and Gail E. Dennison. *The Brain Gym® Teacher's Edition.* 1.

[8] Paul E. Dennison, Master In-Depth Course, 21 Apr. 2009.

[9] Dennison, Paul E. "Brain Gym®, Attention, and Brain Science. 72.

[10] Montessori, Maria. *The Absorbent Mind.* New York: Henry Holt, 1995. 272.

Chapter 11 ~ Ready for Reading

[1] Dehaene, Stanilsaus. *Reading in the Brain.* New York: Viking. 2009. 2.

[2] Dennison, Paul E. Personal communication. 2 Feb. 2011.

[3] Dennison, Paul E. and Gail E. Dennison. *The Brain Gym® Teacher's Edition.* 9.

[4] Dennison, Paul E. Personal communication. 2 Feb. 2011.

[5] *Microsoft Word Reference Tools Dictionary.* Microsoft® Word 2004 for Mac, Version 11.5.5 (090513).

[6] Coren, Stanley. *The Left-Hander Syndrome: The Causes and Consequences of Left-Handedness.* New York: The Free Press, 1992. 30-32.

[7] Dennison, Paul E. Personal communication. 2 Feb. 2011.

[8] Christopher H. Chase et. al., editors. *Developmental Dyslexia: Neural, Cognitive, and Genetic Mechanisms.* Baltimore, MD: York Press. 1996. 89-106.

[9] Carla Hannaford. *Smart Moves.* 170-171.

[10] Dennison, Paul E. *Brain Gym® and Me.* 94.

[11] Dennison, Paul E. and Gail E. Dennison. . *The Brain Gym® Teacher's Edition.* 90.

[12] Ayres, A. Jean. *Sensory Integration and the Child.* Los Angeles: Western Psychological Services. 1979. 177.

[13] Nicholas Wade. *Psychologists in Word and Image.* Cambridge, Massachusetts: The MIT Press. 1995. 195.

[14] Dennison, Paul E. Personal communication. 15 Sept. 2009.

[15] Dennison, Paul E. *Brain Organization Profiles Teacher Training Course.* 27 Jan. 2002.

[16] Dennison, Paul E. *Brain Gym® & Me.* 151.

[17] Dennison, Paul E. Personal communication, 30 Sept. 2009.

[18] Ibid.

[19] Dennison, Paul E. Personal communication, 15 Sept. 2009.

[20] Dennison, Paul E. *Brain Gym® & Me.* 76.

Chapter 12 ~ Make Lasting Change through Edu-K Balancing

[1] Dennison, Paul E. "Running Your Business Like a Balance." *Brain Gym® Journal* 17.1 (May 2003): 3.

[2] Dennison, Paul E. *Brain Gym® & Me.* 119.

[3] Dennison, Paul E. "Drawing Out Each Person's Best," *Brain Gym® Journal* 21.1 (Mar. 2007): 3.

[4] Dennison, Paul E. *Brain Gym® & Me.* 76.

[5] Dennison, Gail E. "Toward an Ecology of Learning." *Brain Gym® Journal*, March 2005. 3.

[6] Dennison, Paul E. "Running Your Business Like a Balance." 13.

Chapter 13 ~ A Selection of Brain Gym Movements

[1] Dennison, Paul E. and Gail E. Dennison. The Brain Gym® Teacher's Edition. 30-31.

[2] Ibid. 32-33.

[3] Ibid. 34-35.

[4] Ibid. 56-57.

[5] Ibid. 54-55.

[6] Ibid. 66-67.

[7] Ibid. 60-61.

[8] Ibid. 74-75.

[9] Ibid. 82-83.

[10] Ibid. 76-77.

[11] Ibid. 69.

[12] Ibid. 68-69.

[13] Ibid. 70-71.

Chapter 14 ~ Brain Gym in the Workplace

[1] Dennison, Paul E., Gail E. Dennison, and Jerry Teplitz. *Brain Gym® for Business.* Ventura: Edu-Kinesthetics, 2000. i.

[2] Teplitz, Jerry V. "A Revolution in Training: Bottom Line Results of the Switched-On Selling Seminar." *Brain Gym® Journal* 15.1-2 (Jul. 2001): 18-20. Additional information on this research can be found at www.teplitz.com.

Chapter 15 ~ Brain Gym and Physical Activity

[1] Bentley, Ross and Ronn Langford. *Inner Speed Secrets Race Driving Skills, Techniques, and Strategies.* Osceola: MBI, 2000. 8, 52-53.

[2] Erickson, Carol Ann. "Comments and Insights." Personal communication.

Chapter 16 ~ Brain Gym in the Classroom

[1] Dennison, Paul E. and Gail E. Dennison. *The Brain Gym® Teacher's Edition.* xv.

[2] Dennison, Gail E. "Toward an Ecology of Learning." *Brain Gym® Journal* 19.1 (Mar. 2005): 3.

[3] Dennison, Gail E. "The Noticing Bridge." 2.

[4] Ibid.

[5] Dennison, Paul E. "Drawing Out Each Person's Best." *Brain Gym® Journal* 21.1 (Mar. 2007): 3.

[6] Franck, Jeannette. "PACED for Listening." *Edu-K Update* 50 (Oct. 1998): 4.

[7] Dennison, Gail E. "The Playful Teaching of Language and Reading Skills." *IAK-Kongress 2009 mit Edu-K® -Gathering: Bewegung, Lernen und Gehirn.* Kirchzarten bei Freiburg, Germany: IAK Institute für Angewandte Kinesiologie GmbH, 2009. 59.

Appendix D

[1] Reichmanis, Maria, Andrew A. Marino, and Robert O. Becker. "Skin conductance variation at acupuncture loci." *American Journal of Chinese Medicine* 4.1 (1976): 69-72.

[2] Heine, H. "The morphological basis of the acupuncture points." *Acupuncture* 1 (1990): 1-6.

[3] Human Anatomy Department of Shanghai Medical University. "A relationship between points of meridian and peripheral nerves." *Acupuncture Anaesthetic Theory Study.* Shanghai: Shangai People's Publishing, 1973: 251-264.

[4] Dung, H.C. "Anatomical features contributing to the formation of acupuncture points." *American Journal of Acupuncture,* 12.1 (1984): 139-143.

[5] Shang, Charles, M.D. "Mechanism of Acupuncture – Beyond Neurochemical Theory." *Medical Acupuncture: A Journal for Physicians by Physicians* 11.2 (Fall 1999-Winter 2000). Accessed 13 Jun. 2012. http://www.medicalacupuncture.com/aama_marf/journal/vol11_2/conduct.html.

[6] Scott-Mumby, Keith. *Virtual Medicine.* Orem: Timpanogos, 2004. 37.

[7] Vernejoul, Pierre, Pierre Albarade, and Jean-Claude Darras. "Editorial; Nuclear Medicine and Acupuncture Message Transmission." *The Journal of Nuclear Medicine* 33.3 (Mar. 1992): 409-412. http://jnm.snmjournals.org/cgi/reprint/33/3/409.pdfm. Accessed 13 Jun. 2012..

[8] Frost, Robert. *Applied Kinesiology: A Training Manual and Reference Book of Basic Principles and Practices.* Berkeley: North Atlantic Books, 2002.

[9] Ibid. 107-108.

Glossary

analytic brain — the expressive or language-processing cerebral hemisphere (usually the left)

anchor — a way of deeply realizing or *noticing* that learning has occurred; in Edu-K, noticing or muscle checking

Asymmetrical Tonic Neck Reflex (ATNR) — A primitive (infant) reflex wherein turning of the infant's head causes immediate extension (straightening) of the arm and leg on the side of the body the head is facing and immediate flexion (bending) of the opposite arm and leg. Experienced sufficiently, ATNR wires the body for intentional movement of one side of the body without automatic motor involvement of the other side, as well as the ability to choose "detail" or "global" mental processing. When retained in older children or adults, causes motor control and perceptual issues and learning challenges, resulting in unconscious compensations.

at-risk — a term applied to individuals whose behaviors put them at risk of academic failure, physical danger, or negative social consequences

attention deficit disorder (ADD) — a term now in wide use to label children who have difficulty sustaining attention or who behave impulsively (see also ADHD)

attention deficit hyperactivity disorder (ADHD) — a term now in wide use to label children who have difficulty sustaining attention or who behave impulsively (as in ADD) but whose behavior is also characterized by excessive activity (see also ADD)

axon — a long, slender projection of a neuron (nerve cell) that conducts electrical impulses away from the neuron's cell body

balance, balancing, balance process — utilizing Edu-K's Five Steps to Easy Learning to lessen or resolve challenges and blocks to learning

behavioral model — a model for explaining mind-body function based on observable behaviors

bilaterality — the ability to coordinate the body's two sides to function as a single unit

bioelectricity — an electrical current that is generated by living tissue, such as nerve and muscle

blending eye — the non-dominant (non-leading) eye that offers supplemental visual information to the dominant (leading) eye

blocked — in brain organization, an inefficient pattern that prevents full access to abilities

brain bridge — see *corpus callosum*

Brain Gym® — a series of specifically conceived movements that address the physical skills of learning (ex: visual, auditory). Brain Gym activities contain three categories of movements: **The Energy Exercises** to develop awareness of the body as the central reference for all directional movements; **The Lengthening Activities** to facilitate skills of focus and attention; and **The Midline Movements** for physical coordination as well as accessing of both analytical and spatial information. (see *Educational Kinesiology*)

Brain Gym® International — the nonprofit foundation holding the registered trademark that represents and protects the quality and consistency of the above materials as set forth by Paul and Gail Dennison

brain organization — the process whereby the whole brain (the cerebral hemispheres, midbrain, and brain stem) continually develops new patterns of connection, or organizes and fires existing patterns, in response to a change in environment, new learning, or the task at hand

brain organization profile — in Edu-K, an individual's specific pattern of sensory-motor interrelationships (eyes, ears, hands, feet, hemispheres) that is evident in response to stress or new learning when we access our unique gifts (see *lead*)

brain stem — the area of the brain formerly known as the back brain or hindbrain. The brain stem controls the automatic, reflexive, and learned functions that support physical survival, including breathing, circulation, the physical senses, and the movement patterns

centering — the ability to cross the dividing line between emotional content and abstract thought; also, the organization of body reflexes

Centering Dimension — the communication pathways and neural activity along them creating reciprocal relationship between upper and lower portions of the brain and the postural system; the ability to cross the dividing line between emotional content and abstract thought; see *dimensions*

centering midline — the horizontal plane dividing the upper and lower portions of the brain and postural system; also called the organization midline

cerebellum — structure at the back of the brain stem that coordinates voluntary motor control, balance, equilibrium, and muscle tone

cerebrum — the largest, most visible structure of the brain that controls the higher functions of the body, consisting of the cerebral cortex, white matter, and subcortical gray matter

cerebral cortex — the outer layer of the brain's cerebrum

cognitive — of, relating to, or involving the process of knowing, including both awareness and judgment

compensation — a strategy one develops in order to complete an activity one may otherwise struggle to achieve

compensatory approach — the outmoded approach to education for learning disabilities that emphasizes that children must accept their situation and learn to adjust to it by maximizing a strength and compensating for any weakness

convergence — our two eyes' ability to aim at the same point, so that binocular fusion is possible

core muscles — muscles of the (mostly lower) torso that align and stabilize the spine, ribs, and pelvis and provide for efficient distribution of weight, absorption of external force (ex: recovering from a blow), and transfer of ground reaction forces (ex: foot hitting the ground when you walk or run). Most full-body movement originates in the core. Toned core muscles hold internal organs in place; engaged core muscles provide internal pressure to expel substances (ex: bowel movements, breath exhalation, vomiting) and are used in lifting and childbirth.

corpus callosum — the structure that connects right and left hemispheres of the cerebrum

crawling — moving about on all fours, with the tummy elevated off the floor (Child development experts use the term "creeping" to describe this movement.)

creeping — the infant's first locomotive "tummy-scooting" activity, with torso in contact with the floor. (Child development experts use the term "crawling" to describe this movement.)

cross crawl — 1) any contralateral movement whereby one side of the body moves in co-ordination with the other side, requiring bihemispheric brain activation; 2) **The Cross Crawl** — in Edu-K, the Brain Gym movement wherein the knee and opposite elbow or hand are brought together, alternating between left knee and right hand, and vice versa

dendrite — a tree-like extension of the neuron (nerve cell), through which electrical impulses travel to the neuron's body

Dennison Laterality Repatterning (DLR) — a five-step process that simulates key stages of laterality development from infancy through walking, and that helps to free compensatory visual or postural habits (see *Edu-K for Kids* by Dennison and Dennison)

detail brain — a phrase used to describe the language/linear functions of the brain, typically the left hemisphere

dimensions — in Edu-K, communication pathways between various areas of the brain and postural system, along with their functions (Laterality Dimension: left/right; Centering Dimension: top/bottom; Focus Dimension: front/back)

dominance — see *lead*

drawing out — a model of learning based on the teacher's ability to interact with the student in such a way that he or she becomes the initiator and discoverer of his or her own learning experience

dyslexia — the perceived inability to read or to decode printed symbols due to the inhibition of the receptive centers of the brain; broadly, any learning disability that causes confusion and requires compensatory movement patterns, often of the eyes or eye-hand coordination – see *reversal*

Edu-Kinesthetics — the application of kinesthetics (movement) to the study of whole-brain integration for purposes of eliminating stress and maximizing full learning potential

Edu-Kinesthetics, Inc. – the publishing house for many Brain Gym books

Educational Kinesiology (Edu-K) — the study of movement and its relationship to whole-brain learning; a process for drawing out innate learning abilities through the understanding of movement and its relationship to whole-brain learning patterns; the application of kinesthetics (movement) to the study of whole-brain integration for purposes of alleviating stress and maximizing the full learning potential. While not specifically accurate, the terms *Brain Gym* and *Edu-K* are often used interchangeably.

Educational Kinesiology Foundation — a nonprofit public-benefit corporation that is responsible for training Brain Gym instructors and consultants and for dissemination of Brain Gym® and Educational Kinesiology information worldwide (also known as Brain Gym® International)

Educational Kinesiology Foundation — see *Brain Gym*

Edu-K in Depth: Seven Dimensions of Intelligence — an advanced Edu-K course exploring the relationship of physical structure to function and offering a priority system for integrating movement patterns to support personal goals

EEG — electroencephalograph machine; a graphical measure of the electrical activity of the brain, produced by an electroencephalograph

Energy Exercises, The — a series of Brain Gym activities designed to facilitate an awareness of the body as the central reference for all directional movement, thus providing a kinesthetic bridge for skills of organization and abstract thought

executive function — a cluster of higher-order capacities that include the ability to form concepts and think abstractly, anticipate outcomes and adapt to changing situations, initiate and stop actions, monitor and change behavior as needed, and plan future behavior when faced with novel tasks and situations

eye-hand coordination — visual-motor skill: the basis for working with any aspect of written language, including reading, spelling, and mathematics

eye-teaming — the process whereby both eyes share information and coordinate movement for such things as eye tracking and reading

eye-tracking — the ability to move the eyes across the midline from the left to the right visual fields and back

Five Steps to Easy Learning — a process unique to Edu-K that anchors new learning to movement experiences

focus — the ability to concentrate on one part of one's experience, differentiating it from other parts through awareness of its similarities and differences

Focus Dimension — the communication pathways and neural activity along them creating reciprocal relationship between front and back portions of the brain and the postural system; the ability to concentrate on one part of one's experience, differentiating it from other parts through awareness of its similarities and differences (see *dimension*)

focus midline — the plane dividing the front and back of the body, also called the participation midline

forebrain — the front 30 percent of the cerebral cortex associated with awareness, noticing, choice making, and social behavior. Also known as the frontal lobes and prefrontal cortex.

foundational issue — the traumatizing event in a person's past that is causing sensitivity to a current event, typically subconsciously

frontal eminence — prominence (rounded elevation) of the skull above either eye. In some people, the frontal eminence is quite prominent; in others, it is barely discernable.

frontal lobe — that part of the cerebral cortex in either hemisphere of the brain lying directly behind the forehead

gestalt — pertaining to the perception of reality as a whole or totality without attention to analysis of its separate parts

gestalting — spontaneously perceiving a complete picture (idea, mental image) from the details (letters, words) as we read

gestalt hemisphere — the lateral hemisphere of the brain whose functions include the holistic, global, and receptive (usually the right)

hemisphere — a lateral half of the cerebrum

high gear — In Edu-K, when integrated, the state of being able to move and think at the same time; in the flow of the already familiar pattern and structure *(Got it!)*; integrated high gear provides a learned context for integrated low gear; the "switched-on" state; the known and familiar. When unintegrated, the state of being unable to move and think at the same time; out of touch with the pattern and structure *(Lost it!)* (see *low gear*).

homeplay — In Edu-K, movements done on one's own on the days following a balance as a continuation of the integration process

homolateral — a normal developmental stage which nurtures each hemisphere separately; the involuntary state where one is able to access only one cerebral hemisphere at any given moment, thereby blocking integrated thought and movement; without an awareness of the center, midfield, and midline

integration — the lifelong process of realizing one's physical, mental, and spiritual potential, the first step being the simultaneous activation of both cerebral hemispheres for specific learning; the act of making whole and complete; in the world of infant reflexes, that aspect of a reflexively-triggered movement blending seamlessly into the overall movement patterns in the body, so the trigger is "inhibited" or no longer active

kinesthesia — sensory system that allows us to be aware of where our different body parts are in space/time and how they are moving in relation to each other and the space around them, through a combination of tactile (touch), vestibular (balance), and proprioceptive (muscle state) feedback

kinesthetic — of, related to, or experienced by bodily movements and tensions, and sensations

K-27s — another name for the "Brain Buttons" points, which comes from the study of meridians and their subtle energy flows; the 27th points on the kidney meridians

laterality — the communication pathways between the left/right areas of the brain and postural system

Laterality Dimension — the communication pathways and neural activity along them creating reciprocal relationship between left and right portions of the brain and the postural system

laterality midline — the plane separating left and right sides of the body, also called the *communication midline*

lateral skills — communication, language, and near-point skills that require left-to-right spatial orientation

learning menu — a list of Brain Gym movements or other activities from which one may choose, to integrate new learning into the mind-body system

lead — the body's tendency to consistently call on either the specialized or adept right or left eye, ear, hand, foot, or brain hemisphere for specific functions. Commonly referred to as "dominance."

leading eye — the eye that does primary pointing, and receiving of visual stimuli; also called dominant eye

learner — an individual who actively participates in his or her own learning process

Lengthening Activities, The — a series of Brain Gym activities designed to facilitate the ability to cross the back-front midline of the brain and postural system, thus integrating meaningful intention with habituated movement responses

linear — that which is processed sequentially, over time, rather than gestalted spontaneously

low gear — In Edu-K, when integrated, the state of being able to stop and think; able to learn and create a new pattern *(I'm getting it!)*; integrated low gear provides the ability to make new experience familiar as a context for integrated high gear; when unintegrated, the state of being unable to stop and think; unable to create a new pattern *(I'm not getting it!)* (see *high gear*)

limbic system — a portion of the brain that controls emotions and instincts and perceives odors

lobes — sections of the cerebrum: occipital, parietal, frontal, prefrontal, temporal

logic hemisphere — the lateral hemisphere of the brain whose functions include the concrete, linear, and symbolic; typically the left hemisphere

membrane potential — the difference in voltage between the interior and exterior of a cell. In nerve cells, "low membrane potential" slows down the transmission speed of impulses.

meridian system — a system of distinct pathways of energy flow in the body, as identified by Chinese medicine

midfield — see *visual midfield*

midline — the line that separates one visual field and hemispheric awareness from the other

midline (midfield) issues — challenges resulting from inability to function comfortably on or across the *laterality midline* (ex: eyes traveling across a page of print, eyes and hand moving across a page to write, two hands joining cooperatively to perform tasks in front of one), indicating the degree of hemispheric communication which is present

Midline Movements, The — a series of Brain Gym activities designed to facilitate the ability to cross the midline of the body for improved reading, writing, listening, and coordination skills

mind-body system — the entirety of a human being, including the brain and the rest of the body and its many communication systems, as well as consciousness, sensory awareness, emotions, and cognitive functioning

mixed-dominance — a brain profile consisting of a dominant hemisphere with one or more dominant functions on the same side of the body and one or more on the opposite side, often resulting in confusion of sensorimotor processing, delayed processing, or longer response time. See *brain organization*.

motor cortex — the area of the cortex involved in the planning, control, and execution of voluntary motor functions; the portion of the brain that registers movement of and sensory reception from other body parts and controls gross- and fine-motor expressions

motoring — aiding another person in accomplishing a movement he or she is unable to do completely, smoothly, or at all on his or her own through direct physical means

myelin — the white fatty substance that provides a sheath around some neural axon fibers

neocortex — the brain's large, six-layered dorsal region, unique to mammals and, phylogenetically, the most recently developed area of the brain

neuron — a nerve cell that is specialized to carry nerve impulses

neurovascular points — the points on the head where light contact stimulates blood flow in another specific location of the body

noticing — attention to one's state of being: self-observation

PACE — an acronym (Positive, Active, Clear, Energetic) for a four-step learning-readiness technique that an individual may use to settle in to his or her own best rate of learning

PET — Positron Emission Tomography, a highly specialized imaging technique that uses short-lived radioactive substances to produce three-dimensional colored images of those substances functioning within the body. These images are called PET scans, and the technique is termed PET scanning.

plasticity — the term used to describe how communication within the brain can reorganize for efficiency and how portions of the brain can take on new roles (ex: in recovering from physical damage)

postural system — combined use of skeletal, muscular, and sensory systems to maintain intended posture

pre-activity / post-activity — performance of an activity both before and after a balance, to measure changes in behavior

profile — see *brain organization profile*

proprioception — the awareness of ourselves gained through proprioceptors in muscles, joints, and other receptors within the body

proprioceptors — the "brain cells" in the muscles; from the Latin word "proprio," which translates to "within the body," and the English word "receptive"

reflex — in Edu-K, used as a modifier to suggest the movements initiated by the gestalt brain when one is one-sided (homolateral) and not yet integrated

reflex (infant) — an automatic movement the infant is neurologically prompted to make for survival or to develop patterns of communication in the brain so that certain kinds of movements become automatic, supporting higher skill development; to act without conscious thought and with instinctual self-preservation

reticular activating system (RAS) — structure housed in the brain stem, in charge of alerting us to incoming sensory signals and filtering out less necessary ones

repatterning — see *Dennison Laterality Repatterning* and *Three Dimension Repatterning*

reversal — in writing, forming letters in reverse image (ex: writing "d" for "b") or reading a word, phrase, or line from the end rather than the beginning

scanning — movement of the eyes about the environment to gestalt information without conscious visual fixation

sensory cortex — the portion of the brain that registers sensory information from other body parts

sensory integration — the process of taking in, coordinating, and organizing the various senses (ex: vision, touch, hearing, taste, smell, movement, and muscle proprioception), allowing for comfortable interaction efficiency in play, in work, and the care of ourselves and others

soft-focus — the ability to take in our visual environment without actively pointing the eyes on a single focal point

spatial — a descriptor for perceptions characteristic of the receptive cerebral hemisphere (usually the right)

switched-off — the involuntary inhibiting of one cerebral hemisphere in order to better access the other, due to stress or lack of integration (used interchangeably with *low gear*)

switched-on — a term used to describe a state of simultaneous processing through the use of both hemispheres; high-gear

Symmetrical Tonic Neck Reflex (STNR) — A primitive (infant) reflex wherein moving the head back of the central midline causes immediate extension (straightening) of the arms and flexing (bending) of the legs; and moving the head forward of the central midline causes immediate flexing of the arms and extension of the legs. Experienced sufficiently in a tummy-down position, STNR eventually brings the infant into position for crawling. When retained in older children or adults, manifests in any (standing, sitting) position as challenges in maintaining postural control and diverse learning issues, resulting in unconscious compensations.

synapse — the microscopic gap between one neuron's axon and another neuron's dendrite

tendon guard reflex — a physiological response to stop, contract the tendons, and freeze when it is not safe to move or take action; when the tendons are chronically tight due to this reflex, the muscles foreshorten and lose flexibility

terminal — the somewhat enlarged, club-shaped endings by which axons make synaptic contacts with other nerve cells or effector cells

Three Dimension Repatterning (3DR) — a variation of Dennison Laterality Repatterning applied to integration of the back/front, top/bottom, and left/right brain hemispheres

TMJ — Temporal Mandibular Joint (jaw joint) and associated issues of stress in that area. In the *Total Core Repatterning* course, TMJ tension is seen as an indicator of homolateral stresses in the body causing postural misalignment and unconscious compensations of jaw tightening (clenching) to maintain equilibrium.

Total Core Repatterning — An upper-level Edu-K course developed by Paul E. Dennison that focuses on the recognition of two specific primitive homolateral reflexes (STNR and ATNR) as well as TMJ misalignment (often caused by homolateral stresses), which interfere with learning and mature motor control, and teaches specific techniques for integrating them through addressing the status of core muscles of the body

tracking — see *eye tracking*

trauma — any physical or emotional experience that leaves one with a residual fear-based pattern

tummy time — the time an infant spends lying with his or her stomach in contact with a stable horizontal surface, supporting development of many important systems in the body through moving against gravity in that position

vestibular system — the sensory system with receptors in the inner ear that helps us keep our balance by responding to changes in head position; this system is constantly coordinating with our eyes, muscles, and joints to keep us oriented to gravity and to how we balance and move the body

Visioncircles — an advanced Edu-K course that explores eight areas of perceptual development, especially as they apply to vision

visual midfield — the area where a person's two visual fields overlap for binocularity and integrated learning

white matter — whitish nerve tissue, especially of the interior of the cerebrum and spinal cord, chiefly composed of myelinated nerve fibers and containing few or no neuronal cell bodies or dendrites

whole-brain learning — learning that involves the full potential of the student to access and store memories, experiences, and skills that are meaningful and relevant to optimal growth and development

whole-brain organization — in Edu-K, an individual's most efficient and functional pattern of sensory-motor interrelationships (eyes, ears, hands, feet, brain hemispheres) that occurs when not under stress

Index

Kathy Brown, M.Ed., has been a Licensed Brain Gym® Instructor/Consultant since 1998, and wishes she'd had the tools of this innovative system during her 23 years as a classroom K-6 educator.

Too often, Kathy could see students struggling to learn, though she could also see that they were clearly intelligent—just stuck. Through her journey with Brain Gym she has come not only to understand where many learning challenges come from, she's learned techniques that help to resolve those challenges.

She now shares her enthusiasm for Brain Gym with others through courses, workshops, school consulting, conference presentations, and private sessions.

Kathy is a prolific writer of articles about the Brain Gym process. She teaches the Brain Gym® 101 course, Optimal Brain Organization, Visioncircles, and Educate Your Brain workshops. She is also the creator of Total Team Effectiveness™ trainings for businesses groups.

She lives with her husband, Laird, and two cats in Phoenix, Arizona.